EUROPEAN COMMUNITY FUNDING FOR BUSINESS DEVELOPMENT

A Complete Guide to Sources, Grants and Application Procedures

second edition

Rona Michie
Kevin Allen

KOGAN PAGE

First published in 1991
Second edition published in 1993

Kogan Page Limited
120 Pentonville Road
London N1 9JN

British Library Cataloguing in Publication Data

A CIP record for this book is available from the British Library.

ISBN 0 7494 0962 2

Typeset by DP Photosetting, Aylesbury, Bucks
Printed in England by
Clays Ltd, St Ives plc

CONTENTS

LIST OF FIGURES ix

LIST OF TABLES ix

ACKNOWLEDGEMENT x

INTRODUCTION xi

PART ONE: INVESTMENT SUPPORT 1

1.0 **Overview** 3

1.1 **Problem Area Development** 13
ECSC: Conversion Loans 15
Exchange Risk Guarantee Scheme 21
European Investment Bank (EIB) 23
European Regional Development Fund (ERDF) 25
ERDF Community Initiatives:
ENVIREG (Environmental Protection in the Regions) 31
INTERREG (Development of Border Areas) 33
LEADER (Rural Development) 35
PRISMA (Preparing for the Single Market) 39
RECHAR (Coal Producing Areas) 41
RENAVAL (Shipbuilding Areas) 44
RESIDER (Steel Producing Areas) 47
RETEX (Textile Producing Areas) 49
STRIDE (Regional Research and Development) 51
TELEMATIQUE (Advanced Telecomms Services) 54
Transport Infrastructure Action Programme 55

1.2 **Sectoral Support** 59
ECSC: Industrial Loans to Promote Coal Consumption 61
ECSC: Industrial Loans to Promote Steel Consumption 63
EAGGF: Marketing and Processing of Agricultural Products 65
EAGGF: Marketing and Processing of Fishery and Aquaculture Products 68
EURATOM Loans 71

1.3 **Capital Provision/Joint Ventures** 73
EUROTECH Capital and INNVEST 75
International Investment Partners (Joint Ventures) 77
Venture Consort Pilot Scheme 81

1.4	**Support for Eastern Europe**	83
	PHARE	85
	JOPP	88
	TEMPUS	90
	European Investment Bank – *see* Problem Area Development (p 23)	
1.5	**Environmental/Energy Projects**	93
	ENVIREG – *see* Problem Area Development (p 31)	
	LIFE (Financial Instrument for the Environment)	95
	Regional and Urban Energy Planning Programme	97
1.6	**Support for the Arts and Heritage**	99
	KALEIDOSCOPE	101
	MEDIA	103
	Pilot Conservation Projects (Architectural Heritage)	106
PART TWO:	EMPLOYMENT AND TRAINING	109
2.0	**Overview**	111
2.1	**Employment and Training**	113
	European Social Fund	115
	Community Initiatives:	
	EUROFORM	118
	HORIZON	120
	NOW	122
	COMETT II	124
	ERASMUS	128
	EUROTECNET	130
	FORCE	131
	LINGUA	134
	PETRA II	137
	TEMPUS – *see* Support for Eastern Europe (p 90)	
	Executive Training in Japan	139
	Support Programme for Employment Creation (SPEC)	141
	Women's Local Employment Initiatives	143
2.2	**Scientific Training**	147
	Human Capital and Mobility Programme:	
	Access to Large-Scale Facilities	149
	R & D Euroconferences	151
	Research Training Fellowships	152
	Scientific and Technical Research Networks	154
	STA Fellowship Programme in Japan	156
	S&T Fellowships in Japan	158

PART THREE: RESEARCH AND DEVELOPMENT/ INNOVATION 161

3.0 **Overview** 163

3.1 **Innovation/Research Dissemination and Evaluation** 169
SPRINT 171
VALUE II 173

3.2 **Information Technology/Communications** 177
ESPRIT III 179
IMPACT II 182
RACE II 184
TEDIS II 187
Telematic Systems Programme 189

3.3 **Industrial and Materials Technologies/Measurement and Testing** 195
BRITE/EURAM II 197
Steel Research Programme 200
Measurements and Testing Programme 203

3.4 **Energy** 207
3.4.1 **Nuclear Energy** 207
TELEMAN 209
Controlled Thermonuclear Fusion Programme 211
Nuclear Fission Safety Programme 213

3.4.2 **Non-Nuclear Energy** 217
THERMIE 219
Coal Research Programme 221
Non-Nuclear Energies Programme 223

3.5 **Environmental Research** 227
Environment Programme 229

3.6 **Biotechnology/Healthcare** 233
Biotechnology Programme 235
Biomedicine and Health Programme 237

3.7 **Agriculture and Fisheries Research** 241
MAST II 243
Agriculture and Agro-Industries Programme (AIR) 246
Life Sciences and Technologies for Developing Countries 249

3.8 **Programmes with Fully Allocated Budgets** 253
Decommissioning of Nuclear Installations 255
EPOCH 255
EURET 255
MONITOR 256
Management and Storage of Radioactive Waste 256

ALPHABETIC INDEX 259

LIST OF FIGURES

Figure 1: Objective 1 Designated Areas 5
Figure 2: Objective 2 Designated Areas 6
Figure 3: Objective 5(b) Designated Areas 7

LIST OF TABLES

Table 1: Budget for Structural Action 1993–99 10
Table 2: Third Framework Programme 1990–94 164
Table 3: Proposed Fourth Framework Programme 1994–98 165

ACKNOWLEDGEMENT

European Community Funding for Business Development provides a guide to the financial incentive programmes operated by the European Commission and other European Community institutions. Individual programme information has been drawn from the online AIMS database, a continually updated information service on financial assistance schemes for businesses located in the United Kingdom. The information on AIMS and in this book is structured and presented in such a way as to enable business managers and their advisers to identify quickly assistance which could be of relevance to their particular activities and requirements.

In the ongoing maintenance and development of the information on AIMS (and subsequently reproduced in this book) we have received a great deal of help from a variety of sources. In particular, we are grateful to the departments and agencies which administer the various programmes. As ever, they have dealt with our requests for information and queries about changes with courtesy, patience and efficiency. The majority have also read through our final drafts and provided invaluable comments and suggestions on the presentation of the detailed texts.

We are also grateful for the encouragement and feedback received from the practitioners themselves, ie those who have direct experience applying for assistance under the individual programmes.

Finally, we would like to thank our colleagues in EPRC, without whose help this book would never have been possible.

A book such as this is bound to have its shortcomings. As with previous editions, we would welcome any comments which may help us to improve future editions and the ongoing coverage of the online service. As always, responsibility for any shortcomings and errors of fact or judgement rests entirely with us.

Rona Michie
Kevin Allen

January 1993

INTRODUCTION

Promoters of business projects and their advisers are often aware that funding may be available from European sources but are unsure of exactly what assistance is on offer. This book considers the financial incentive programmes operated by the European Community funding authorities (ie those funded from the General Budget of the European Communities) in addition to the activities of the European Coal and Steel Community (ECSC), European Investment Bank (EIB) and European Atomic Energy Community (EURATOM).

The book is structured into three main parts, each of which is concerned with a key area of current EC policy: Investment Support; Employment and Training; and Research and Development/Innovation. Within each part, a separate overview explains the policy background and main operational features of the Community's support mechanisms. This is followed by a detailed description of the individual programmes currently in operation. Generally speaking, the administration of EC programmes is consistent throughout the different Member States. Where this is not the case, the programme is described in terms of its operation in the UK. Where required, further guidance should be sought from the relevant public authority in the Member State concerned.

This volume, together with its companion guide, *Government Funding for United Kingdom Business*, provides a comprehensive overview of all business incentive programmes available from both UK and European Community sources. Both books benefit directly from their association with the AIMS online grants information service. By providing continuously updated information on financial assistance programmes, together with a separate news update file, AIMS overcomes the difficulties of keeping up-to-date with the constantly changing incentives field. Accompanying search software tackles the complexity of the field by facilitating the identification of assistance programmes relevant to the specific characteristics of an individual business/concern. In commercial operation since 1983, AIMS is now widely acknowledged as the most authoritative source of up-to-date information on financial incentives available in the UK and is used extensively by many of the intermediary organisations which firms would commonly turn to for advice (ie government departments,accountancy practices, TECs, LECs, local authorities, development agencies, trade associations, etc).

For those who want to keep up-to-date on changes in the incentives field following publication of the book, a fortnightly hard-copy Newsletter is available on subscription from EPRC Ltd. This should be of particular relevance to those interested in following the Commission's Research and Technological Development (RTD) Programmes, which are characterised by very short application deadlines. Details of calls for proposals under the various RTD programmes are generally in the AIMS News file within three or four days of their publication in the Official Journal.

The presentation of the information on individual EC programmes in this volume retains the structure adopted in previous editions. Each programme is set out in such a way as to enable business managers and their advisers to identify easily the aspects which concern them most. This structure is designed to answer a logical series of questions:

- What is it? – is it a grant, shared cost contract, soft loan, mobility grant, etc?
- Who qualifies for it? – what location, type of organisation, size of firm etc is eligible for support?
- What is it worth? – what is the form and value of the support, eg the percentage contribution, loan subsidy etc, and what expenditure is it paid on?
- What is the catch? – what other conditions must be fulfilled in order to qualify?
- How is it obtained? – what is the application procedure and where is more information available?

The information provided on each programme is presented in fourteen Sections as follows:

1. Summary:
Specifies the form of the incentive (ie grant, shared cost contract, soft loan, etc), the objectives of the programme and the main eligibility restrictions, together with the way in which it is administered (ie direct or via a national public sector intermediary). In the case of Research and Technological Development (RTD) programmes the current status of the programme is described in terms of budget provision and calls for proposals, where relevant.

In most instances, this Section will allow the reader to recognise quickly whether the programme is of any interest.

2. Awarding Body:
Gives the name of the funding institution, and where relevant, the body which administers the programme within the UK.

3. Location Restrictions:
This is the first in a series of 'eligibility filters'. Others follow in Sections 4 to 8 below. Location restrictions indicate whether the programme is available only in specified areas – such as coal and steel closure areas, regions designated under the European Regional Development Fund, etc – or whether it is available throughout the European Community. Where appropriate, specific location restrictions, as defined for the UK, are provided in detail.

4. Sectoral Restrictions:
Details industrial sectors supported under the programme, or conversely, any sectors which are excluded and, where relevant, the type of organisations (eg public, private, nationalised industries, research institutes etc) eligible to participate.

5. Size Restrictions:
Lists any size restrictions or priorities, specified in terms of firm size or project size, applied under the programme.

6. Programme Duration:
Specifies the announced duration of the programme and, if known, its expected continuance beyond this terminal date.

7. Submission of Applications:
Covers any deadlines for the submission of applications under multiannual programmes and, where appropriate, provides details of when the next call for proposals is expected.

8. Other Restrictions:
Highlights a variety of additional eligibility conditions, usually specific to the particular programme under review.

9. Eligible Expenditure:
Specifies items or elements of expenditure which qualify for support.

10. Rate of Award:
The rate of award is generally expressed as a proportion of eligible costs. Any differences in rates, determined on the basis of priority size groups, areas or industries, would also be noted here. In the case of loan schemes, this Section gives an indication of interest rates, concessions and repayment holidays.

11. Payment Procedure:
Explains whether grants are paid in line with expenditure, on project completion or with delays. For loan schemes, the repayment systems adopted are specified.

12. Points to Note:
Covers other important aspects such as broader objectives of the programme and its relationship with other EC initiatives.

13. Application Procedure:
Indicates the method of application and gives details of any other aspects of the application procedure.

14. Further Information:
Gives contact addresses and telephone numbers where further information can be obtained. Where appropriate, the relevant addresses in the UK and at the European Commission are provided.

An overview of how the different programmes fit into general EC policy objectives and how the budget allocations are channelled into business activity, whether directly by application to the Commission or indirectly through national authorities, is provided in the introductory chapter to each of the three main parts of the book. As already noted, these deal in turn with Investment Support, Employment and Training and Research and Development/Innovation. Readers can also go directly to a known programme by referring to the alphabetic index of EC programmes at the end of the book, which includes acronyms as well as full programme names.

PART ONE

INVESTMENT SUPPORT

1.0 OVERVIEW 3

1.1 PROBLEM AREA DEVELOPMENT 13

1.2 SECTORAL SUPPORT 59

1.3 CAPITAL PROVISION/JOINT VENTURES 73

1.4 SUPPORT FOR EASTERN EUROPE 83

1.5 ENVIRONMENTAL/ENERGY PROJECTS 93

1.6 SUPPORT FOR THE ARTS AND HERITAGE 99

1.0 OVERVIEW

European Community financing for productive investment and infrastructure projects is channelled primarily through the national or regional authorities which are responsible for economic development within the Member States concerned. To a large extent, the areas designated as eligible for investment aid under each Member State's own regional policy (eg the Assisted Areas in the UK) coincide with those targeted for European money. Most European grant-aid for investment projects cannot be distinguished from that awarded under a Member State's own regional aid programmes. For many firms, therefore, the emphasis when considering investment support will be on the opportunities available under the relevant regional aid programmes on offer at the national level (eg Regional Selective Assistance and Regional Enterprise Grants in the UK). However, additional European lending facilities are available which may provide extra funding on attractive terms for certain projects. These include loan facilities operated by the European Coal and Steel Community (ECSC) and the European Investment Bank (EIB).

Although direct investment support to firms from the European Community tends to be limited – being focused either on designated problem regions or on particular sectors – it is nevertheless of considerable strategic value to firms to keep informed about European Community industrial policy and related funding mechanisms. EC policy not only influences any nationally administered grant-aid for which firms might be eligible, but also helps determine the relative growth and future prosperity of different regions. Furthermore, for sectors like construction, the considerable sums of money allocated to infrastructure financing under current EC regional policy measures represents a clear business opportunity.

The detailed programme descriptions which follow this overview are divided into six broad headings. Section 1.1 focuses on support for problem area development, most of which falls under the auspices of the European Regional Development Fund (ERDF), one of the Community's three Structural Funds. Section 1.2 then considers sectoral support, primarily via the ECSC and a second of the Structural Funds, the European Agricultural Guidance and Guarantee Fund: Guidance Section (EAGGF). (The third Structural Fund is concerned with employment and training measures and is discussed further in Part 2). The remaining four Sections cover a number of less well-known programmes: Section 1.3 concentrates on EC-level assistance for capital provision and joint ventures; Section 1.4 considers support mechanisms for Eastern Europe; Section 1.5 deals with assistance for both environmental and energy-related projects; and Section 1.6 covers support for the arts and heritage projects.

Given the prominence and complexity of the Structural Funds, they form the subject matter of most of the remainder of this overview. The Funds' objectives and their complex administrative procedure are outlined, followed by a brief description of the Community Initiatives, which are funded from the Structural Fund budget. Future developments are then discussed, including the new Cohesion Fund agreed at Maastricht in 1991. There then follows a discussion of several of the other major Community financing instruments. The overview concludes with a brief review of one of the Commission's more recent areas of activity – support for Eastern Europe.

The Structural Funds

Current EC policy objectives were established with the passing of the Single European Act in 1987. Not only did the Act provide the legislative framework necessary for the Single European Market, but it also led to the reform of the three Structural Funds in line with five priority Objectives which aimed to counter the risks of regional imbalances resulting from market liberalisation, and to reinforce the need to speed adjustment in the structurally weak regions and countries of the Community.

The five Structural Fund Objectives are:

1. Promoting the development and structural adjustment of the regions whose development is lagging;
2. Converting the regions, frontier regions or parts of regions (including employment areas and urban communities) seriously affected by industrial decline;
3. Combating long-term unemployment (European Social Fund);
4. Facilitating the occupational integration of young people (European Social Fund);
5. With a view to the reform of the Common Agricultural Policy:
   (a) speeding up the adjustment of agricultural structures;
   (b) promoting the development of rural areas.

Measures funded under Objectives 1, 2 and 5(b) are restricted to particular regions of the Community. Objective 1 regions (structurally underdeveloped regions) are targeted to receive 80 percent of the total Structural Fund budget. Regions designated under Objective 1 for the period 1989-93 are: Northern Ireland, Ireland, southern Italy, southern Spain, Portugal, Greece, the French overseas departments and Corsica. Figure 1 (page 5) shows the regions designated under Objective 1.

Objective 2 regions (regions in industrial decline) agreed for the UK for the period 1989–93 correspond roughly with the current British Assisted Areas map which determines eligibility for regional assistance. Figure 2 (page 6) shows the areas designated under Objective 2 for the whole Community.

Objective 5(b) regions are rural areas, disadvantaged because of their dependence on agricultural production for which they are not ideally suited, and/or because of their peripherality, lack of infrastructure and business environment required to attract new economic development. Objective 5(b) regions in the UK cover the Highlands and Islands and Borders regions of Scotland, rural Wales and parts of Devon and Cornwall. Figure 3 (page 7) shows the map of areas eligible under Objective 5(b) for the whole Community.

Taken as a group, the Structural Funds were allocated a total budget of approximately 17.6 billion ECU in 1992, accounting for roughly 27 percent of the total Community budget and making them second in importance only to the Common Agricultural Policy (CAP). The largest of the three Funds is the European Regional Development Fund (ERDF), accounting for roughly

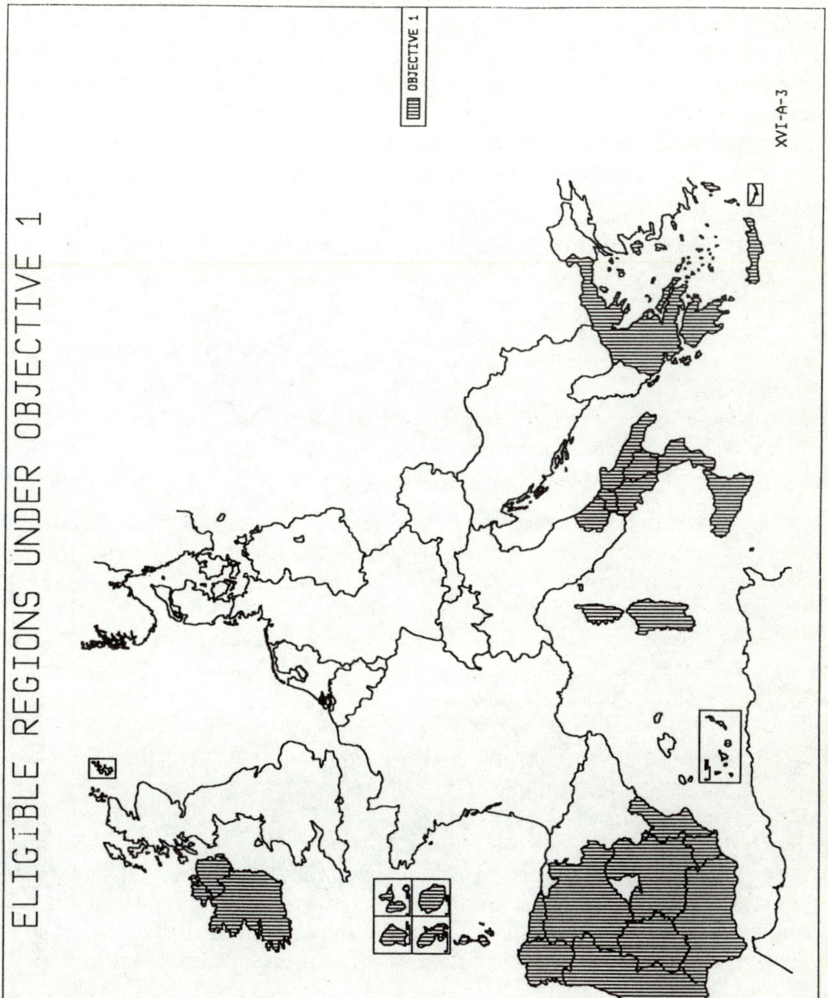

Figure 1: Objective 1 Designated Areas
Source: Commission of the European Communities (DG XVI)

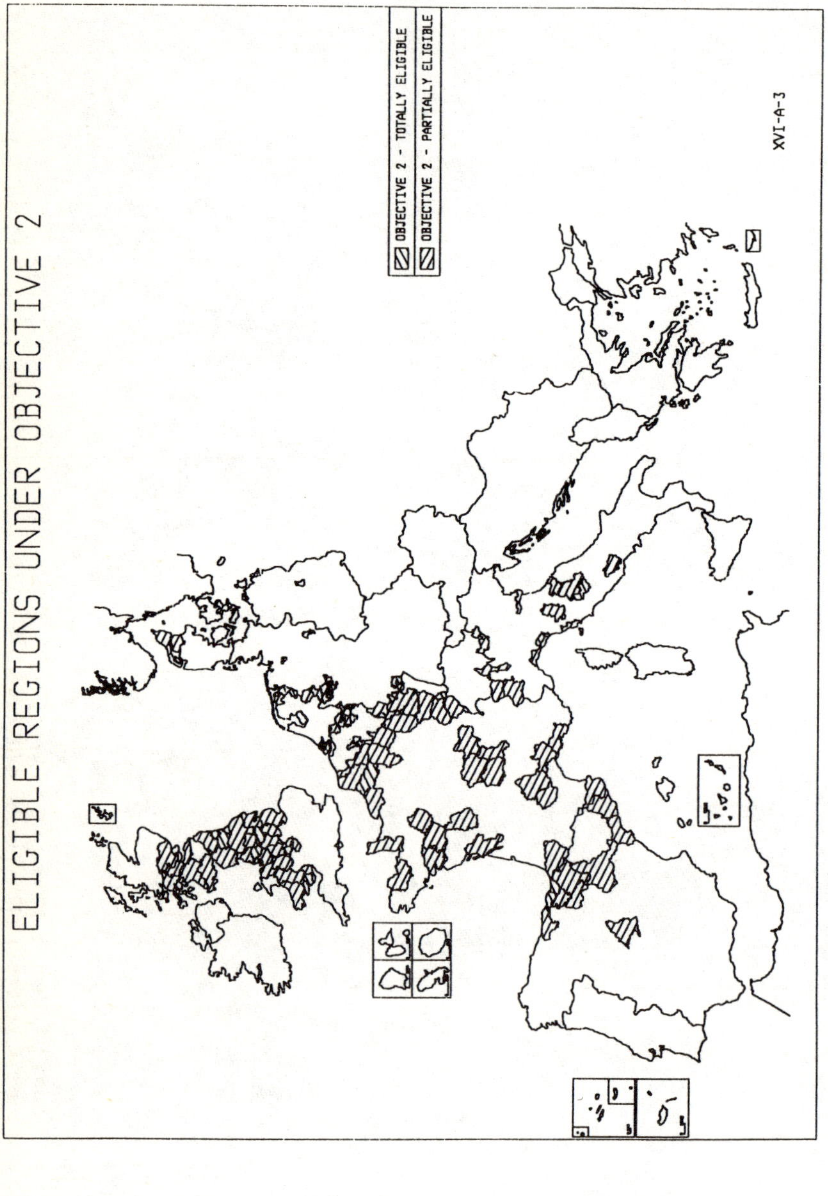

Figure 2: Objective 2 Designated Areas
Source: Commission of the European Communities, (DG XVI)

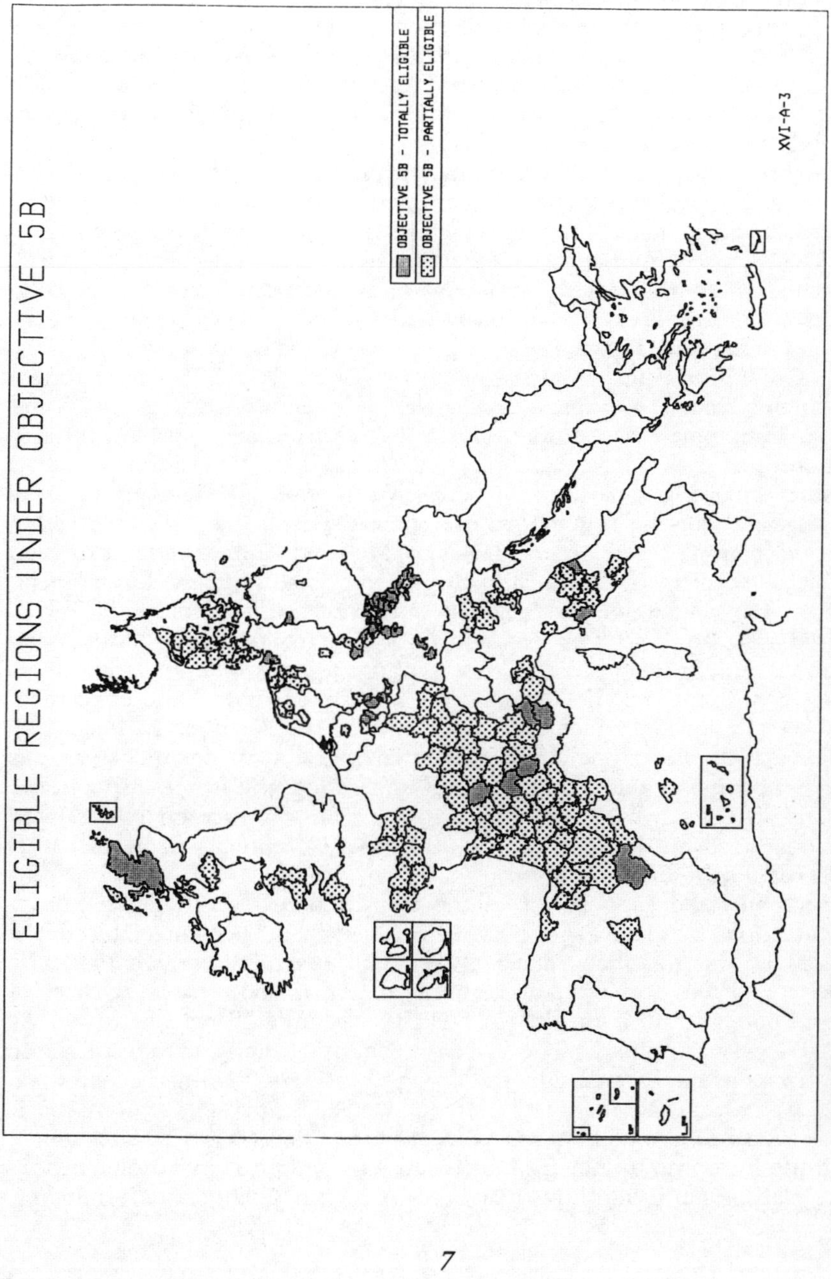

Figure 3: Objectives 5(b) Designated Areas
Source: Commission of the European Communities, (DG XVI)

half of the total Structural Fund budget. The ERDF is the Community's principal instrument for promoting regional economic development through the funding of infrastructure and productive investment. Over 75 percent of the ERDF budget allocation is assigned to Objective 1 regions. Of the remainder, roughly 16 percent is intended for Objective 2 regions, 3 percent for Objective 5(b) regions and 5 percent to fund transitional measures and innovative operations without any specific regional restriction.

Following agreement on the Single European Act, new reforming legislation governing the operation of the Structural Funds was introduced in 1989 to target them more effectively on the objective of promoting the economic and social cohesion of the Community's regions. Objective 1 regions will, as a result of the reforms, receive double their 1987 commitment appropriations by 1993 (in real terms).

One central aspect of the reforming legislation was that it strengthened a process already underway of shifting Fund support away from individual project financing to a 'programme' financing basis (ie the funding of a consistent series of multiannual measures designed to tackle specific objectives associated with the particular problems of an individual region). A second feature of the reforming legislation was that it required coordination in the activities of the three Funds, both with each other, and with the activities of the other Community financing instruments – ECSC and EIB. To a certain extent, this type of coordination was already underway through the 'Integrated Development Operations' (IDOs) which had been approved prior to the introduction of the reforming legislation. Each IDO consisted of a set of measures involving a partnership between a number of regional and local organisations working together to overcome the problems associated with a particular region's development. IDOs could include infrastructure provision as well as specific support schemes to promote small business development, tourism, etc. The reforming legislation has channelled almost all ERDF funding into an IDO-type concept through agreement on 'Community Support Frameworks' (CSFs). CSFs comprise a series of multiannual measures, agreed between the Commission and the Member State concerned, which are designed to tackle the problems of specific regions. Each CSF consists of a number of operational programmes dealing with particular aspects of the problem region (eg communications, training, tourism, transportation, etc) and involves, where appropriate, one or more Structural Funds, with additional financing available through the other Community financial instruments (discussed further below).

Structural Fund support within the context of CSFs can range from a maximum of 75 percent (Objective 1 regions) to 50 percent (Objective 2 regions) of the Member State's own public expenditure on a particular measure. All projects/operations must attract financial backing from a national public sector authority to be eligible for any European grant-aid. As a result, local authorities and Government departments play a very central role in the award of European funding. Although European funding is meant to be additional to each Member State's intended expenditure on its regions, much criticism has been levied in recent years at the fact that Member States simply substitute European money for money already committed in national expenditure plans. Even though this may be the case, the Commission's influence over spending continues to increase as Member States are compelled to formulate their own expenditure plans in line with Commission priorities in order to maximise returns from Europe.

Aside from the ERDF, the other EC Structural Fund which focuses particularly on investment and infrastructure financing is the European Agricultural Guidance and Guarantee Fund: Guidance Section (EAGGF), which promotes economic development activity within the poorer agricultural regions of the Community. The Guarantee Section of the EAGGF accounts for over 50 percent of the total Community budget and is used to fund the wide range of income support measures available under the Common Agricultural Policy. The Guidance Section of the EAGGF, accounting for roughly 18 percent of the total Structural Fund budget (or just over 4 percent of the total Community budget) is used to promote development in Objective 5(b) regions, and also fund measures to promote the marketability of agricultural products by offering grants for marketing and processing investments in agriculture, forestry, aquaculture and fishery products.

Community Initiatives

Apart from the CSFs agreed with each of the Member States, the Commission has introduced, within the Structural Fund budget, a number of special Europe-wide 'Community Initiatives' which are designed to tackle specific aspects of structural change. These include RECHAR for coal producing areas, RENAVAL for shipbuilding areas, RESIDER for steel producing areas and RETEX for textile producing areas. Where appropriate, funding under these Community Initiatives is amalgamated with other measures agreed under the relevant CSF. The funding allocated under these programmes is, however, additional to that which would normally be allocated. A number of other Community Initiatives deal with other aspects which impede the development of specific regions. These include: STRIDE, to promote research and development in disadvantaged regions; ENVIREG, to address environmental problems affecting specific regions; INTERREG, to promote cross-border cooperation; LEADER, to promote rural development; PRISMA, preparing underdeveloped regions for the Single Market; and TELEMATIQUE, promoting advanced telecommunications services.

Knowledge of operational programmes agreed under CSFs and under these special Community Initiatives is of direct relevance to any assessment of market opportunities being created in Europe. At the most immediate level, both types of measure result in the concentration of substantial expenditure on the provision of major infrastructure installations. Specific operational programmes defined within the CSFs indicate both the type, location and funding of any intended infrastructure investments and are open to tender from any firm based within the European Community. At a more indirect level, the concentration of European funding on certain regions of the Community is bound to accelerate the development of these regions, create new markets and generally improve the business environment within these regions.

Maastricht, the Cohesion Fund and Future Developments

The Maastricht Treaty on European Union agreed at the end of 1991 amended the Treaty of Rome and signalled a new phase in the development of the European Community. The Treaty set a framework for the creation of

European Political Union and Economic and Monetary Union (EMU). The Maastricht Treaty emphasised the importance of economic and social cohesion for the development of the Community as a whole and made provision for the establishment of a 'Cohesion Fund' to assist the poorer Member States in adjusting to Economic and Monetary Union. The Fund will provide support for environmental projects and transport infrastructure projects in Ireland, Greece, Spain and Portugal, at a Community co-financing rate of between 80 and 85 percent. The Cohesion Fund is due to come into operation during 1993.

It should be noted that the current Regulations governing the operation of the Structural Funds are due to expire in December 1993, and are currently under review. The same basic principles will underlie the operation of the Funds, but some changes are likely, including a simplified administrative procedure. Reinforcing the effect of the new Cohesion Fund, particular importance will still be placed on the development of the Community's weakest regions (Objective 1 regions). The budget to be allocated to the Structural Funds and Cohesion Fund over the period 1993–99 is shown in Table 1.

TABLE 1
BUDGET FOR STRUCTURAL ACTION 1993–99

	Structural Funds and Other Structural Operations[1]	Cohesion Fund[1]	Total Structural Actions[1]	Resources Allocated to Objective 1 regions[1]
1993	19,777	1,500	21,277	12,328
1994	20,135	1,750	21,885	13,220
1995	21,480	2,000	23,480	14,300
1996	22,740	2,250	24,990	15,330
1997	24,026	2,500	26,526	16,396
1998	25,690	2,550	28,240	17,820
1999	27,400	2,600	30,000	19,280
Totals	161,248	15,150	176,398	108,674

[1]in MECU (1992 prices)
Source: Commission of the European Communities

Other Community Financing Instruments

As already mentioned, other Community financing instruments which are closely coordinated with the investment and infrastructure activities of the Structural Funds are the European Investment Bank (EIB) and the European Coal and Steel Community (ECSC). Although the former offers loan financing on commercial terms, it is able to pass on the benefits of being rated as 'AAA' in raising finance for onlending in international markets. Where ECSC loans are available, they generally offer attractive lending terms for individual investment projects. Projects meeting certain employment creation conditions can qualify for substantial interest rebates. For loans up £500,000, the Department of Trade and Industry also operates an Exchange Risk Guarantee Scheme which covers against exchange risk loss for non-sterling loans. In addition to these 'Conversion Loans', the ECSC also operates two loan schemes designed to promote the consumption of European Community steel and coal.

A number of changes to the administration of ECSC Conversion Loans were made during 1992. The changes were designed to improve the coordination of Conversion Loans with the Structural Funds, and fell into three main categories: a regional allocation of the interest rebates available; changes to the supervisory structure; and an increased sectoral and geographical concentration of the loans and interest rebates. A distinction was made between ECSC employment areas eligible for Structural Fund assistance and those which were not. From 1 January 1993, interest rebates in non-Structural Fund areas will only be granted according to a strict 'social clause' (interest rebates will be calculated on the number of ex-ECSC workers effectively employed). Where ECSC areas are covered by a Community Support Framework (CSF), the CSF Monitoring Committee will be involved in the approval process for direct loans and for indirect loans of over 10 MECU. Conversion Loans will also be increasingly coordinated with the regional development priorities of the CSFs.

In addition, a number of sectoral restrictions have been introduced. In principle, Conversion Loans will not be granted in the following sectors: retail (except for centralised services); hospitals (with some exceptions); leisure, sport and cultural centres not linked to tourism promotion; general education establishments (with a number of exceptions); construction/renovation of housing; finance and banking (except for centralised services); and agriculture, forestry and fisheries (except agricultural food industries). Investment projects must not have started before the loan application is submitted.

A new source of regional funding was made available in 1991 under the PERIFRA programme. Unlike the Community Initiatives, PERIFRA was launched at the initiative of the European Parliament rather than the European Commission. Funding is provided under a special credit line, rather than from the Structural Fund budget.

The programme was launched as a one-off initiative to assist regions suffering from the negative effects of four developments during 1990 – the reduction in defence-related activities following international disarmament agreements, new trade concessions to Central and Eastern Europe, the accession of the German Democratic Republic to the Community and the Gulf crisis. Although originally launched as a one-year programme with a very limited budget, the initiative was subsequently extended for 1992 to assist particular areas suffering from structural problems due to arms industry conversion and cuts in military installations, and areas with industries (such as textiles) affected by the trade concessions to Central and Eastern Europe. Given the one-off nature of this initiative, and its focus on local and regional authorities, it has not been included among the programme descriptions which follow.

Support for Eastern Europe

One of the most significant developments in European assistance over the last few years has been the involvement of the Commission in the provision of aid to the emerging democracies of Central and Eastern Europe.

The PHARE programme was launched in 1989 to promote the economic reform process in the countries of Central and Eastern Europe, and a full description appears in the following chapter, along with descriptions of two subprogrammes – JOPP and TEMPUS.

It should be noted that the Commission recently launched a programme to support economic reform and development in the Commonwealth of Independent States (CIS) and Georgia. TACIS (Technical Assistance to the Commonwealth of Independent States and Georgia) has been described as the world's largest aid programme of its kind, with a budget of 450 million ECU in 1992.

Organisations located within the European Community cannot submit individual project proposals under TACIS, but they can work with potential aid recipients, assisting with the implementation of projects already defined and chosen by the European Commission and the beneficiary States. Funding is primarily available to the eligible States for policy advice, institution building, the design of legal or regulatory frameworks and training in five priority sectors: energy; transport; financial services; food distribution; and training. The funding is allocated within integrated programmes for the development of specific areas or regions.

A further source of finance for firms interested in investment in Central and Eastern Europe is the European Bank for Reconstruction and Development (EBRD). Founded in 1991 to provide advice, loans, equity investment and debt guarantees for projects promoting development in Central and Eastern Europe, the EBRD seeks to fund projects which: develop the private sector; implement privatisation of state-owned enterprises; encourage direct foreign investment; create and strengthen financial institutions; restructure the industrial sector; create a modern infrastructure for private sector development and transition to a market economy; promote small and medium-sized firms; and improve the environment. It should be noted, however, that the EBRD offers funding on a market, rather than a subsidised or concessionary basis. Neither the EBRD nor TACIS are therefore included in the programme descriptions which follow.

PART ONE

INVESTMENT SUPPORT

1.1 PROBLEM AREA DEVELOPMENT

ECSC: Conversion Loans	15
Exchange Risk Guarantee Scheme	21
European Investment Bank (EIB)	23
European Regional Development Fund (ERDF)	25
ERDF Community Initiatives:	
ENVIREG (Environmental Protection in the Regions)	31
INTERREG (Development of Border Areas)	33
LEADER (Rural Development)	35
PRISMA (Preparing for the Single Market)	39
RECHAR (Coal Producing Areas)	41
RENAVAL (Shipbuilding Areas)	44
RESIDER (Steel Producing Areas)	47
RETEX (Textile Producing Areas)	49
STRIDE (Regional Research and Development)	51
TELEMATIQUE (Advanced Telecomms Services)	54
Transport Infrastructure Action Programme	55

1.1 PROBLEM AREA DEVELOPMENT

ECSC: CONVERSION LOANS

1. Summary:

Loans at favourable market rates are available under Article 56 of the Treaty establishing the European Coal and Steel Community for approved investment projects which are associated with the creation of employment opportunities in areas affected by the restructuring of the coal and steel industries. The employment opportunities arising must be suitable for former ECSC workers. The proposed investment for which the loan is sought must permit the expansion or the creation of new economic activities leading to the creation of additional jobs.

Conversion loans may be granted either in the form of direct loans or in the form of sub-loans administered by intermediary financial institutions to which the ECSC has granted a global loan. Subject to the availability of budgetary resources, an interest rebate related to the number of new jobs created by the investment may also be awarded (see 10).

Applications must relate to an investment which has not yet started and can be completed within a normal maximum of three years from the date of financing (or, exceptionally, in the case of direct loans, within five years).

Loans of up to £500,000 may qualify for cover under the Exchange Risk Guarantee Scheme.

2. Awarding Body:

European Coal and Steel Community (ECSC).

Loans of less than 7.5 MECU equivalent are advanced through one of the intermediaries appointed by ECSC, subject to their normal lending criteria. In the UK, sub-loans are available through the following: Bank of Scotland plc; Barclays Bank plc; Clydesdale Bank plc; Midland Bank plc; National Westminster Bank plc; Royal Bank of Scotland plc; TSB Scotland plc; Welsh Development Agency; and 3i plc.

3. Location Restrictions:

Loans are available in designated ECSC employment areas ie areas particularly affected by the restructuring of ECSC industries, where ECSC conversion operations have not as yet resulted in the creation of new jobs equal to the ECSC jobs lost between 1 January 1978 and the end of the restructuring process in the relevant area. Also eligible are regions designated under the RECHAR initiative for the conversion of coal-mining areas.

In the UK, eligible areas are:

- In the North East: the counties of Cleveland, Durham, Northumberland and Tyne and Wear;
- In the North West: the counties of Greater Manchester and Merseyside, and the Travel-to-Work-Area (TTWA) of Workington, Copeland district in Cumbria;
- Yorkshire and Humberside: Scunthorpe TTWA, West Yorkshire (Leeds, Wakefield and Castleford TTWAs) and South Yorkshire;

- Midlands: the counties of Derbyshire, Nottinghamshire, Staffordshire and the West Midlands, Coalville TTWA (Leicestershire), Corby TTWA (Northamptonshire) and in Warwickshire, the boroughs of North Warwickshire, Nuneaton and Bedworth;
- South East: Dover and Thanet districts of Kent;
- Wales: Gwent, Mid Glamorgan, South Glamorgan, West Glamorgan, Clwyd (Wrexham and Shotton TTWAs), and Dyfed (Llanelli TTWA);
- Scotland: Local authority areas of Strathclyde, Lothian and Fife; the Objective 2 part of Stirling; the part of Cumnock and Sanquhar TTWA in Dumfries and Galloway; and Clackmannan LAD.

From 1 January 1993, for loans granted in ECSC employment areas which are not also eligible for assistance under the Community's Structural Funds, interest rebates will be calculated on the basis of the number of former ECSC workers effectively re-employed.

4. Sectoral Restrictions:

Conversion loans can be granted to businesses (and, in the case of direct loans, to certain public bodies) for economically sound investment projects in most industrial and service sectors which create new jobs, with a number of exceptions. These are as follows: retail (except for the creation/development of central production, storage or distribution services); hospitals and related activities (except in Objective 1 regions, or establishments reserved for ECSC/former ECSC workers and their families); leisure, sport and cultural centres, services or activities not linked to the promotion of tourism; general educational establishments (with the exception of those in Objective 1 regions, and technical, specialised or vocational training establishments, including those at university level); the construction or renovation of housing; finance and banking (including insurance) except for the creation or development of central services; agriculture, forestry and fisheries (except agricultural and food industries). In exceptional circumstances in regions eligible for assistance from the Structural Funds, unsubsidised loans may be considered in the above sectors, where they meet development priorities outlined in the region's Community Support Framework (CSF). Workers in the coal and steel industries who have been, or are to be, made redundant and who would like to set up on their own account are also eligible.

In industries whose activities relate to the coal and steel industries, investment projects are eligible only if they substantially modify the activity of the undertaking concerned by providing an entirely new employment-creating activity. In these cases, projects protecting existing jobs under threat may also be considered. In the case of investments carried out by a steel company, an interest rebate may only be granted if the new activity is outside the steel sector.

The establishment of industrial estates with advance factories and the redevelopment of industrial sites, particularly those formerly occupied by ECSC industries, may also be eligible for a conversion loan, provided that such investment is closely linked to the creation of new activities and employment opportunities. However, at this time ECSC cannot grant interest rebates for such projects.

5. Size Restrictions:

Within an overall limitation of 50 percent of capital investment, the maximum sub-loan (ie onlent through an intermediary financial institution) is 7.5 MECU (approximately £5 million). For larger loans, application is made direct to the ECSC.

Exchange risk cover provided under the Exchange Risk Guarantee Scheme is limited to the first £500,000 of any sub-loan.

6. Programme Duration:

There is no specified terminal date for this loan facility.

7. Submission of Applications:

Application must relate to an investment which has not yet started, and which can be completed within a normal maximum of three years from the date of financing (or exceptionally, in the case of direct loans, within five years).

After normal lending considerations have been completed, sub-loan applications handled by financial intermediaries will either be approved under their own delegated authority or approved by ECSC. (Some financial intermediaries have the ability to approve loans of up to 1 MECU on behalf of ECSC.) Where delegation applies response time will be immediate, where cases are considered by ECSC, the average response time is six weeks. Applications in sensitive areas may take longer; where an application requires referral for sectoral or other reasons, approval may take four months or longer.

Approval of direct loan applications requires a formal process, and normally takes up to six months from the date of receipt of the application by the European Commission.

Applications should therefore be submitted as early as possible.

8. Other Restrictions:

The interest rebate (see 10), granted on the basis of the number of jobs actually created or maintained, may be reduced if the durability of the jobs is considered to be inadequate.

The recipients of ECSC Conversion Loans will be given guidance on how they must notify the new jobs resulting from the project being financed to the relevant employment offices and the undertakings which are liable to shed workers (which could include notification to recognised trade unions where appropriate).

For sub-loans, loans will only be granted where the financial intermediary's normal lending criteria are met.

In the case of a direct loan application the following elements must be considered. The social objective of the ECSC loan facility is to facilitate the re-employment of workers made redundant by the ECSC industries. An assessment is made of the employment situation in the area in which the investment project is located, and in particular the ECSC jobs which have been lost or are likely to be lost, the vocational training opportunities available in that area and the project's potential for the creation of new jobs suitable for the productive re-employment of former ECSC workers.

Appraisal of the economic aspects of the project will take account of the contribution of the investment to the development of the region, its financial viability, its level of technology, market prospects and the situation in the sector concerned. In addition, an assessment is made of the financial situation of the borrower and that of its parent companies, and of the value of guarantees.

9. Eligible Expenditure:

Eligible expenditure generally relates to the capital expenditure on an approved project and may include intangible assets such as patents, licences, know-how, and research and development expenditure directly linked to the investment concerned. Relocation expenses and installation costs are also eligible. Working capital and training costs are not eligible.

Straightforward relocation will not qualify for ECSC support, unless it results in an overall increase in jobs in the Community.

10. Rate of Award:

The rate of award and interest rebate are as follows:

(i) Loan Amount: Loans to businesses are available for up to 50 percent of the fixed investment needed to implement the project.

- Loans with exchange risk cover (ie loans of up to £500,000): Loans of up to £500,000 which meet the eligibility criteria may qualify for exchange risk cover under the Exchange Risk Guarantee Scheme.

  For loans with exchange risk cover, interest rates will be fixed for the life of the loan and the term will be eight years with no capital repayments until the fifth year.
- Loans of between £500,000 and £5 million are available from financial intermediaries in sterling or other currency directly raised from ECSC. Some projects may be awarded exchange risk cover for the first £500,000, and not the remainder. Loans of less than £500,000 which have failed the criteria for exchange risk cover can also be funded through this route, although agents would normally apply a limit of £200,000.

  For loans without exchange risk cover, interest rates may be on a fixed or floating basis as required by the borrower, and the nominal term will be five years with one capital repayment at the end of the fifth year.
- Larger Loans: Loans of over £5 million are funded directly by the ECSC at a rate similar to that available from financial intermediaries. Except for major blue-chip companies, the ECSC will require a bank guarantee to secure the direct lending.

(ii) Interest Rebate: An interest rebate of 3 percent is payable during the first five years of any loan, and is directly linked to the total number of jobs created by the project. The normal basis for calculating the interest rebate is as follows: amount of rebate (in ECU) payable per annum is equal to the number of new jobs x 2/3 x 20,000 x 3 percent, ie in total, over five years each job will provide rebate income of 2,000 ECU. This formula can vary at the ECSC's sole discretion, although normally only where direct loans are concerned.

In very exceptional circumstances, where the CSF Monitoring Committee is involved in the loan approval process (see 12) a rebate of 1–2 percent higher than the usual maximum may be awarded.

In the case of direct loans, the maximum 3 percent rebate will only be awarded to the following: productive investments in manufacturing (except in sensitive/crisis sectors), or eligible productive investments by ECSC-sector companies (see 4).

The budget available for interest rebates is allocated on a regional basis. The allocation for the period 1992–1993 is based on the criteria used for allocation of Structural Fund resources.

From January 1993, for loans granted in ECSC employment areas which are not eligible under the Structural Funds, the interest rebate is calculated on the basis of the number of former ECSC workers effectively re-employed. For public sector loans, the Government provides exchange risk cover. Cover is restricted to loans in excess of £25 million equivalent except in cases where they are associated with grants from the European Community, eg in the case of integrated operations.

11. Payment Procedure:

Interest rebates are paid to the borrower in three instalments, in months 12, 42 and 54 after borrowing commences.

12. Points to Note:

An environmental impact assessment of the proposed investment is made on the basis of the national and Community legislation in force, and this will be reflected in the borrower's loan agreement. In ECSC regions eligible for Structural Fund assistance and covered by a Community Support Framework (CSF), the CSF Monitoring Committee will be involved in approval of applications for direct loans and indirect loans of over 10 MECU. Where appropriate, an ECSC Loans Committee may be set up.

The Commission requires annual reports from borrowers on the implementation of investments, jobs created, jobs filled and the number of former ECSC workers re-employed. Investment projects for which loans have been granted may be inspected by the Commission to check that they are being implemented in accordance with the contract. The interest rebate may be redetermined for projects in ECSC employment areas if the number of jobs created within three years of the disbursement of the loan is less than the number first specified in the contract. In other areas, the interest rebate may be redetermined if the specified number of jobs has not been created and filled with ex-ECSC workers.

Fundamental changes to a project must be notified to ECSC (via the intermediary where appropriate) to ensure that there is no negative impact on eligibility, and that interest rebate provisions are not restricted.

13. Application Procedure:

Application for an indirect loan is made to an intermediary financial institution to which a global loan has been granted (see 2).

Application for a direct loan is sent to the ECSC through the Department of Trade and Industry, Scottish Office Industry Department or Welsh Office Industry Department, as appropriate.

However, nominated ECSC intermediaries may be able to assist applicants with preparation of their submission.

14. Further Information:

European Commission
DG XVIII – Division B-2
Batiment Jean Monnet
L-2920 Luxembourg
Tel: (010 35 2) 43011

For information on Exchange Risk Cover:

Department of Trade and Industry
Investment and Development Division
Kingsgate House
66–74 Victoria Street
London SW1E 6SW
Tel: (071) 215 2604/5
Fax: (071) 215 8779

Scottish Office Industry Department
Industrial Development Division
Alhambra House
45 Waterloo Street
Glasgow G2 6AT
Tel: (041) 248 2855

Welsh Office Industry Department
New Crown Building
Cathays Park
Cardiff CF1 3NQ
Tel: (0222) 825111

For Regional Policy Considerations:

European Commission
DG XVI – Division C-3
Rue de la Loi 200
B-1049 Brussels
Tel: (010 32 2) 235 8468

Bank of Scotland plc
61 Grassmarket
Edinburgh EH1 2JF
Tel: (031) 442 7777

Barclays Bank plc
European Loans Unit
PO Box No 256
7th Floor, Fleetway House
25 Farringdon Street
London EC4A 4LP
Tel: (071) 489 1995

Clydesdale Bank plc
30 St Vincent Place
Glasgow G1 2HL
Tel: (041) 248 7070

Royal Bank of Scotland plc
29 Gresham Street
London EC2
Tel: (071) 623 4356

TSB Scotland plc
120 George Street
Edinburgh EH2 4TS
Tel: (031) 225 4555

3i plc
Trinity Park
Bickenhill
Birmingham B37 7ES
Tel: (021) 782 3131
Fax: (021) 782 6161

Midland Bank plc
Courtwood House
Silver Street Head
Sheffield S1 1RD
Tel: (0742) 752 394

National Westminster Bank plc
Level 14
National Westminster Tower
London EC3
Tel: (071) 920 5555

Welsh Development Agency
Investment Division
Pearl House
Greyfriars Road
Cardiff CF1 3XX
Tel: (0222) 222666

EXCHANGE RISK GUARANTEE SCHEME

1. Summary:
To encourage industry to take advantage of the low interest foreign currency loans available from the European Coal and Steel Community (ECSC), the UK Government runs the Exchange Risk Guarantee Scheme under which borrowers take on only a sterling liability and the Government takes the exchange risk in return for an annual premium.

2. Awarding Body:
Responsibility for the Exchange Risk Guarantee Scheme lies with the Department of Trade and Industry (DTI), the Welsh Office and the Scottish Office, as appropriate. For ECSC loans of up to £5.25m and exchange risk cover on them, companies should contact any of the following intermediaries: 3i plc, Bank of Scotland, Barclays Bank, Clydesdale Bank, Midland Bank, National Westminster Bank, Royal Bank of Scotland, Trustee Savings Bank Scotland, or the Welsh Development Agency (WDA). All of the agencies and intermediaries for ECSC loans apply for exchange risk cover from the DTI on behalf of the applicant. If the project is not eligible for cover, the loan may still be available but it is open to the applicant to take a loan in sterling or bear the exchange risk cover himself on a foreign currency loan. Loans of more than £5.25m are negotiated direct with the ECSC.

3. Location Restrictions:
ECSC loans are only available to firms located in areas designated by the European Commission as being affected by steel or coal plant closures or run-downs.

4. Sectoral Restrictions:
The scheme applies mainly to manufacturing industry projects but may also apply to tourism and service projects.

5. Size Restrictions:
Exchange risk cover is only available on loans of up to £500,000 for each project supported.

6. Programme Duration:

There is no specified terminal date for this scheme.

7. Submission of Applications:

Application must be made as early as possible and certainly before the start of the project.

8. Other Restrictions:

Exchange risk cover on private sector loans is only available with respect to European Coal and Steel Community loans. Therefore, any restrictions applicable to these loans must also be observed.

To be eligible for exchange risk cover projects must create new jobs. In addition it must be shown that the project would not take place on the basis proposed without assistance (ie assistance must lead to a significant change in the nature or scale of the project or to a significant advancement in time).

9. Eligible Expenditure:

Exchange risk cover is available on ECSC loans of up to £500,000 for each project supported. Such loans can be in respect of the fixed capital costs of projects which provide new employment opportunities in coal or steel closure areas.

10. Rate of Award:

ECSC loans are medium term for ERGS loans, generally around eight years though usually five years for sterling loans. They cover 50 percent of eligible capital costs and are at a fixed rate of interest. The interest rate is determined by the currency of the loan raised by the ECSC in the international money market, plus a premium for exchange risk cover, plus the intermediary's margin.

11. Payment Procedure:

Loans are repayable normally in half-yearly instalments, with repayment of principal starting in year 5.

12. Points to Note:

None.

13. Application Procedure:

Application is made to the appropriate Department at the same time as a loan is negotiated.

14. Further Information:

In England:
Department of Trade and Industry
Investment and Development Division
Kingsgate House
66-74 Victoria Street
London SW1E 6SW
Tel: (071) 215 2604/5
Fax: (071) 215 8779

In Wales:
Welsh Office Industry Department
New Crown Building
Cathays Park
Cardiff CF1 3NQ
Tel: (0222) 825111

In Scotland:
Scottish Office Industry Department
Industrial Development Division
Alhambra House
45 Waterloo Street
Glasgow G2 6AT
Tel: (041) 248 2855

EUROPEAN INVESTMENT BANK

1. Summary:

The European Investment Bank (EIB) offers loan financing on flexible terms for private and public sector capital investment projects meeting its eligibility and lending criteria. Loans are related to asset life and may be offered for projects in infrastructure, transport, telecommunications, energy, industry and tourism.

EIB loans are at fixed or floating rates at close to the EIB's cost of borrowings; other interest rate formulae can be considered. The rates reflect market conditions and are unaffected by the type or location of the project, by the nationality or nature of the borrower or by the size of the loan.

2. Awarding Body:

The European Investment Bank (EIB).

3. Location Restrictions:

Available in any Member State of the European Community.

For private sector loans, industrial projects costing up to £14 million from small and medium-sized enterprises (companies with assets of less than about £50 million and fewer than 500 employees) may be eligible irrespective of location through an EIB intermediary (currently Barclays Bank, 3i Group and the Allied Irish Bank in the UK); public or private sector projects costing £14 million or more are financed in industry, energy or infrastructure if they help regional development (normally in the Assisted Areas, Northern Ireland, Wales, the Scottish Highlands, or a recognised textile, steel, shipbuilding or fisheries zone), improve communications (transport and telecommunications), enhance the competitiveness of industry (introduction of advanced technology), protect and improve the environment, or help energy security (production, transportation, saving).

In countries outside the Community, EIB financing falls under protocols and agreements negotiated between the EC and countries in the Mediterranean region, as well as under the Lome Convention with 70 African, Caribbean and Pacific countries. Loans under these agreements are made with the consent of the governments of the countries concerned. Projects of direct benefit to the EC may also be supported outside the Community.

In Eastern Europe, EIB loans are currently available in Poland, Hungary, the Czech and Slovak Federal Republics, Bulgaria, Romania, Albania, Estonia, Latvia and Lithuania.

4. Sectoral Restrictions:

None, finance is available to nationalised industries, local authorities, companies or any sound borrower for capital investment projects in industry, energy, infrastructure, tourism, transport and telecommunications. Priority for private sector loans is given to independent companies.

5. Size Restrictions:

The minimum directly negotiated loan is around £7 million (ie minimum project costs of about £14 million); there is no absolute maximum. Certain location restrictions apply according to project and company size (see 3).

6. Programme Duration:

There is no specified terminal date for this facility.

7. Submission of Applications:

Application can be made after project start but must be made before completion of the project.

8. Other Restrictions:

A corporate guarantee from a well-diversified parent company may be adequate support for an EIB facility; if not then security may be needed from an outside guarantor such as from a bank, a banking syndicate or other acceptable party. The EIB often acts as a source of funding within a financing agreement put together in close collaboration with other banks. The EIB may sometimes take as security a charge on specific assets or an assignment of revenues.

Loans to local authorities are secured by a charge on future revenues and/or government guarantee.

In June 1991, an experimental facility was introduced to provide funds for equity participation in productive investments by small and medium-sized firms in regional development areas. The system will operate for two years, with an annual ceiling of 15 MECU, and funds will be disbursed by existing EIB intermediaries.

9. Eligible Expenditure:

Loans usually cover between 25 and 30 percent (maximum 50 percent) of the cost of a project, including permanent working capital requirements and intangible assets.

Minimum project cost for direct loans is normally about £14 million; there is no absolute maximum. Finance below this level is handled by an EIB intermediary (see 12 for further details).

10. Rate of Award:

EIB loans are at fixed or floating rates at just above the EIB's cost of borrowings; other interest rate formulae can be considered (eg adjustable fixed rates). Interest rates reflect market conditions and are not influenced by the type or location of the project, by the nationality or nature of the borrower or by the size of the loan.

EIB loans are in pounds sterling or in other currencies according to the borrower's preference. Disbursements can be in a single currency or a mixture of currencies.

Loan maturities are usually from 4 to 12 years for industry and up to 20 years for infrastructure and energy projects.

The EIB does not usually charge any arrangement fees, commitment fees or other expenses.

11. Payment Procedure:

Borrowers can drawdown loans in one or a number of instalments with flexibility on their timing.

Repayment is normally by yearly or half-yearly instalments of principal and interest, after a capital repayment holiday to suit the needs of the project or borrower. There are early repayment possibilities for both floating and fixed-rate loans.

12. Points to Note:

The European Investment Bank is a banking institution whose shareholders are the Member Countries of the European Community. It raises most of its funds by borrowing on capital markets where it has an 'AAA' credit rating. The EIB can structure a facility in a flexible way to suit the debt financing requirements.

The facility can take the form of a loan or a guarantee; it can be made available on a direct basis, through an intermediary or through a lessor.

The EIB has arranged loan facilities for Barclays Bank, 3i Group and the Allied Irish Bank to help promote the long term financing of capital investment made by small and medium-sized enterprises (ie businesses with fewer than 500 employees, fixed assets up to £50 million and investment projects of up to £14 million) in the industrial and service sectors. Loans available as a result of this arrangement are made on the standard commercial terms set at the time of application by the intermediary financial institution concerned.

13. Application Procedure:

Application is made direct to the EIB.

14. Further Information:

Jos Van Kaam
European Investment Bank
100 Bvd. Konrad Adenauer
L-2950 Luxembourg
Tel: (010 35 2) 4379 5406
Telex: 0402 3530 BANKEU LU
Fax: (010 35 2) 43 77 04

Guy Baird
European Investment Bank
Liaison Office for the UK
68 Pall Mall
London SW1Y 5ES
Tel: (071) 839 3351
Telex: 919159 BANKEU G
Fax: (071) 930 9929

EUROPEAN REGIONAL DEVELOPMENT FUND (ERDF)

1. Summary:

The European Regional Development Fund (ERDF) is the European Commission's principal funding instrument for correcting regional imbalances within the Community. The basic tasks of the ERDF are as follows:

promoting the development and structural adjustment of underdeveloped regions (Objective 1); converting regions seriously affected by industrial decline (Objective 2); and participating in measures to promote the development of rural areas (Objective 5(b)). The ERDF can co-finance the following types of activities: productive investment linked to job-creation/maintenance; infrastructure investment; the development of indigenous potential (ie local development initiatives and services for small and medium-sized enterprises (SMEs)); operations planned in the context of regional development at Community level (eg frontier regions); studies and assessment measures. Activities financed by the ERDF can be undertaken within the context of regional operational programmes, the part-financing of national regional aid schemes, through individual project financing (infrastructure and productive investment – see 5), the provision of global grants to intermediaries (primarily in relation to local development initiatives) and direct support for studies and assessment measures related to ERDF operations.

ERDF financing is disbursed primarily through existing national aid schemes or through public sector intermediaries.

2. Awarding Body:
European Regional Development Fund (ERDF).

3. Location Restrictions:
Support is restricted to measures undertaken within regions designated by the Commission under one of the three Objectives with which the ERDF is concerned (see 1):

- Objective 1 regions (structurally backward) are generally designated at NUTS level II (equivalent to regions in the UK), and are targeted to receive 80 percent of the total budget of the three Structural Funds (see 12). Regions designated under Objective 1 for 1989–93 include: Northern Ireland, Southern Ireland, southern Italy, southern Spain, Portugal, Greece, the French overseas departments and Corsica.
- Objectives 2 (in industrial decline) and 5(b) (rural) regions are designated at NUTS level III (county or district in the UK).

In the UK, Objective 2 assistance for the period 1989–93 is restricted to the most seriously affected parts of the following Travel to Work Areas:

- In England: Alnwick & Amble, Morpeth & Ashington, Newcastle-upon-Tyne, South Tyneside, Sunderland, Bishop Auckland, Darlington, Durham, Hartlepool, Stockton-on-Tees, Middlesbrough, Doncaster, Goole & Selby (Selby portion excluded), Grimsby, Hull, Scunthorpe, Barnsley, Rotherham & Mexborough, Sheffield (excluding part in Derbyshire), Castleford & Pontefract, Wakefield & Dewsbury, Ashfield, parts of North-East Derbyshire district and Bolsover district in Alfreton and Ashfield TTWA; Gainsborough, Mansfield, Nottingham (urban programme area), Retford, Worksop, Chesterfield, Manchester, Oldham, Rochdale, Bolton & Bury, Wigan & St. Helens, Accrington & Rossendale, Blackburn, Burnley, Pendle, Liverpool, Widnes & Runcorn, Wirral & Chester, Birmingham, Coventry & Hinckley (Hinckley part excluded), Dudley & Sandwell (excluding part in Hereford), Wolverhampton, Walsall, Telford & Bridgenorth, Workington, Whitehaven;

- In Wales: Ebbw Vale & Abergavenny, Merthyr & Rhymney, Newport, Pontypool & Cwmbran, Aberdare, Pontypridd & Rhondda, Bridgend (excluding part in South Glamorgan), Neath & Port Talbot, Swansea, Llanelli, Flint & Rhyl, Wrexham, Cardiff (part only);
- In Scotland: Dunfermline, Kirkcaldy, Dundee, Arbroath, Alloa, Falkirk, Bathgate, Stirling, Glasgow, Dumbarton, Greenock, Irvine, Kilmarnock, Girvan, Ayr, Cumnock & Sanquhar, Lanarkshire, Midlothian Local Authority District (LAD) and part of East Lothian LAD (wards of East, Central, West and South Musselburgh, Tranent North, Tranent Ormiston, Carberry, West and East Prestonpans and Cockenzie).

Objective 5(b) assistance for the period 1989–93 is restricted to the following areas:

- In Scotland: Highlands and Islands Enterprise administrative area; Intermediate Areas of Dumfries and Galloway (excluding parts designated under Objective 2);
- In Wales: the counties of Dyfed, Powys and Gwynedd, excluding Llanelli, that part of the Conway and Colwyn TTWA in Gwynedd, and parts already designated under Objective 2;
- In England: Assisted Areas of Devon and Cornwall.

Separate provision has been made for ERDF financing to be available in the inner London boroughs of: Hackney, Islington, Lambeth, Tower Hamlets, Southwark, Lewisham and Newham.

Additional conditions apply to certain types of projects, depending on the particular Objective under which the region in question is designated (see 9).

4. Sectoral Restrictions:

Measures supported by the ERDF are jointly funded with an appropriate public authority eg local authorities, regional authorities, national governments.

Regulation (EEC) No 4254/88 requires that a significant proportion of applications submitted by each Member State is in respect of investment in industry, craft industry and services, particularly through the part-financing of aid schemes. Infrastructure investment is eligible provided it is financed wholly or partly by a public authority, or organisation responsible for infrastructure investment in the same way as a public authority. Investment in public buildings that is not linked to productive investment (eg social welfare, administrative, education and health), leisure not linked to tourism promotion, and house building is generally not eligible, although in Objective 1 regions it may be considered where a need is demonstrated (see 9).

Further restrictions to infrastructure investment also apply depending on the severity of the regional problem (ie whether designated Objective 1, 2 or 5(b) (see 9).

5. Size Restrictions:

For operational programmes submitted in respect of Objective 1 regions, the total cost must generally reach 100 million ECU, with annual average costs greater than 15 million ECU.

Direct assistance from the ERDF may be provided in respect of major projects provided the total project cost exceeds 15 million ECU for infrastructure investments or 10 million ECU for productive investments. Measures relating to the development of indigenous potential should be tailored to the requirements of small and medium-sized firms.

6. Programme Duration:

There is no specified terminal date for the activities of the ERDF. The scope of its operations are, however, reviewed periodically. The current Regulation (EEC) 4254/88 came into force on 1 January 1989.

7. Submission of Applications:

A Community Support Framework, drawn up on the basis of a regional development plan submitted by the national Government must be agreed before any applications for grant-aid can be considered. Thereafter, applications relating to expenditure incurred under an approved measure must generally be lodged with the Commission on or before the date the expenditure was incurred, except in the case of part-financing of projects and aid schemes, where applications must be submitted within six months of the date the expenditure was incurred.

8. Other Restrictions:

The relevant public authority (designated by the Member State) is required to draw up a regional development plan in relation to one or several regions designated under a particular Objective (see 3). Regional development plans are subsequently approved within the context of a Community Support Framework which specifies the measures eligible for assistance from the ERDF, and in the case of integrated programmes, from all participating Structural Funds and Community financial instruments (see 12). Assistance covered by a Community Support Framework is provided predominantly in the form of operational programmes.

Regional plans submitted in respect of Objectives 1 (structurally underdeveloped), 2 (industrial decline) and 5(b) (rural) regions must include employment and vocational training measures which are not covered under a plan submitted in respect of Objectives 3 (long-term unemployment) and 4 (youth unemployment – Social Fund applications). Plans may be revised on an annual basis.

Fund assistance must represent a genuine additional economic impact in the regions concerned and result in an equivalent increase in the total volume of official structural aid in the Member State concerned.

9. Eligible Expenditure:

Eligible expenditure for ERDF part-financing includes:

(a) productive investment linked to the creation or maintenance of permanent jobs;

(b) infrastructure investment: in Objective 1 regions, must increase economic potential, development or structural adjustment although where a need is demonstrated, certain non-economic facilities (eg health and education) may also be supported; in Objective 2 regions, must relate to the regeneration of the area concerned or provide the basis for the creation or development of economic activity; in Objective 5(b) regions, must be linked directly to economic activity which creates jobs other than in agriculture;

(c) indigenous potential – services for SMEs, technology transfer, improving access to the capital market (through guarantees and equity participation), direct investment aid (where no aid scheme exists), the provision of small-scale infrastructure.
(d) operations planned in the context of regional development at Community level (eg frontier regions);
(e) preparatory, accompanying and assessment measures necessary for the implementation of the ERDF Regulation carried out by the Commission or outside experts;
(f) productive investment and infrastructure investment aimed at environmental protection where such investment is linked to regional development.

10. Rate of Award:

The rate of award in respect of the various Objectives (see 1) is subject to the following ceilings:

- in Objective 1 regions, a maximum of 75 percent of total costs and, as a general rule, at least 50 percent of public expenditure on qualifying activities (not applicable to revenue-bearing investment);
- in Objective 2 and 5(b) regions, a maximum of 50 percent of total costs, and, as a general rule, at least 25 percent of public expenditure on qualifying activities.

Fund contributions to investments in firms may not exceed 50 percent of the total cost of the regions covered by Objective 1 and 30 percent of the total cost in other regions.

Rates of award for individual measures forming part of operational programmes are differentiated in accordance with agreements concluded in the relevant Community Support Framework. In determining the rate of support, the revenue generating capability of the investment is taken into account.

Preparatory studies and technical assistance measures undertaken on the initiative of the Commission may be financed at 100 percent of total costs in exceptional cases.

11. Payment Procedure:

Payment is normally made over to the public authority concerned (national or local) as a partial reimbursement for its contribution to the project.

For operations carried out over a period of two or more years, budgetary commitments are generally effected in annual instalments with the first instalment being made at the time the decision approving the operation is adopted by the Commission. An advance payment of up to 50 percent of the amount committed can be made at the start of the particular year. A second advance such that the total amount advanced does not exceed 80 percent may be made after the responsible authority has certified that at least half of the first advance has been used up and the operation is progressing satisfactorily. Payment of the balance is conditional upon the submission of a request for payment within six months of the end of the year concerned, or on the completion of the operation concerned, together with the necessary documentation to fulfil the Commission's reporting requirements.

In the case of studies, payments will be determined on a case-by-case basis.

12. Points to Note:

On the initiative of the Member State or the Commission, operational programmes which are the subject of an agreed Community Support Framework, may take the form of an 'integrated' operation where the programme involves financing by more than one Structural Fund or at least one Fund and one financial instrument other than a loan instrument.

Structural Funds which may participate in an integrated operation include the ERDF, the European Social Fund and the European Agricultural Guidance and Guarantee Fund: Guidance Section (EAGGF). Financial instruments include the European Coal and Steel Community and European Investment Bank. The relevant Community Support Framework will take in all acting partners within a single agreement. Framework Regulation (EEC) No 2052/88 governs the tasks of the Structural Funds and sets out the basic tasks of the ERDF in relation to the five Objectives agreed in the Single Act. Implementing Regulation (EEC) No 4254/88 specifies the activities which the ERDF can co-finance.

13. Application Procedure:

Applications and expenditure claims are submitted by the public authority concerned to the ERDF.

14. Further Information:

General Information:
Department of Trade and Industry
Investment, Development and Accountancy Services Division
Kingsgate House
68–72 Victoria Street
London SW1E 6SW
Tel: (071) 215 8517

Information on Opportunities in other Member States:
World Aid Section
Room 042
Department of Trade and Industry
1 Victoria Street
London SW1H 0ET
Tel: (071) 215 4279/5615
Fax: (071) 215 5637

In England:
(infrastructure projects)
Department of the Environment
Regional Policy B
2 Marsham Street
London SW1P 3EB
Tel: (071) 276 3815/3813

In Scotland:
Scottish Office Industry Department
Regional Policy Branch 3
New St Andrew's House
Edinburgh EH1 3TA
Tel: (031) 556 8400 Ext.5086/5309/5400

In Wales:
Welsh Office Industry Department
ERP2 (A)
New Crown Building
Cathays Park
Cardiff CF1 3NQ
Tel: (0222) 825111

In Northern Ireland:
Department of Economic Development
Netherleigh
Massey Avenue
Belfast BT4 2JP
Tel: (0232) 63244 Ext.297

ENVIREG (ENVIRONMENTAL PROTECTION IN THE REGIONS)

1. Summary:

ENVIREG offers grants and loans for projects tackling the environmental problems of the European Community's less developed regions. In particular, ENVIREG aims to: reduce pollution in coastal areas whose economies depend on tourism; provide land use planning in coastal areas to preserve natural beauty and protect and enhance biotopes; improve the control and management of toxic and hazardous industrial waste; and strengthen know-how relating to the above.

Measures funded under ENVIREG are only available in designated Objective 1 regions (Northern Ireland in the UK) and Mediterranean coastal regions covered by Objectives 2 and 5(b) (see 3).

ENVIREG has been allocated a budget of 500 MECU for the period 1990-93, and is implemented through operational programmes submitted by Member States, run mainly at a local level.

2. Awarding Body:

ENVIREG is funded from the budgets of the European Community's Structural Funds, ie the European Regional Development Fund (ERDF), European Social Fund (ESF) and European Agricultural Guidance and Guarantee Fund (EAGGF), in conjunction with Member State governments. Loans may also be available from the European Investment Bank (EIB).

3. Location Restrictions:

Assistance for pollution reduction, the promotion of land-use planning and related know-how will be available in Objective 1 coastal regions, and Mediterranean coastal regions covered by Objectives 2 and 5(b). (The eligible area being a zone starting at the coastline and extending inland not more than 10 km, except in duly justified cases.) Assistance for the control of toxic and hazardous industrial waste and related know-how is restricted to Objective 1 regions. Northern Ireland is the only region in the UK currently designated under Objective 1.

4. Sectoral Restrictions:

The programme is implemented mainly by local authorities in regions concerned.

5. Size Restrictions:

None.

6. Programme Duration:

ENVIREG is set to run from 1990 to 1993.

7. Submission of Applications:

Member States had until November 1990 to submit proposals for operational programmes to the European Commission. The operational programmes are implemented mainly by local authorities in the regions concerned.

8. Other Restrictions:

Possible actions under ENVIREG include:

1. Pollution reduction in coastal areas whose economies depend on tourism. Priority will be given to Mediterranean regions, especially areas experiencing rapid economic growth with serious environmental problems and subject to sharp sectoral population fluctuations. Actions may include: the construction or modernisation of infrastructure and equipment for the treatment of waste water (priority will be given to urban areas with less than 10,000 residents); the construction of infrastructure and equipment for the collection, treatment, storage, recycling and disposal of solid waste in urban areas; studies, soil analyses, technical assistance, agricultural extension services and demonstration projects relating to the agricultural use of compost/sludge from urban sewage; and port installations for storing and treating ships' ballast/washing/bilge water. (Priority will be given to projects undertaken jointly by more than one local authority.)
2. Land use planning for coastal areas: studies leading to regional land-use plans for coastal areas; schemes protecting biotopes while providing for tourism development; and the protection of biotopes in relation to agriculture;
3. Control and management of toxic and hazardous industrial waste: the construction of infrastructure and productive investments relating to the collection, treatment, storage and recycling of hazardous or toxic industrial waste; and studies to identify industrial activities giving rise to pollution;
4. Strengthening of know-how in connection with actions 1 to 3 above: feasibility studies determining appropriate treatment processes; service centres assisting local authorities with plant and equipment; facilitating the transfer of know-how between regional experts; and training measures.

9. Eligible Expenditure:

Eligible expenditure relates to the total cost of approved measures.

10. Rate of Award:

The rate of award is specified in the Commission decision on an operational programme, and depends on the quality of the programme and importance of the problems to be tackled.

11. Payment Procedure:

The Member State concerned is responsible for claiming payments from the Commission in respect of expenditure incurred under an agreed programme.

12. Points to Note:

The ENVIREG guidelines, and invitation for Member States to submit operational programmes were published in OJ C115; 9.5.90.

13. Application Procedure:

The UK government is required to apply to the Commission to receive approval for its own national programmes of assistance under ENVIREG. The Department of the Environment is coordinating UK projects.

14. Further Information:
Mr E Landaburu
DG XVI (Regional Policy)
European Commission
Rue de la Loi 200
B-1049 Brussels
Tel: (010 32 2) 235 1111

INTERREG (DEVELOPMENT OF BORDER AREAS)

1. Summary:

INTERREG offers grants and loans to assist border areas of the European Community overcome development problems arising from their isolated position. INTERREG promotes the creation and development of cooperation networks across internal borders, assists the adjustment of external border areas to their new role as border areas within the Single Market, and promotes cooperation with non-EC countries across external borders. Three types of action are undertaken: cross-border programmes; measures improving information flows; and initiatives to promote cooperation.

In the UK, Northern Ireland (excluding Belfast) and Kent are eligible for support.

INTERREG has been allocated a budget of 800 MECU for the period 1990–93 and is implemented through operational programmes submitted by Member States (see 8 for further details of the UK operational programmes).

2. Awarding Body:

INTERREG is funded from the budgets of the European Regional Development Fund (ERDF), European Social Fund (ESF), and European Agricultural Guidance and Guarantee Fund (EAGGF), in conjunction with Member State governments. Loans may also be available from the European Investment Bank (EIB).

3. Location Restrictions:

Eligible areas include all Objective 1, 2 and 5(b) regions along internal and external Community land borders delineated at sub-regional level. In the UK, Northern Ireland qualifies as an Objective 1 region (although Belfast is excluded).

Limited assistance may be offered to border areas not eligible under Objectives 1, 2 and 5(b); in the UK, Kent falls into this category. Within Kent, the coastal districts of Ashford, Canterbury, Dover, Shepway and Thanet are involved in the initiative.

4. Sectoral Restrictions:

The Commission gave priority to proposals made by Member State governments in cooperation with regional and local authorities in border areas including the establishment/development of shared institutional or administrative structures intended to extend cross-border cooperation between public agencies, private organisations and voluntary bodies.

5. Size Restrictions:
None.

6. Programme Duration:
INTERREG is set to run from 1990 to 1993.

7. Submission of Applications:
Member States had until February 1991 to submit proposals for operational programmes to the European Commission (or amendments to the previously agreed Community Support Frameworks, which outline Structural Fund spending in eligible regions).

8. Other Restrictions:
The INTERREG initiative in Kent involves a joint programme with Nord-Pas-de-Calais in France, covering the four coastal employment catchment areas of Boulogne, Calais, Dunkerque and St Omer. The programme has a budget of £15.4 million, and will be managed by a transfrontier committee made up of representatives of both British and French national and local government and the EC. Five sub-programmes are envisaged: Economic Development, promoting links and inter-trading between SMEs on both sides of the Channel and joint promotion of both regions; Education and Training, furthering educational links; Tourism, covering a number of initiatives; Transport and Telecommunications, including investment to harmonise standards such as road safety, and the installation of more efficient cable links; and Environment, including a range of projects.

9. Eligible Expenditure:
Eligible expenditure relates to the Member State's total public expenditure on eligible activities.

10. Rate of Award:
The rate of award is specified within each operational programme, and will depend on the quality of the programme and importance of the problems to be tackled.

11. Payment Procedure:
The Member State concerned is responsible for claiming payments from the Commission in respect of expenditure incurred under an agreed programme.

12. Points to Note:
The INTERREG guidelines, and invitation for Member States to submit operational programmes were published in OJ C215; 30.8.90.

13. Application Procedure:
Proposals relating to internal border areas in the Community had to be submitted in the form of a single operational programme by the two or more Member States concerned.

14. Further Information:

Mr Bill Smith
DG XVI/A/1
European Commission
Rue de la Loi 200
B-1049 Brussels
Tel: (010 32 2) 236 5255
Fax: (010 32 2) 236 2568

In Northern Ireland:
Department of Finance and Personnel
Parliament Buildings
Stormont
Belfast BT4 3UW
Tel: (0232) 63210

In Kent:
Kent County Council
Economic Development Department
Springfield
Maidstone
Kent ME14 2LT
Tel: (0622) 671411

LEADER (RURAL DEVELOPMENT)

1. Summary:

The LEADER initiative supports the promotion of networks of Local Rural Development Action Groups funding innovative solutions to rural development problems, which serve as a model for all rural areas. Three types of measure are eligible: those of direct benefit to the inhabitants and economy of the rural areas concerned; those concerning the establishment, equipment and management of the Local Groups; and those ensuring the operation of the network of groups.

The programme operates through global grants awarded to the Local Groups, who administer the funds and select projects for support (see 8 for further details). Thirteen Local Groups have been selected in the UK to administer LEADER funds.

LEADER is set to run from 1990 to 1993, with a budget allocation of 400 MECU.

2. Awarding Body:

LEADER is funded from the budgets of the European Regional Development Fund (ERDF), European Social Fund (ESF), and European Agricultural Guidance and Guarantee Fund (EAGGF), in conjunction with Member State governments.

3. Location Restrictions:

The programme applies to rural areas designated under Objectives 1 (underdeveloped) and 5(b) (rural) of the Structural Funds. In the UK, Northern Ireland is the only Objective 1 region; Objective 5(b) regions are as follows:

- In Scotland: Highlands and Islands Enterprise administrative area; Intermediate Areas of Dumfries and Galloway (excluding parts designated under Objective 2);
- In Wales: the counties of Dyfed, Powys and Gwynedd, excluding

Llanelli, that part of the Conway and Colwyn TTWA in Gwynedd, and parts already designated under Objective 2;

– In England: Assisted Areas of Devon and Cornwall.

The selected Local Rural Development Action Groups should cover a rural area with a population of between 5,000 and 100,000 people. Within this area, individual initiatives undertaken by the Groups may concern rural communities of a smaller size. Selected initiatives should serve as a model for all Objective 1 and 5(b) areas.

4. Sectoral Restrictions:

The Local Rural Development Action Groups taking part should: have expertise in the field of rural development; be local in character (ie local organising bodies or local branches of a regional body); and involve leading figures in the local economy and society. They may be in either the private or public sector.

5. Size Restrictions:

Local Groups should cover a rural area with a population of between 5,000 and 100,000 people.

6. Programme Duration:

LEADER is set to run from 1990 to 1993.

7. Submission of Applications:

Guidelines for integrated global grants were published in OJ C73; 19.3.91; Member States had to submit proposals for global grants, including a list of proposed Local Groups, within six months.

8. Other Restrictions:

Thirteen Local Groups have been selected to administer LEADER global grants in the UK:

In England: West Cornwall LEADER Group; and the North Tamar LEADER Group (covering North Cornwall/Devon);

In Wales: South Pembrokeshire Partnership, Menter Powys; Antur Teifi; and the South Gwynedd Enterprise Network;

In Scotland: Western Isles Enterprise and Skye and Lochalsh Enterprise; Caithness and Sutherland Enterprise; Shetland Enterprise; Lochaber Limited; Argyll and the Islands Enterprise; and Scottish Borders Enterprise;

In Northern Ireland: the Rural Development Council.

Three types of measure are eligible:

A. Measures benefitting the rural areas concerned, including:

1. Technical Support for rural development: technical assistance; and promotion of links with other EC measures/finance encouraging rural development in the area;
2. Vocational training and assistance for recruitment;
3. Rural tourism: identifying local project promoters, and facilitating: investment; measures to extend the tourist season; adaptation of small public works; listing, restoration and development of buildings and rural sites; market studies and promotion; reservation systems;
4. Small firms, craft enterprises and local services: identifying local project promoters, and facilitating assistance for working from home; access to

business services for small firms and craft enterprises; start-up aid for the establishment of local services needed in the area; and investment in craft industries (including those carried out in conjunction with farming and forestry);

5. Exploitation and marketing of local agriculture, forestry and fishery products; including market studies; plant and technical assistance for the production of local specialities; technology transfer; promotion of quality; and marketing. Priority will be given to collective and cooperative projects;
6. Other measures devised by the Groups, which contribute to rural development;

B. Measures concerning the establishment, equipment and management of the Local Groups themselves;

C. Measures concerning the operation of the transnational network of Groups.

9. Eligible Expenditure:

The rural development programme agreed with Local Groups outlines the types of measures which may receive assistance.

10. Rate of Award:

When allocating global grants to Member States, the Commission based its decision on: the extent of the rural areas of the regions proposed; the number of farm workers and farms; low population density; and geographical features of the areas concerned.

The rural development programme agreed with the Local Group outlines the rates for granting assistance.

11. Payment Procedure:

Global grants are paid over to appropriate national level bodies; the management of these grants is then delegated to the Local Groups, on the basis of the agreed local rural development programme. The agreed programme covers the types of measures to be undertaken, the criteria for selecting beneficiaries, the conditions and rates for granting assistance, and the specific provisions for monitoring utilisation of the global grant.

12. Points to Note:

Consideration must be given to the environmental impact of investments supported; those which generate pollution or damage rural landscapes are not eligible for support. Action supported under LEADER should complement measures under the relevant Community Support Framework for the region. An invitation to tender for the provision of technical assistance with the implementation of LEADER was published in OJ C76; 21.3.91; the deadline for tenders was 2 May 1991.

13. Application Procedure:

Further information on assistance programmes (if any) run in eligible areas is available from the Local Groups.

14. Further Information:

In England:

West Cornwall:
Mr Bill Bawden
West Cornwall LEADER Project
Rosewarne
Cambourne
Cornwall TR14 0AB
Tel: (0209) 716674

North Tamar:
Miss Jo Talbot
North Tamar LEADER Group
Bude
Cornwall EX23 8LG
Tel: (0288) 356888

In Wales:

South Gwynedd Enterprise Network:
Dafydd Wyn Jones
Antur Dwyryd Enterprises
11 Osmond Terrace
Penrhyndeudraeth
Gwynedd LL48 6PA
Tel: (0766) 771345
Fax: (0766) 771396

South Pembrokeshire Partnership for Action with Rural Communities (SPARC):
Mrs Joan Asby
The Old School
Station Road
Narbeth
Dyfed SA5N 8DU
Tel: (0834) 860965
Fax: (0834) 361547

Menter Powys:
Ms Liz Bickerton
Agriculture House
Royal Welsh Showground
Builth Wells
Powys
Tel: (0982) 552 224
Fax: (0982) 552 872

Antur Teifi:
Mr Wynford James
Teifi Valley Business Centre
Aberarad
Newcastle Emlyn
Dyfed SA38 9DB
Tel: (0239) 710238
Fax: (0239) 710358

In Scotland:

Skye & Lochalsh Enterprise
Bridge Road
Portree
Isle of Skye IV51 9GR
Tel: (0478) 2841
Fax: (0478) 2164

Caithness & Sutherland Enterprise
2 Princes Street
Thurso
Caithness KW14 7EQ
Tel: (0847) 66115
Fax: (0847) 63369

Shetland Enterprise
Toll Clock Shopping Centre
20 North Road
Lerwick
Shetland ZE1 0PE
Tel: (0595) 3177
Fax: (0595) 32081

Lochaber Limited
5 Cameron Square
Fort William PH33 6AJ
Tel: (0397) 702160/704326
Fax: (0397) 705309

Argyll & the Islands Enterprise
Stag Chambers
Lorne Street
Lochgilphead
Argyll PA31 8LU
Tel: (0546) 602281/602563
Fax: (0546) 603964

Scottish Borders Enterprise
Wheatlands Road
Galashiels TD1 2HQ
Tel: (0896) 58991
Fax: (0896) 58625

Western Isles Enterprise
3 Harbour View
Cromwell Street Quay
Stornoway
Isle of Lewis PA87 2DF
Tel: (0851) 703905
Fax: (0851) 704130

In Northern Ireland:
Rural Development Council
Newry Tel: (0693) 63053
Enniskillen Tel: (0365) 325004
Ballymeena Tel: (0266) 44121

PRISMA (PREPARING FOR THE SINGLE MARKET)

1. Summary:
The PRISMA initiative (Preparing Enterprises for the Single Market) aims to help firms in Objective 1 regions of the Community adapt to the completion of the Single Market so that they can fully benefit from any opportunities arising. The specific objectives are: to support the development of certification and testing infrastructures (in particular, creating or strengthening calibration and metrology services enabling business to have access to or possess facilities and services needed to show potential clients that they are able to comply with technical quality standards) and the preparation of small and medium-sized firms for the opening up of public procurement and the Single Market (see 8 for further details). Grants and loans will be available within the framework of operational programmes drawn up by Member States.

PRISMA is set to run from 1991 to 1993 with a budget of 100 MECU. Northern Ireland has been allocated a budget of £4 million.

2. Awarding Body:
Commission of the European Communities.

3. Location Restrictions:
In the UK, Northern Ireland is the only region eligible for assistance under PRISMA.

4. Sectoral Restrictions:
None.

5. Size Restrictions:
None.

6. Programme Duration:
PRISMA is set to run from 1991 to 1993, although the programme may be extended after 1993.

7. Submission of Applications:

Assistance takes place within the framework of operational programmes drawn up by Member States. Guidelines for the drawing up of operational programmes were published in OJ C33; 8.2.91; Member States had six months in which to submit programmes to the Commission for approval.

8. Other Restrictions:

Member States should choose a more limited set of measures from the following list:

1. Creation and strengthening of structures for calibration and metrology and related services: the creation or modernisation of installations for testing laboratories; expenditure related to the control, by accredited bodies, of technical equipment in testing laboratories and enterprises; start-up costs for accreditation bodies for calibration and metrology laboratories; and consultation fees paid by businesses with a view to adjusting production methods so that their products conform to Community policy on certification and quality assurance.
2. Technical assistance to small and medium-sized firms: (a) operating expenditure and facilities for local bodies whose aim it is to set up or develop the following services related to public procurement: selection and distribution of information in a form adapted to the needs and capacities of firms on the basis of TED (Tenders Electronic Daily) and other more detailed sources of public tender information; information on national quality systems, Community testing and certification standards, legal and procedural obligations in other Member States; where appropriate, information on R & D results relating to products intended for public sector markets, information on new market opportunities, exhibitions, seminars or conferences related to public procurement; and other support and advisory services; (b) assistance to SMEs for costs related to cooperation with other firms in the field of public tenders; registration and admission to lists of qualified tenderers; translation and other costs related to a response to public tenders outside the area where firms are located; (c) other assistance designed to improve competitiveness of SMEs in Objective 1 regions.

9. Eligible Expenditure:

Eligible expenditure will vary according to the measure undertaken.

10. Rate of Award:

The amount of the EC contribution to an operational programme will depend on the quality of the programme and the needs of the region, taking into account the additional facilities and services required to enable the region's industry to participate fully in the Single Market.

11. Payment Procedure:

Payment procedure will vary according to the measure undertaken.

12. Points to Note:

Guidelines for the operational programmes established by Member States were published in OJ C33; 8.2.91.

Loans from the European Investment Bank may also be made available under PRISMA. Operational programmes should be drawn up with regard for measures relating to industry already financed within the Community Support Frameworks outlining Structural Fund assistance (ie the European Regional Development Fund, the European Social Fund, and the European Agricultural Guidance and Guarantee Fund).

13. Application Procedure:
Operational Programmes are submitted by Member States to the European Commission for approval.

14. Further Information:

Mr E Landaburu
European Commission
DG XVI
200 rue de la Loi
B-1049 Brussels
Tel: (010 32 2) 299 1111

Department of Economic Development
The Arches Centre
11/13 Bloomfield Avenue
Belfast BT5 5HD
Tel: (0232) 732411

RECHAR (COAL PRODUCING AREAS)

1. Summary:
RECHAR, a Community Programme financed from the European Regional Development Fund (ERDF), aims to assist the restructuring of coal mining areas.

The objective of RECHAR is to regenerate local economies through support for small and medium-sized firms and the introduction of new technologies and alternative industries in mining areas. It operates by co-financing public sector measures undertaken by Member State public authorities. In the UK, RECHAR will contribute to expenditure on Regional Enterprise Grants, a £14 million scheme of business support measures (in England), and business development schemes run by Local Enterprise Companies (LECs) in Scotland (see 8 for further details).

RECHAR has been allocated a budget of 300 MECU for the period 1990–94. This budget has now been fully allocated between Member States. Of the total, the UK was allocated 174.9 MECU (£124.2 million).

2. Awarding Body:
RECHAR is funded by the European Regional Development Fund (ERDF) and European Social Fund (ESF), through the Department of Trade and Industry, Scottish Office and Welsh Office.

The European Coal and Steel Community (ECSC) also provides funding in the form of redeployment aids and interest subsidised loans, under Article 56 of the ECSC Treaty.

3. Location Restrictions:
Available in coal mining areas located in areas eligible under Objectives 1, 2 or 5(b) of the Structural Funds which meet the following criteria:

1. strong dependency of the area's economy on coal mining activity;

2. significant job losses in the coal mining industry in the past and/or expected job losses which are likely to worsen the regional unemployment situation.

RECHAR may also apply in areas not eligible under Objective 1, 2 or 5(b) provided they meet the above criteria and have an unemployment rate at or above the Community average, taking into account likely increases in unemployment as a consequence of expected job losses.

Eligible UK areas include:

In England:

- Derbyshire/Nottinghamshire: part of North-East Derbyshire District; Mansfield TTWA; Worksop TTWA; Chesterfield TTWA; the part of Bolsover District in Alfreton and Ashfield TTWA; Ashfield District; Retford TTWA; and part of Nottingham City;
- Durham/Tyne and Wear: part of Newcastle-upon-Tyne TTWA (excluding the urban programme areas of Newcastle-upon-Tyne and Gateshead); Sunderland TTWA; part of Hartlepool TTWA (Easington District); Durham TTWA; and South Tyneside TTWA;
- Greater Manchester/Merseyside: Wigan and St Helens TTWA; Knowsley District; and part of Salford District;
- North and West Yorkshire: Castleford and Pontefract TTWA; Wakefield and Dewsbury TTWA;
- Northumberland: part of Alnwick District; part of Castle Morpeth District; Morpeth and Ashington TTWA;
- South Yorkshire: Doncaster TTWA; Rotherham and Mexborough TTWA; Barnsley TTWA; part of Sheffield TTWA (Rotherham District);
- Staffordshire: the Objective 2 part of Cannock Chase District; part of Lichfield District; part of Wolverhampton TTWA; and part of South Staffordshire District (the part in Walsall TTWA);
- Warwickshire: North Warwickshire District and Nuneaton and Bedworth District;

In Wales:

- Dyfed: Llanelli TTWA; Swansea TTWA (except Swansea District);
- Gwent: Blaenau Gwent District; Islwyn District; Torfaen District;
- Mid Glamorgan: part of Bridgend TTWA; part of Cardiff TTWA (Rhymney Valley District); Merthyr and Rhymney Valley TTWA; Pontypridd and Rhondda TTWA;
- Powys: Aberdare TTWA and Swansea TTWA;
- West Glamorgan: Neath and Port Talbot TTWA; Lliw Valley District;

In Scotland:

- Central: the Part of Stirling LAD (Local Authority District) eligible under Objective 2; Clackmannon LAD;
- Dumfries: Cumnock and Sanquhar TTWA;
- Fife: Kirkcaldy LAD; Dunfermline LAD;
- Lothian: Bathgate TTWA; Midlothian LAD; and part of East Lothian LAD;
- Strathclyde: Cumnock and Doon Valley LAD; part of Motherwell LAD; part of Clydesdale LAD; and part of Kyle and Carrick LAD.

4. Sectoral Restrictions:
Assistance under RECHAR is targeted at small and medium-sized firms.

5. Size Restrictions:
Support channelled to the private sector is available for the promotion of small and medium-sized firms.

6. Programme Duration:
RECHAR has been adopted to run for the period 1990 to 1994.

7. Submission of Applications:
Member States had to submit their proposals for eligible areas to the Commission by 27 February 1990; the Commission then determined and published a list of eligible areas (OJ C177; 18.7.90). Member States with eligible areas were required to submit detailed proposals for operational programmes within six months.

8. Other Restrictions:
In the UK, the following measures are co-financed by RECHAR:
- In England, a new £14 million scheme of business support measures will be set up, subject to EC approval. DTI Regional Offices will be able to select the most suitable assistance to meet each coalfield area's needs, from a range of authorised measures. These include support for: economic promotion agencies and local community initiatives (eg local task forces, business clubs); the provision of common services and feasibility studies relating to the provision of managed workspace and business accommodation; encouragement of innovation in industry and its commercial application in SMEs; assistance of risk appraisal by non-profit making organisations; and information provision to SMEs to improve access to markets;
- In Scotland, the LECs have been invited to promote business development schemes of their own, tailored to local circumstances;
- In Wales, Regional Enterprise Grants (Investment) have been extended to cover designated RECHAR areas;
- In addition, Regional Enterprise Grants (Innovation) have been extended to cover designated RECHAR areas throughout the UK.

9. Eligible Expenditure:
Eligible expenditure co-financed under RECHAR relates to the Member State's total public expenditure on eligible activities.

10. Rate of Award:
RECHAR contributes 50 percent of the costs of agreed measures undertaken by the national government concerned.

11. Payment Procedure:
The national government concerned is responsible for claiming payments from the European Commission in respect of expenditure incurred under an agreed programme.

12. Points to Note:
The distribution of RECHAR funds in the UK has been allocated as follows: South Yorkshire £22.9 million; East Midlands £21.7 million; South Wales

£21.1 million; Southeast, Tyne and Wear and Northumberland £12.3 million; Mid Yorkshire £11.7 million; Eastern Scotland £11.4 million; County Durham £8.7 million; Lancashire £5.9 million; Southern Staffordshire £3.6 million; Western Scotland £2.8 million; Northern Warwickshire £2.1 million.

13. Application Procedure:

The UK Government is required to apply to the Commission to receive approval for its own national programmes of assistance under RECHAR and undertake their complete administration. For individual firms, in respect of whose projects the DTI may subsequently be reimbursed, application procedure is as set out under the relevant assistance scheme.

14. Further Information:

In England, DTI Regional offices:

North East (091) 232 4722	East Midlands (0602) 506181
North West (061) 236 2171	West Midlands (021) 631 6181
York & Humber (0532) 443171	South East (071) 215 5000
East (0223) 461941	South West (0272) 272666

Welsh Office Industry Department (0222) 825111
Scottish Office Industry Department (041) 248 2855

European Commission
DG XVI – RECHAR
Rue de la Loi 200
B-1049 Brussels
Tel: (010 32 2) 299 1111
Telex: 21877 COMEU B

Department of Trade and Industry
Kingsgate House
68–72 Victoria Street
London SW1E 6SW
Tel: (071) 215 8517

RENAVAL (SHIPBUILDING AREAS)

1. Summary:

RENAVAL, a Community Programme financed from the European Regional Development Fund (ERDF), aims to assist the conversion of declining industrial regions adversely affected by the restructuring of the shipbuilding industry. It operates by co-financing public sector measures undertaken by Member State public authorities.

The purpose of RENAVAL is to contribute to the development of new, job-creating economic activities through measures to improve infrastructure and environment in the areas concerned, as well as the establishment of new activities, the growth of small and medium-sized enterprises, the development of innovation, and investment in tourism activities. Under RENAVAL, the ERDF may contribute to schemes to aid industry and infrastructure projects. In the UK, RENAVAL will contribute to expenditure on infrastructure projects and Regional Enterprise Grants and the Enterprise Initiative.

2. Awarding Body:

European Regional Development Fund through the Department of Trade and Industry, Department of the Environment and the Scottish Office.

3. Location Restrictions:

Available in regions of the European Community adversely affected by the restructuring of the shipbuilding industry. To be eligible for RENAVAL funding, the area must satisfy certain criteria relating to job losses in the shipbuilding industry, dependency on the shipbuilding industry for employment, and the extent to which the socio-economic situation in the region in which the area is located is characterised by particular employment difficulties.

Member States were required to submit to the European Commission applications supporting the designation of areas eligible under RENAVAL as and when areas satisfied the criteria set out in Article 3 of the RENAVAL Regulation. In the UK, the following areas are eligible:

- Plymouth TTWA (Travel to Work Area): Plymouth City, part of the district of South Hams, Caradon and West Devon;
- Fife: Kirkcaldy TTWA, Dunfermline TTWA (excluding West and East Kinross wards) and the Kincardine/Culross ward of Alloa TTWA;
- Strathclyde: Glasgow and Greenock TTWAs;
- Teesside: Tyne and Wear, Middlesbrough and Langbaurgh districts.
- Merseyside: Wirral and Sefton districts.

4. Sectoral Restrictions:

The purpose of RENAVAL is to support diversification from the shipbuilding sector into other activities. Activities in the shipbuilding sector are not, therefore, eligible for assistance. Private firms cannot qualify directly under RENAVAL; assistance is provided, in the first instance, to public, local and regional authorities.

Local and regional development corporations, other businesses, cooperatives or self-employed persons may benefit indirectly through participation in measures and projects undertaken by those authorities.

5. Size Restrictions:

Support channelled to the private sector is available for the promotion of small and medium-sized enterprises. In the UK this will generally be those firms with fewer than 500 employees but in certain instances fewer than 25 employees. Local and public authorities are not so restricted.

6. Programme Duration:

RENAVAL is set to run from 16 August 1988 to 31 December 1993. Member States had until 30 April 1990 to submit applications supporting the designation of areas eligible under RENAVAL.

7. Submission of Applications:

Member States are required to submit a programme of assistance within six months of the Commission's decision on the application for eligibility of a given area.

The Member State administers any regional aid schemes approved under the programme and reclaims the ERDF contribution against its expenditure. Applications for infrastructure projects can be submitted at any time.

8. Other Restrictions:

In the UK, RENAVAL will be used to contribute to national aid schemes to industry, and infrastructure projects which satisfy the criteria set out in the

RENAVAL Regulation (EEC) No 2506/88 (published in Official Journal No L33; 5.02.88).

9. Eligible Expenditure:

Eligible expenditure co-financed under RENAVAL relates to the Member State's total public expenditure on eligible activities.

10. Rate of Award:

Assistance under RENAVAL may not exceed 55 percent of the total public expenditure taken into account in a programme. With respect to infrastructure projects, ERDF participation is restricted to 50 percent of public expenditure.

11. Payment Procedure:

The national government concerned is responsible for claiming payments from the ERDF in respect of expenditure already incurred under an agreed programme.

12. Points to Note:

None.

13. Application Procedure:

The UK Government is required to apply to the Commission to receive approval for its own national programmes of assistance under RENAVAL and to undertake their complete administration. For individual firms, in respect of whose projects the DTI may subsequently be reimbursed, application procedure is as set out under the relevant assistance schemes.

14. Further Information:

Merseyside:
DTI North-West
Sunley Tower
Piccadilly Plaza
Manchester M1 4BA
Tel: (061) 838 5000
Fax: (061) 228 3740

Teeside:
DTI North-East
Stanegate House
2 Groat Market
Newcastle upon Tyne
NE1 1YN
Tel: (091) 232 4722
Fax: (091) 232 6742

Plymouth:
DTI South-West
5th Floor
The Pithay
Bristol BS1 2PB
Tel: (0272) 272666
Fax: (0272) 299494

Strathclyde and Fife:
Scottish Office Industry Department
European Fund Division
New St Andrews House
St James Centre
Edinburgh EH1 3TA
Tel: (031) 244 4611
Fax: (031) 244 4785

RESIDER (STEEL PRODUCING AREAS)

1. Summary:

RESIDER, a Community Programme financed from the European Regional Development Fund (ERDF), aims to assist the conversion of industrial regions affected by the restructuring of the steel industry. It operates by co-financing public sector measures undertaken by Member State public authorities.

The purpose of RESIDER is to contribute to the development of new, job-creating economic activities through measures to improve infrastructure and the environment in the areas concerned, as well as the establishment of new activities, the growth of small and medium-sized enterprises, the development of innovation, and investment in tourism activities.

In the UK, RESIDER contributes to expenditure on infrastructure projects, Regional Enterprise Grants and the Enterprise Initiative.

2. Awarding Body:

European Regional Development Fund through the Department of Trade and Industry and the Department of the Environment.

3. Location Restrictions:

Available in regions of the European Community adversely affected by the restructuring of the steel industry. To be eligible for RESIDER funding, the area must satisfy certain criteria relating to the number of jobs in the steel industry, dependency on the steel industry for employment, major job losses in the steel industry, and the extent to which the socio-economic situation in the region in which the area concerned is located is characterised by particular employment difficulties.

Member States were required to submit to the European Commission applications supporting the designation of areas eligible under RESIDER as and when areas satisfied the criteria set out in Article 4.1 of the RESIDER regulation.

In the UK, the county of South Yorkshire (including the Sheffield Travel to Work Area) and the Scunthorpe TTWA are the only areas which met the criteria of the RESIDER Regulation.

4. Sectoral Restrictions:

The purpose of RESIDER is to support diversification from the steel sector into other activities. Activities in the steel sector are not, therefore, eligible for assistance. Private firms cannot qualify directly under RESIDER, assistance is provided, in the first instance, to local and regional authorities. Local and regional development corporations, other businesses, cooperatives or self-employed persons may benefit indirectly through participation in measures and projects undertaken by those authorities.

5. Size Restrictions:

Support channelled to the private sector is available for the promotion of small and medium-sized enterprises. In the UK this will generally be those with fewer than 500 employees but in certain instances fewer than 25 employees. Local and public authorities are not so restricted.

6. Programme Duration:

RESIDER is set to run from February 1988 to 31 December 1992. Member States had until 30 April 1990 to submit applications supporting the designation of areas eligible under RESIDER.

7. Submission of Applications:

Member States were required to submit a programme of assistance within six months of the Commission's decision on the application for eligibility of a given area.

The Member State administers any regional aid schemes approved under the programme and reclaims the ERDF contribution against its expenditure. Applications for infrastructure projects can be submitted at any time.

8. Other Restrictions:

In the UK, RESIDER will be used to contribute to national aid schemes to industry and infrastructure projects which satisfy the criteria set out in the RESIDER regulation (EEC) No 328/88 (published in Official Journal No L33; 5.02.88).

The programme is used to extend Regional Enterprise Grants (REGs) for investment and innovation to eligible companies located in the Barnsley, Sheffield and Doncaster Intermediate Areas of South Yorkshire. REGs are normally only available in the Development Areas of Great Britain.

9. Eligible Expenditure:

Eligible expenditure co-financed under RESIDER relates to the Member State's total public expenditure on eligible activities.

10. Rate of Award:

Assistance under RESIDER may not exceed 55 percent of the total public expenditure taken into account in a programme. With respect to infrastructure projects, ERDF participation is restricted to 50 percent of public expenditure.

11. Payment Procedure:

The national government concerned is responsible for claiming payments from the ERDF in respect of expenditure already incurred under an agreed programme.

12. Points to Note:

None.

13. Application Procedure:

The UK Government is required to apply to the Commission to receive approval for its own national programmes of assistance under RESIDER and undertake their complete administration. For individual firms, in respect of whose projects the DTI may subsequently be reimbursed, application procedure is as set out under the relevant assistance scheme.

14. Further Information:

European Commission
DG XVI
Rue de la Loi 200
B-1049 Brussels
Tel: (010 32 2) 299 1111
Telex: 21877 COMEU B

DTI Yorkshire and Humberside
25 Queen Street
Leeds LS1 2TW
Tel: (0532) 443171
Fax: (0532) 338301

RETEX (TEXTILE PRODUCING AREAS)

1. Summary:

The RETEX programme aims to promote the diversification of economic activities in regions heavily dependent on the textiles and clothing sectors. The objective is to enable the regions to become less dependent on the sector, and encourage the adjustment of business.

RETEX has been allocated a budget of 100 MECU for 1993, and an estimated budget of 400 MECU for the period 1994 to 1997. The programme will be implemented through operational programmes submitted by Member States; assistance is likely to be channelled through regional or local authorities.

2. Awarding Body:

European Regional Development Fund (ERDF).

3. Location Restrictions:

Available in regions of the European Community which are heavily dependent on the textile and clothing sector, and which are already eligible for assistance from the ERDF under Objectives 1, 2 and 5(b).

Each Member State will decide on the precise demarcation of recipient areas.

4. Sectoral Restrictions:

None specified.

5. Size Restrictions:

None specified.

6. Programme Duration:

RETEX is set to run from 1993 to 1997.

7. Submission of Applications:

Member States are required to submit an operational programme within six months of the publication of the RETEX guidelines (OJ C142; 4.6.92).

8. Other Restrictions:

Possible measures under RETEX include:

(i) improving know-how by providing business with aid to pay for advisory services, and the equipment (excluding machines for production) to put the advice into practice, in the fields of design, quality control, computer-aided manufacturing and planning, marketing and internal business organisation, and health and safety;

(ii) aid for the formation of local associations of businesses and other cooperation schemes to: improve know-how as described under (i) above; accelerate the spread of innovative production methods and new forms of business organisation; research and development; marketing and product diversification; strengthening links between firms and their suppliers and customers; improving information on market trends; and creating networks of contacts;

(iii) the setting-up of a team to provide ideas and advice to SMEs;

(iv) temporary contributions towards paying engineers, technical staff and managers recruited to help implement modernisation plans drawn up with the assistance of outside experts;

(v) vocational training schemes for staff of businesses, associations of businesses and providers of joint services in eligible regions, and for staff in textile or clothing firms faced with redundancy or already unemployed;

(vi) the rehabilitation of industrial wasteland, including restoring redundant industrial buildings; aid to reduce pollution caused by industry, especially aid to facilitate the treatment and recycling of liquid effluent and industrial waste, and for technical assistance to promote the development of less polluting production and maintenance processes;

(viii) improving access to venture capital and loans.

9. Eligible Expenditure:

Not specified.

10. Rate of Award:

The level of assistance provided by the EC to each Member State will depend on the current level of employment in the textiles and clothing sector in eligible regions.

11. Payment Procedure:

The national government concerned will be responsible for claiming payments from the Commission in respect of expenditure incurred under an agreed programme.

12. Points to Note:

Qualifying measures in a given area will complement the measures already undertaken in the relevant Community Support Framework.

13. Application Procedure:

Assistance is likely to be channelled through public-sector organisations in the region concerned.

14. Further Information:

European Commission
DG XVI
Rue de la Loi 200
B-1049 Brussels
Tel: (010 32 2) 299 1111

Department of Trade and Industry
Kingsgate House
68–72 Victoria Street
London SW1E 6SW
Tel: (071) 215 8517

STRIDE (REGIONAL RESEARCH AND DEVELOPMENT)

1. Summary:

STRIDE supports the improvement of regional capabilities for research and technological development and innovation.

Three categories of projects are eligible for grant support: A. Strengthening the research facilities in Objective 1 regions; B. Promoting greater participation in EC and other international research programmes and networks; and C. Promotion of linkages between research centres and industry. STRIDE has been allocated a budget of 400 MECU for the period 1990–93. The UK budget is £11.5 million for Objective 2 regions and £10 million for Northern Ireland. STRIDE is implemented through operational programmes submitted by Member States (see 8 for further details of implementation in the UK).

2. Awarding Body:

STRIDE is funded from the budgets of the European Community's European Regional Development Fund (ERDF) and European Social Fund (ESF) in conjunction with Member State governments. Loans may also be issued to further the objectives of the programme through the European Investment Bank (EIB) and European Coal and Steel Community (ECSC).

3. Location Restrictions:

Assistance for measures A and B (see 8) will be available in regions eligible under Objective 1 of the Structural Funds (structurally underdeveloped regions). Northern Ireland is the only region in the UK currently designated under Objective 1.

Assistance for measure C will be available in regions eligible under Objectives 1 and 2 (regions in industrial decline). For a full list of UK Objective 2 regions, see European Regional Development Fund (ERDF). Organisations applying for funding do not have to be located in Objective 2 regions, but the benefits of the project must be. Projects can also cover non-Objective 2 regions, but only those parts within Objective 2 regions will be eligible for funding.

4. Sectoral Restrictions:

Assistance is available to industrial, commercial, educational and research establishments.

5. Size Restrictions:

None.

6. Programme Duration:
STRIDE is set to run from 1990 to 1993.

7. Submission of Applications:
The last deadline for applications from organisations in Objective 2 regions was 2 October 1992; the next closing date is expected in early 1993. The deadline for applications in Northern Ireland was 27 March 1992.

8. Other Restrictions:
In Northern Ireland, assistance is available for a wide range of projects, including: research facilities; promotion of participation in international research programmes and networks; collaboration between research centres and companies; improvements in technology transfer from research project through to the production process.

In Objective 2 regions, grants are available for projects under the following four measures (Great Britain budget allocation in brackets):

1. Encouraging small and medium enterprise to make greater use services and specialist expertise in Higher Education Institutions and other research centres (8.88 MECU);
2. Expansion of the activities of local centres set up to support regional innovatory and technology transfer capacity (8.88 MECU);
3. Promoting a greater level of regional R&D activity (2.95 MECU); and
4. Assisting education and training activities which facilitate the other three measures (2.18 MECU).

Emphasis is placed on meeting regional and local needs through pump-priming and making existing networks more effective. The programme will concentrate on objectives which are most directly aimed at promoting technology transfer and innovation.

9. Eligible Expenditure:
Eligible expenditure includes labour costs, overheads (limited to 100 percent of direct labour costs) and materials consumed during the project. Ineligible costs include input VAT, audits, and legal and non-essential costs.

10. Rate of Award:
The rate of award is between 50 and 75 percent of costs in Objective 1 regions, and up to 50 percent of costs in Objective 2 regions. The minimum funding in Objective 2 regions is £50,000, ie eligible costs of the project must be £100,000.

11. Payment Procedure:
Member States are responsible for claiming payments from the Commission in respect of expenditure incurred under an agreed operational programme.

Funding may also take the form of a global grant disbursed to an intermediary in the Member State concerned.

12. Points to Note:
STRIDE will complement and coordinate with other Community activities supporting research and development, especially those within the regional Community Support Frameworks (CSFs), the Framework Programme for RTD, and the SPRINT and COMETT programmes.

The STRIDE guidelines and invitation to Member States to submit operational programmes were published in OJ C196; 4.8.90.

13. Application Procedure:

Application details are available from the UK coordinators (see 14).

14. Further Information:

Ms S Platteuw
STRIDE Programme Secretariat
DTI
Bay 317
Kingsgate House
66–74 Victoria Street
London SW1E 6SW
Tel: (071) 215 2555
Fax: (071) 215 8779

In Yorkshire and Humberside:
Mrs G Timmons
DTI
25 Queen Street
Leeds LLS1 2TW
Tel: (0532) 443171 Ext.341
Fax: (0532) 338301/2

North East:
Mr A Reed
DTI
Stanegate House
3 Groat Market
Newcastle-upon-Tyne NE1 1YN
Tel: (091) 232 4722 Ext.2235
Fax: (091) 232 6742

East Midlands:
Mr D Jones
DTI
Severns House
20 Middle Pavement
Nottingham NG1 7DW
Tel: (0602) 506323
Fax: (0602) 587074

North West:
Mr J Law
DTI
Sunley Tower
Piccadilly Plaza
Manchester M1 4BA
Tel: (061) 236 2171 Ext.5315
Fax: (061) 228 3740

West Midlands:
Dr A Hickman
DTI
77 Paradise Circus
Queensway
Birmingham B1 2DT
Tel: (021) 212 5175
Fax: (021) 212 1010

In Northern Ireland:
Mrs Pat Gorman
Technology Division
Department of Economic Development
Netherleigh
Massey Avenue
Belfast BT4 2JP
Tel: (0232) 763244 Ext.2498

In Scotland:
Mr D Fennessey
SOID
Alhambra House
45 Waterloo Street
Glasgow G2 6AT
Tel: (041) 242 5560
Fax: (041) 242 5404

TELEMATIQUE (ADVANCED TELECOMMS SERVICES)

1. Summary:

The TELEMATIQUE initiative promotes the use of advanced telecommunications services in disadvantaged regions, particularly through improving access to advanced services available elsewhere in the Community. The initiative will reinforce action undertaken through the STAR programme, and will support the setting up of data communications services of value to SMEs, and assist SMEs to create or develop such services themselves. TELEMATIQUE also supports the development of telecommunications in the public sector, where they will contribute to regional development. The emphasis of the initiative is on services rather than infrastructure investment, except where this is directly linked to the promotion of services. The implementation of TELEMATIQUE in each Member State will depend on the priorities agreed with the European Commission in an Operational Programme. In the UK, Northern Ireland is the only region eligible for assistance.

TELEMATIQUE is set to run from 1991–1993 with a budget of 200 MECU. Northern Ireland has been allocated a budget of £4 million.

2. Awarding Body:

Operational Programmes are funded jointly by the Industrial Development Board for Northern Ireland and the European Regional Development Fund.

3. Location Restrictions:

In the UK, Northern Ireland is the only region eligible for assistance under the TELEMATIQUE programme.

4. Sectoral Restrictions:

None.

5. Size Restrictions:

None.

6. Programme Duration:

TELEMATIQUE is set to run from 1991 until 1993.

7. Submission of Applications:

The Industrial Development Board for Northern Ireland is responsible for the implementation of the programme, for issuing contracts and for claiming assistance from the ERDF.

8. Other Restrictions:

The implementation of TELEMATIQUE in each Member State will depend on the priorities outlined in the Operational Programme agreed with the European Commission. Measures may relate to the following areas:

1. Development of the use by SMEs of services linked to advanced telecommunications systems and of the supply of such services to SMEs;
2. Development of services in the public sector for data communication likely to contribute to regional development;
3. Development of networks in Objective 1 regions and between these regions and the rest of the Community.

9. Eligible Expenditure:
Operational Programmes are jointly financed by the European Commission and the Member State.

10. Rate of Award:
Assistance from the ERDF may not exceed 55 percent of the total public expenditure taken into account in the programme.

11. Payment Procedure:
Payment will be made over to the Industrial Development Board in Northern Ireland to be passed on as appropriate.

12. Points to Note:
Guidelines for Member States drawing up Operational Programmes were published in OJ C33; 8.2.91.

13. Application Procedure:
Not relevant.

14. Further Information:

Mr Alan Hingston
Industrial Development Board
IDB House
64 Chichester Street
Belfast BT1 4JX
Tel: (0232) 233 233

Fernando Toledano
European Commission
DG XIII
Rue de la Loi 200
B-1049 Brussels
Tel: (010 32 2) 236 0235

TRANSPORT INFRASTRUCTURE ACTION PROGRAMME

1. Summary:
The European Commission's action programme in the field of transport infrastructure aims to coordinate and promote infrastructure projects of Community interest, creating a modern and efficient EC transport network. Financial assistance is aimed at: the elimination of bottlenecks; the integration of landlocked or peripheral areas; the reduction of costs associated with transit traffic; the improvement of links on land/sea routes; and the provision of high-quality links between the major urban centres, including high-speed rail links with a view to the completion of an integrated transport market in 1992. The programme funds: feasibility studies or preparatory work for infrastructure projects; related schemes; and the development of part or the whole of a project. Support for transport infrastructure projects takes the form of subsidies, or in exceptional cases, any other form of support felt to be appropriate.

Project proposals are put forward by central governments of Member States, who then place contracts with industry for projects approved by the Commission.

2. Awarding Body:
Commission of the European Communities.

3. Location Restrictions:
Specific individual projects selected for support must be components of the following major projects:

1. Contribution to the high-speed rail network linking: Paris–London–Brussels–Amsterdam–Cologne and connecting lines to other Member States; Seville–Madrid–Barcelona–Lyons–Turin/Milan–Venice and from there to Tarvisio and Trieste; Oporto–Lisbon–Madrid;
2. The Alpine transit route (Brenner route);
3. Contribution to the combined transport network of Community interest;
4. International trans-Pyrenean road links (Somport);
5. The road link with Ireland (A5/A55 North Wales coast road) and the improvement of the Dublin–Belfast cross-border railway line;
6. The Scanlink;
7. The strengthening of land communications in Greece.

4. Sectoral Restrictions:
None.

5. Size Restrictions:
Support is limited to projects of such a scale that they present particular difficulties for financing, and cannot be financed by national or regional authorities alone.

6. Programme Duration:
The programme was due to terminate on 31 December 1992; however, an extension to the programme has been proposed.

7. Submission of Applications:
Funds awarded under the programme are allocated to central governments in Member States, who then place contracts with industry.

8. Other Restrictions:
Transport infrastructure projects are assessed on the basis of the following criteria:

- the benefit of the project to international Community traffic and broad programme objectives. Among the factors which must be included are: the importance of present or potential intra-Community international traffic; the importance of exchanges between the Community and third countries on the route involved in the project; and the extent of the project's contribution to the creation of a homogeneous and balanced network within the Community framework, geared to existing and future transport needs;
- the socio-economic return on the project;
- the project's consistency with other Community policies and national transport policies;
- particular difficulties in raising finance;
- inability of national or regional authorities to carry out the project alone.

9. Eligible Expenditure:
Eligible expenditure is decided on a case-by-case basis.

10. Rate of Award:
The rate of award is decided on a case-by-case basis but grant-aid generally covers up to 25 percent of total project costs (or costs of that part of the project granted assistance) and up to 50 percent for preparatory studies for construction work. Where a specific project forming part of one of the approved major projects (see 3) is already being granted non-repayable EC support, that project may only receive aid in the form of loans.

11. Payment Procedure:
Funds under the programme are disbursed to central governments within the relevant Member States, who then place contracts with industry. An advance payment of no more than 40 percent of the Community contribution may be provided to accelerate the execution of projects.

12. Points to Note:
Council Regulation (EEC) 3359/90 adopting the programme was published in OJ L326; 24.11.90.

Projects may only receive support if all EC public procurement requirements are met. Where a project receiving support has not been carried out as planned, or where conditions imposed are not fulfilled, financial support may be reduced or cancelled.

13. Application Procedure:
Projects are submitted by the governments of Member States to the Commission for approval, with an indication of anticipated total costs, a work schedule, information necessary for the evaluation of the Community interest of the project, and an environmental impact assessment.

14. Further Information:
European Commission
DG VII/C-2
Rue de la Loi 200
B-1049 Brussels
Tel: (010 32 2) 299 1111
Telex: 21877 COMEU B

PART ONE

INVESTMENT SUPPORT

1.2 SECTORAL SUPPORT

ECSC: Industrial Loans to Promote Coal Consumption 61
ECSC: Industrial Loans to Promote Steel Consumption 63
EAGGF: Marketing and Processing of Agricultural Products 65
EAGGF: Marketing and Processing of Fishery and Aquaculture Products 68
EURATOM Loans 71

1.2 SECTORAL SUPPORT

ECSC: INDUSTRIAL LOANS TO PROMOTE COAL CONSUMPTION

1. Summary:

Loans are available under Article 54(2) of the Treaty establishing the European Coal and Steel Community for investment projects which promote the consumption of European Community coal. Loans may be granted directly or indirectly through financial agents under a global ECSC loan (although at present no agents have been appointed).

Applications must normally relate to investment projects on which work has not been started, and which can be completed within three years.

2. Awarding Body:

European Coal and Steel Community (ECSC).

3. Location Restrictions:

Available in any Member State of the European Community.

4. Sectoral Restrictions:

Loans are available to businesses, public bodies or local authorities.

5. Size Restrictions:

There is no limit on the size of direct loans. Unless prior agreement is reached with the Commission, the total investment value of projects for which an individual loan is sought under a global loan may not exceed 15 MECU.

6. Programme Duration:

There is no specified terminal date for the granting of these loans, although they are subject to the availability of funds.

7. Submission of Applications:

Applications must normally relate to investment projects on which work has not been started, and which can be completed within three years.

8. Other Restrictions:

The following types of investment projects may qualify: installations and equipment relating to the combustion, transformation, handling and preparation of coal, and to the treatment and disposal of effluents, whose purpose is to promote the consumption of Community coal. The Commission will assess the economic aspects of the industrial project, principally in terms of the contribution the investment will make to the consumption of Community coal and of the technical and financial prospects for its implementation. The Commission will also assess the financial situation of the borrower and of any parent companies, and the value of the guarantees offered.

An analysis will be made of any significant effects on the environment from emissions and waste produced by the project. Projects must in any event meet the requirements of Community legislation on the environment. It is a condition of an industrial loan that Community coal only is used for a period of five years from the date the project is completed.

9. Eligible Expenditure:

Eligible expenditure relates to the investment value of the project (excluding working capital requirements).

10. Rate of Award:

The maximum loan is set at 50 percent of the investment value of the project. Unless there is specific agreement by the ECSC to the contrary, this maximum will be reduced proportionately if any non-Community coal is used in the period of five years after the project is completed. The interest rate on the loan is set by the Commission in line with the cost of borrowed funds.

A rebate of 3 percent per annum may be granted for a period of five years on the interest payable on the loans, except for projects relating to power stations and coking plants. The rebate is calculated on the total amount of the loan expressed in ECU. The amount of rebated loan is linked to the consumption of Community coal and may therefore, in some circumstances, be lower than the loan granted.

11. Payment Procedure:

An industrial loan is granted direct to the promoter of the project. The rebate is paid direct to the borrower in the relevant national currency on the date the interest falls due.

12. Points to Note:

In determining any interest rebate, the Commission takes account of any national aid granted to the project, and ensures in particular that the cumulative effect of national and Community aid does not distort competition in a way which is contrary to the public interest. Borrowers must send the Commission periodical reports on the progress of investment projects and the consumption of Community coal. The Commission will make selective inspection visits to the projects to ensure that they are being carried out as planned.

Loans are also available from the ECSC towards the cost of converting gas or oil fired boiler systems to coal. Loans are usually made in foreign currencies and repayment is required in the same currencies; they are available directly or through 3i plc. However, no loans have been made by 3i plc under this facility for several years, since the abolition of exchange risk cover.

13. Application Procedure:

Loan applications should be directed to the European Commission.

14. Further Information:

Ms Judith Elles
European Commission
DG XVIII/Division B3
Batiment Wagner
L-2920 Luxembourg
Tel: (010 35 2) 4301 6368

ECSC: INDUSTRIAL LOANS TO PROMOTE STEEL CONSUMPTION

1. Summary:

Loans are available under Article 54(2) of the Treaty establishing the European Coal and Steel Community for investments aimed at promoting the consumption of European Community steel. Loans may be granted directly or indirectly through financial agents under a global ECSC loan (although at present no agents have been appointed).

Applications should relate to investment projects on which work has not been started or is still in progress and which, as a rule, can be completed within three years.

2. Awarding Body:

European Coal and Steel Community (ECSC).

3. Location Restrictions:

Available in any Member State of the European Community.

4. Sectoral Restrictions:

Loans are available to properly constituted enterprises.

Eligible products covered by the term 'steel' are defined in the Annex to the decision (85/C121/03) and include: raw materials for iron and steel production; pig iron and ferro-alloys; crude and semi-finished products or iron, ordinary steel or special steel, including products for re-use and re-rolling; hot finished products of iron, ordinary steel or special steel; and end products of iron, ordinary steel or special steel.

5. Size Restrictions:

There is no limit on the size of direct loans. Unless prior agreement is reached with the Commission, the total investment value of projects for which an individual loan is sought under a global loan facility may not exceed 15 MECU.

6. Programme Duration:

There is no specified terminal date for the granting of these loans, although they are subject to the availability of funds.

7. Submission of Applications:

Applications should relate to investment projects on which work has not been started or is still in progress and which, as a rule, can be completed within three years.

8. Other Restrictions:

The following types of industrial projects may qualify for support: those aimed at introducing new applications for steel or at improving the competitiveness of steel in relation to any other products; projects by undertakings for which the cost of steel purchased, reflected in the price of the finished product, accounts for (a) at least 50 percent of the total cost of raw materials (including steel) or, if this provision cannot be applied for technical reasons, (b) at least 20 percent of the total cost of the constituents (including raw materials) of the finished product or, if this provision cannot be applied for technical reasons,

(c) at least 5 percent of the selling price of the finished product.

Only expenditure on installations directly connected with the continuous use of steel will be considered. Loans are also available for major infrastructure projects of European interest, but for these the continuous use of steel is waived.

The Commission assesses the economic aspects of the project, principally in terms of the contribution the investment will make to the consumption of Community steel and of the technical and financial prospects for its implementation, its viability, the market outlook for the products and the situation in the sector concerned. The Commission also assesses the financial situation of the borrower, of any parent companies and the value of any guarantees offered. An analysis may be made of any significant effects on the environment from emissions and waste produced by the project. Projects must in any event meet the requirements of Community legislation on the environment.

9. Eligible Expenditure:

Eligible expenditure in relation to industrial projects relates to the investment value of the project (excluding working capital requirements).

Eligible expenditure in relation to major infrastructure projects of European interest is limited to the total actual value of the steel used in the project, provided always that the total does not exceed 20 percent of fixed capital investments.

10. Rate of Award:

Loans may be for up to 50 percent of the investment value of projects aimed at increasing or maintaining the level of consumption of Community steel.

Loans of up to 20 percent are available for major infrastructure projects.

The loans are provided in a mixture of foreign currencies. Interest rates are at favourable market rates reflecting the rate paid by the ECSC itself on financial markets on which it has borrowed funds.

11. Payment Procedure:

Payment is arranged between the applicant and the Commission on a case-by-case basis.

12. Points to Note:

Borrowers must send the Commission periodical reports on the progress of investment projects and the consumption of Community steel. The Commission will make selective inspection visits to the projects to ensure they are being carried out as planned.

13. Application Procedure:

Loan applications should be sent to the European Commission.

14. Further Information:

Ms Judith Elles
European Commission
DG XVIII/Division B3
Batiment Wagner
L-2920 Luxembourg
Tel: (010 35 2) 4301 6368

EAGGF: PROCESSING AND MARKETING OF AGRICULTURAL PRODUCTS

1. Summary:

Under Regulation (EEC) 866/90 financial assistance is available from the European Agricultural Guidance and Guarantee Fund: Guidance Section (EAGGF) (sometimes known as FEOGA) for capital investments designed to improve and rationalise the treatment, processing and marketing of agricultural products.

EAGGF financing takes place within the framework of Sectoral Plans drawn up by Member States. Eligible projects conforming most closely to the aims of the Regulation and to Sectoral Plan priorities are incorporated into Operational Programmes for consideration by the European Commission at six-monthly intervals.

2. Awarding Body:

European Agricultural Guidance and Guarantee Fund: Guidance Section. Assistance is disbursed through the relevant Agriculture Ministry/Department: ie the Ministry of Agriculture, Fisheries and Food in England; the Scottish Office Agriculture and Fisheries Department; the Welsh Office Agriculture Department; and the Department of Agriculture for Northern Ireland.

3. Location Restrictions:

Available in any Member State of the European Community. EAGGF Guidance Section funding is also available to promote the development of rural areas – ie those designated eligible under Objectives 1 and 5(b) of the EC's Structural Funds. (For a full list of Objective 1 and 5(b) regions see European Regional Development Fund). Assistance from the EAGGF is combined with funding from the other Structural Funds in Community Support Frameworks (CSFs) agreed between the Government and the European Commission for eligible areas.

4. Sectoral Restrictions:

Support is intended to benefit the primary producer and, as such, investments eligible for assistance must guarantee the producers of the basic agricultural product an adequate and lasting share in the resulting economic benefits.

5. Size Restrictions:

Total project costs must be between £70,000 and £6,000,000.

6. Programme Duration:

Member States are required to submit to the European Commission Sectoral Plans covering the agriculture sector for a period of up to five years. There are currently two UK Sectoral Plans: one covering crops, and one covering livestock and livestock products. The current Plans will expire on 31 December 1993.

7. Submission of Applications:

The last date for receipt of applications under the present scheme arrangements was 30 September 1992.

The scheme is competitive; projects conforming most closely to the aims of the scheme will be shortlisted by Agriculture Ministries/Departments and submitted to the EC for approval.

Applications for individual projects must be received and acknowledged in writing before any work on a project is started. (Exceptions to this are: site purchase; obtaining planning permission; architect/consultancy work; obtaining quotations and ordering (but not taking delivery of) equipment.) This will take approximately four weeks from the date of an application's despatch. The acknowledgement will indicate the earliest date when work may commence.

8. Other Restrictions:

Guidelines published by the European Commission in OJ L91; 6.4.90 outlined the following types of project as eligible for support: rationalising or developing the preparation and processing of agricultural products or recycling of by-products or manufacturing waste; improving marketing channels; applying new processing techniques, including the development of new products and by-products, or opening up new markets and innovative investments; and improving product quality. Priority may be given to projects improving market structures for agricultural products, particularly if they encourage the development of new outlets by facilitating the marketing of new products or of high quality products, including those grown organically.

The two UK Sectoral Plans, Crops and Livestock and Livestock Products cover the following agricultural commodities (including those produced by organic methods):

(1) Crops: Cereals (including straw disposal; potatoes; horticultural produce (including ornamentals); oilseeds; field peas and beans; dried fodder; hops;

(2) Livestock: Utilisation and recycling of waste and by-products; red meat; pigmeat; poultry; eggs; milk and milk products.

Applicants should contact Agriculture Departments for a detailed summary of eligible projects within each of these sectors.

Applicants must be able to justify the need for grant-aid, and each application must refer to a complete project or separate viable part of a project (phasing of projects into viable self-contained parts is acceptable). No more than 80 percent of project inputs may be the applicant's own produce, and at least 80 percent by volume of primary produce used as a result of the project must come from EC countries. Projects should not be solely concerned with hygiene upgrading.

9. Eligible Expenditure:

The following items or areas of expenditure are not eligible: land purchase costs; the purchase of buildings which have previously been used for the same purpose; working capital; items not coming into an applicant's beneficial ownership within four years after award of aid (including hire purchase and leasing arrangements); vehicles for external transportation (forklift trucks, or similar, used for internal transportation and handling are eligible); any second-hand equipment; harvesting equipment (items such as field rigs used to wrap and box vegetables and equipment primarily for processing and packing are eligible); own labour and equipment costs; costs related to the transfer and installation of existing plant and equipment into a new building or other place of work where the project will be realised; consumables; maintenance costs; and one-for-one replacement. The inclusion of any of these items would not normally render the whole project costs ineligible for grant-aid. Apart from land purchase costs, the value of these items must not make up more than 40 percent of total project costs, or the project will be ineligible.

10. Rate of Award:
Successful projects will normally be awarded a grant of up to 25 percent of eligible costs, up to a maximum grant of £900,000 (and up to 50 percent of eligible costs in Objective 1 regions – Northern Ireland in the UK).

Projects must attract a UK grant of not less than 5 percent of eligible costs. Where this cannot be obtained from other sources, the appropriate Agriculture Ministry/Department will be prepared to consider providing a 'back-up' grant, but only if EAGGF assistance is awarded and the subsequent claim approved. Beneficiaries of EAGGF assistance must make a financial contribution of at least 25 percent of project costs in Objective 1 regions and 45 percent in other areas.

11. Payment Procedure:
EAGGF assistance is disbursed via the relevant Agriculture Ministry/ Department. Grant is paid only after proven expenditure has been incurred and claimed.

12. Points to Note:
Regulation (EEC) 866/90 replaced Regulation (EEC) 355/77 (commonly referred to as FEOGA).

13. Application Procedure:
Applications are submitted on form MAP/1 (with one copy). Applicants should contact the relevant Ministry/Department (see 14) for advice and guidance with preparing an application.

14. Further Information:

England:
Ministry of Agriculture Fisheries and Food
Nobel House, Room 721
17 Smith Square
London SW1P 3JR
Tel: (071) 238 6316
Fax: (071) 238 6308

Wales:
Welsh Office Agriculture Department
Crown Buildings, Room 2003
Cathays Park
Cardiff CF1 3NQ
Tel: (0222) 823835
Fax: (0222) 823036/3204

Scotland:
Scottish Office Agriculture and Fisheries Department
Pentland House, Room 259
47 Robb's Loan
Edinburgh EH14 1TW
Tel: (031) 244 6387/8
Fax: (031) 244 6001

Northern Ireland:
Department of Agriculture for Northern Ireland
Room 145
Dundonald House
Upper Newtownards Road
Belfast BT4 3SB
Tel: (0232) 650111 Ext.799
Fax: (0232) 659856

EAGGF: PROCESSING AND MARKETING OF FISHERY AND AQUACULTURE PRODUCTS

1. Summary:

Under Regulation (EEC) 4042/89, financial assistance is available from the European Agricultural Guidance and Guarantee Fund: Guidance Section (EAGGF) (sometimes known as FEOGA) for capital investments designed to improve conditions under which fishery and aquaculture products are processed and marketed. Investment needs have been identified in the following areas: the modernisation and increased efficiency of existing processing and marketing facilities; technical innovation; and improvements in hygiene standards needed to meet the requirements of new EC fish and shellfish hygiene legislation taking effect in 1993.

EAGGF financing takes place within the framework of Sectoral Plans drawn up by Member States. Eligible projects conforming most closely to the aims of the Regulation and to Sectoral Plan priorities are incorporated into Operational Programmes for consideration by the European Commission at six-monthly intervals.

2. Awarding Body:

European Agricultural Guidance and Guarantee Fund: Guidance Section. Assistance is disbursed through the relevant Agriculture Ministry/Department: ie the Ministry of Agriculture, Fisheries and Food in England; the Scottish Office, Agriculture and Fisheries Department; the Welsh Office Agriculture Department; and the Department of Agriculture for Northern Ireland.

3. Location Restrictions:

Available in any Member State of the European Community. EAGGF Guidance Section funding is also available to promote the development of rural areas – ie those designated eligible under Objectives 1 and 5(b) of the EC's Structural Funds. (For a full list of Objective 1 and 5(b) regions see European Regional Development Fund.) Assistance from the EAGGF is combined with funding from the other Structural Funds in Community Support Frameworks (CSFs) agreed between the Government and the European Commission for eligible areas.

4. Sectoral Restrictions:

Priority may be given to investments undertaken by primary producers, producers' groups, associations and cooperatives.

5. Size Restrictions:

Total project costs must be between £25,000 and £6,000,000.

6. Programme Duration:

Regulation (EEC) 4042/89 came into force on 1 January 1990. Under this Regulation, each Member State is required to submit to the European Commission a Sectoral Plan covering the entire fisheries and aquaculture sector. The UK Sectoral Plan will run for three years, from 1991 to 1993. Agriculture Departments will submit Operational Programmes for consideration by the Commission at six-monthly intervals in April and October each year.

7. Submission of Applications:

The last date for receipt of applications under the present scheme arrangements was 31 December 1992. The scheme is competitive; projects conforming most closely to the aims of the scheme will be shortlisted by Agriculture Ministries/Departments and submitted to the EC for approval.

Applications for individual projects must be received and acknowledged in writing before any work on a project is started. This will take at least four weeks from the date of an application's despatch.

8. Other Restrictions:

Guidelines published by the European Commission in OJ L388; 30.12.89 outlined the following priority investment areas: the construction, modernisation and rationalisation of auction markets and halls for the first-hand sale of products landed by EC vessels; the storage, smoking and handling of fishery and aquaculture products; facilities for preparation for the first-hand sale and filleting of fresh fish and the preparation of deep-frozen fish; the preparation of finished products from fish caught by and/or deep-frozen on board EC vessels; technically advanced production units, producing preserved and semi-preserved products; the development of new products and technologies based on the results of research, pilot and demonstration projects; improvement of the quality and hygiene of production and marketing processes; enhancement of the added value of production.

Priority will be given to projects which offer more in terms of investment and producer benefit than simply upgrading to meet legislative requirements.

The following investments are not eligible: investments at the retail level; product processing on board ship; fishery/aquaculture produce intended for purposes other than human consumption (except investments intended solely for the treatment, processing or marketing of fishery wastes); vehicles used for the transport and distribution of fishery/aquaculture products; products not listed in Annex II of the Treaty of Rome, although consideration will be given in cases where the beneficiary has a direct contractual link with producers; projects in respect of which work commenced more than six months before the date on which the Commission receives the Operational Programme for which the project is to be considered; and investments for the production of processed goods for which the existence of realistic potential outlets has not been demonstrated.

Applicants must be able to justify the need for grant-aid, and each application must refer to a complete project or a separate viable part of a project (phasing of projects into viable self-contained parts is acceptable). At least 20 percent of the primary produce to be marketed/processed must come from fishermen other than the applicant, and at least 51 percent by volume of primary produce used as a result of the project must originate from landings by EC vessels.

9. Eligible Expenditure:

The following items or areas of expenditure are not eligible: land purchase costs; the purchase of buildings which have previously been used for the same purpose; working capital; items not coming into an applicant's beneficial ownership within four years after award of aid (including hire purchase and leasing arrangements); any second-hand equipment; own labour and equipment costs; costs related to the transfer and installation of existing plant and equipment into a new building or other place of work where the project will be realised; consumables; maintenance costs; and one-for-one replacement. The inclusion of some of these items would not normally render the whole project ineligible, but their cost would be deducted from the total project costs eligible for grant aid. Apart from land purchase costs, the value of these items must not make up more than 40 percent of total project costs or the project will be ineligible.

10. Rate of Award:

Successful projects will normally be awarded a grant of up to 30 percent of eligible costs, up to a maximum grant of £900,000 (and up to 50 percent of eligible costs in Objective 1 regions – Northern Ireland in the UK).

Projects must attract a UK grant of not less than 5 percent of eligible costs. Where this cannot be obtained from other sources, the appropriate Agriculture Ministry/Department will be prepared to consider providing a 'back-up' grant, but only if EAGGF assistance is awarded and the subsequent claim approved. Beneficiaries of EAGGF assistance must make a financial contribution of at least 25 percent of project costs in Objective 1 regions and 45 percent in other areas.

11. Payment Procedure:

EAGGF assistance is disbursed via the relevant Agriculture Ministry/ Department. Grant is paid only after proven expenditure has been incurred and claimed.

12. Points to Note:

Regulation (EEC) No 4042/89 came into force on 1 January 1990, replacing Regulation (EEC) No 355/77.

13. Application Procedure:

Applications are submitted on form MAP/2 (with one copy).

Applicants should contact the relevant Ministry/Department (see 14) for advice and guidance with preparing an application.

14. Further Information:

England:
Ministry of Agriculture
Fisheries and Food
Room 721
Nobel House
17 Smith Square
London SW1P 3JR
Tel: (071) 238 6316
Fax: (071) 238 6308

Wales:
Welsh Office Agriculture
Department
Room 2003
Crown Buildings
Cathays Park
Cardiff CF1 3NQ
Tel: (0222) 823835
Fax: (0222) 823036/3204

Scotland:
Scottish Office: Agriculture and Fisheries Department
Pentland House
47 Robb's Loan
Edinburgh EH14 1TW
Tel: (031) 244 6387/8
Fax: (031) 244 6001

Northern Ireland:
Department of Agriculture for Northern Ireland
Room 145
Dundonald House
Upper Newtownards Road
Belfast BT4 3SB
Tel: (0232) 650111 Ext.799
Fax: (0232) 659856

EURATOM LOANS

1. Summary:
Loans are available on terms reflecting market rates for promoting the use of nuclear energy, thus reducing the Community's dependence on external energy supplies. Eligible projects are those relating to investment in nuclear power stations and industrial nuclear fuel cycle installations.

2. Awarding Body:
Commission of the European Communities.

3. Location Restrictions:
Available in any Member State of the European Community.

4. Sectoral Restrictions:
Available to any individual, organisation or group of organisations investing in nuclear power stations, or industrial nuclear fuel cycle installations.

5. Size Restrictions:
The ceiling for Euratom loans is 4,000 MECU. There are no specified upper or lower limits to the size of project that can be assisted.

6. Programme Duration:
There is no specified terminal date for the availability of Euratom loans.

7. Submission of Applications:
Application can be made at any time.

8. Other Restrictions:
The decision on whether to issue a loan is at the discretion of the Commission and decisions are made on a case-by-case basis.

9. Eligible Expenditure:
Eligible expenditure covers total project costs.

10. Rate of Award:
The rate of award is at the discretion of the Commission and is normally up to 20 percent of total project costs. The terms and interest rates reflect market conditions.

11. Payment Procedure:
The pattern of payment and repayment is decided on a case-by-case basis.

12. Points to Note:
None.

13. Application Procedure:
Application is made direct to the Commission of the European Communities.

14. Further Information:
European Commission
DG XVIII
Batiment Jean Monnet
L-2920 Luxembourg
Tel: (010 35 2) 43011

PART ONE

INVESTMENT SUPPORT

1.3 CAPITAL PROVISION/JOINT VENTURES

EUROTECH Capital and INNVEST	75
International Investment Partners (Joint Ventures)	77
Venture Consort Pilot Scheme	81

1.3 CAPITAL PROVISION/JOINT VENTURES

EUROTECH CAPITAL AND INNVEST

1. Summary:

Eurotech Capital is a pilot project aiming to stimulate private capital funding of transnational high-technology projects (THTPs). The European Commission will grant the 'Eurotech Capital' label to financial organisations which have an investment capacity of at least 50 MECU, and which agree to earmark at least 20 percent of these resources to acquiring holdings in firms (preferably SMEs) undertaking THTPs. The label carries a number of benefits – a repayable financial contribution which must be invested in THTPs, and preferential access to two EC services – Eurotech Projects (a database of technical and financial information on major transnational high technology projects recognised by the Commission as being technically viable), and Eurotech Data (information on technologies, patents and potential markets in Europe for new high-technology products). Enterprises seeking access to this high technology development funding may apply through INNVEST (see 12 for further details).

2. Awarding Body:

Commission of the European Communities.

3. Location Restrictions:

Available in any Member State of the European Community. The 'reserved part' (see 5) must be invested in companies whose registered office and main area of activity are within the territory of a Member State. THTPs are considered 'transnational' if they stem from an EC or European research programme, or if the R & D phase or industrial exploitation phase is transnational in accordance with the following criteria: 1. If the greater part of the phase is undertaken by a single company, the members of the company's board of directors must not all be resident in a single Member State, and the total number of shares in the company held by shareholders in a single Member State must not exceed 75 percent in relation to the shares held by other Community shareholders; 2. If the major part of the project is undertaken by a joint-venture company or by means of a significant exchange of know-how or high technology components, the partners must not all have their main seat of activity in a single Member State. Projects cannot be considered transnational if only the marketing phase is transnational, or if the partners/shareholders are controlled by a single shareholder or group.

4. Sectoral Restrictions:

Participants must be a company or other legal person, or network of legal persons whose main objective is the acquisition of temporary holdings in companies not quoted on a stock exchange, with the aim of financing their development. The organisation must be managed by directors with wide experience in the relevant field, and must have a management team appropriate for the type and size of scheme. The 'reserved part' (see 5) must be invested in companies which promote THTPs.

5. Size Restrictions:

The 'Eurotech Capital' label may be granted to financial organisations which have an investment capacity of at least 50 MECU, and which agree to earmark at least 20 percent of these resources (the 'reserved part') to acquiring holdings in companies undertaking THTPs. (The Community contribution must also be invested in THTPs.) Priority will be given to investments in SMEs, ie businesses employing fewer than 500 persons, with net fixed assets not exceeding 75 MECU, and not more than one-third of their shares held by large companies. Priority will also be given to the installation and start-up phases of companies promoting THTPs.

6. Programme Duration:

There is no specified terminal date for this scheme.

7. Submission of Applications:

Application may be made at any time.

8. Other Restrictions:

THTPs are defined in a broad and flexible manner. All projects stemming from EC R & D programmes or European R & D programmes are automatically considered THTPs. Other projects may be considered THTPs if they have been financed under a national high-technology research programme during the R & D phase. A project may also be considered to be a 'high technology' project if: it represents a significant step forward in relation to existing technology in the Community (by introducing a new technology); brings about a substantial improvement in the existing situation in the EC (by modifying certain characteristics of a product/production method); and provides a quantifiable price or cost advantage in the markets concerned.

9. Eligible Expenditure:

The EC contribution can be used either together with the 'reserved part' of the funds (see 5) for all investments in THTPs, or it can be used exclusively to provide 50 percent co-finance for the seed-corn phases of THTPs.

10. Rate of Award:

The EC financial contribution will amount to 1/25th of the funds reserved by the financial body for financing THTPs, up to a maximum of 1 MECU. The contribution must be repaid within a maximum period of ten years, together with an amount equivalent to half of the capital gain made (but only if the final value of the 'reserved part' exceeds the initial value, converted to present value).

11. Payment Procedure:

Payment procedure will be in accordance with the agreed contract.

12. Points to Note:

The 'reserved part' (see 5) must be invested within three years of the 'Eurotech Capital' label being granted. When granting the label, the EC may take into account existing investment in THTPs. Financial bodies may choose the THTPs in which they wish to invest; no prior agreement will be required from the Commission, although a full inspection of the portfolio of investments will be carried out at the end of the third year. After that date, if a THTP investment is sold, an amount equivalent to the nominal amount of the 'reserved part' must be invested in new THTPs. Any surplus may be used for other types of investment.

As part of Eurotech Capital, the Commission has also launched INNVEST, a confidential database accessed by a group of European financial institutions committed to investing in high-technology development initiatives. The database is used to link risk capital fund managers with promoters of THTPs. The INNVEST management team processes data supplied by enterprises seeking development funding, and passes information on to investors via the database. When an investor finds a suitable project, contact is made directly with the project developer.

13. Application Procedure:

Applications for the 'Eurotech Capital' label should be submitted to the address below. Once an application has been received, the organisation will be contacted for any further information required. Applications will be dealt with in the order in which they are received (budget permitting). Once an application has been approved, a contract will be drawn up between the Commission and the organisation concerned.

14. Further Information:

Mr Raffaele Liberali
Head of Unit
European Commission
DG XVIII
Batiment Wagner
L-2920 Luxembourg
Tel: (010 35 2) 43011
Fax: (010 35 2) 43 63 22
Telex: 3366 EURFIN LU

INNVEST Team:
Mrs Madeleine Campbell
Project Manager
Longman Cartermill Ltd
Technology Centre
St Andrews
Fife KY16 9EA
Tel: (0334) 77660
Fax: (0334) 77180

INTERNATIONAL INVESTMENT PARTNERS (JOINT VENTURES)

1. Summary:

The European Commission's International Investment Partners (ECIIP) initiative is a trial facility offering grants, interest-free loans and equity loans to promote joint ventures between firms located in EC Member States and firms located in Latin America, Asia and the Mediterranean. Financial support may be awarded for the following types of operation undertaken during the course of a joint investment project: the identification of potential projects and partners; operations prior to launching a joint venture; the financing of capital requirements; and the development of training and management expertise.

2. Awarding Body:

Commission of the European Communities, through approved financial intermediaries. In the UK, the Commonwealth Development Corporation (CDC), the Midland Bank, and Morgan Grenfell act as intermediaries for the scheme.

3. Location Restrictions:

The initiative is open to any national of an EC Member State or eligible country, whose domicile or registered office is located in that country. Firms from more than one EC Member State may apply jointly for support, providing that the third party in the joint venture comes from an eligible country. Eligible countries are:

- Latin America: Argentina, Bolivia, Brazil, Chile, Colombia, Ecuador, Mexico, Paraguay, Peru, Uruguay, Venezuela;
- Central America: Costa Rica, El Salvador, Guatemala, Honduras, Nicaragua, Panama;
- Asia: Bangladesh, Brunei, India, Indonesia, Macau, Malaysia, Maldives, Pakistan, Phillipines, Singapore, Sri Lanka, Thailand, Vietnam;
- the Mediterranean: Algeria, Cyprus, Egypt, Israel, Jordan, Lebanon, Morocco, Malta, Syria, Tunisia, Turkey, Yugoslavia.

4. Sectoral Restrictions:

Individual firms with specific investment projects are eligible for interest-free loans to support the cost of finding suitable partners and for preliminary operations (eg feasibility studies, prototypes, etc). Subsequently, equity loans are available for the financing of capital requirements.

Grants for the identification of potential projects and partners (ie not in relation to any specific investment project) are restricted to financial institutions, Chambers of Commerce, professional associations and public agencies.

The participation of small and medium-sized firms is particularly encouraged.

5. Size Restrictions:

When co-financing a joint venture operation in respect of capital requirements and training and management expertise (through or with a financial institution), the European Commission's contribution will never exceed that of the financial institution in question.

6. Programme Duration:

The scheme is set to run for five years from 1 January 1992.

7. Submission of Applications:

Application is made to an approved financial intermediary, who assesses the proposal and, if successful, forwards it to the Commission. If the application is approved, a response will be received within 20 working days. For studies identifying potential partners and projects, support will be granted directly to the applicant.

8. Other Restrictions:

The following types of operations may receive support:

1. Identification of potential projects and partners: (restricted to financial institutions, Chambers of Commerce, professional associations and

public agencies, ie not for a firm's individual investment project); supports studies identifying countries and sectors suitable for involvement in joint ventures and the identification of local firms which would be suitable as joint venture partners. Grants are provided under an agreement which authorises both the EC and the sponsoring organisation to use the results of the studies undertaken;

2. Operations prior to launching a joint venture: interest-free loans are available to support: a search for partners for an individual investment project; marketing and feasibility studies; the setting up of pilot production units; and the manufacture of prototypes. The loan does not have to be repaid if the sponsor does not proceed with the project with a delay of a maximum of two years after completion of the study and presentation of the report. (However, the Commission will be free to use the results of any study financed under the facility.) If a project resulting from an EC-funded study goes ahead, and the financial intermediary decides to fund the project itself, the loan must either be repaid to the EC, or the sponsoring firm may apply to the EC, via the financial intermediary, to convert it into a loan with equity features (ie an equity loan) or into an equity holding by the EC in the capital of the joint venture;
3. Financing of capital requirements: equity loans and equity holdings are available to support the setting-up of a new joint venture or the renovation and expansion of an existing one. The European sponsor must have, or take, an equity holding of at least 10 percent of the joint venture's capital;
4. Training and management expertise: interest-free loans are available to support the setting up of new joint ventures or the renovation and expansion of existing ones through assistance with staff and management training, eg the training of local technicians and managers; the temporary appointment of consultants; secondments.

9. Eligible Expenditure:

Eligible expenditure depends on the type of project being undertaken (see 8).

10. Rate of Award:

The following rates of award apply:

1. Identification of potential projects and partners: grants covering up to 50 percent of costs, up to a grant ceiling of 100,000 ECU.
2. Operations prior to launching a joint-venture: interest-free loans covering up to 50 percent of costs, up to a maximum loan of 250,000 ECU.
3. Financing of capital requirements: equity holdings or equity loans up to 20 percent of the joint venture's total capital, with a maximum loan of 1 MECU.
4. Training and management expertise: interest-free loans covering up to 50 percent of costs, up to a maximum loan of 250,000 ECU.

When facilities 2, 3, and 4 are combined, the upper limit of financial support available is 1 MECU per investment project.

11. Payment Procedure:

When all terms and conditions surrounding the application have been satisfied, the EC and the financial intermediary concerned draw up a specific financial agreement. The financial intermediary then makes a back-to-back financial agreement with the applicant, after which the funds may be released.

For studies identifying potential partners and projects, support will be granted directly to the applicant.

12. Points to Note:

Applications for assistance may be submitted by a firm in the EC, or a firm in an eligible country (see 3).

The willingness of a financial intermediary to support a project will depend, among other things, on its own investment portfolio at the time the application is made.

The Commission will approve projects on the basis of: the anticipated soundness of the investment and quality of the promoters; the contribution to development; compatibility with the sectoral and geographical aspects of Community policy; and compliance with the eligibility criteria.

13. Application Procedure:

UK applicants should contact one of the EC-approved financial intermediaries who will then assess the proposal and send an application to the European Commission. If the application is approved, a reply will be received within 20 working days.

The Commission would also welcome approaches from development banks, commercial banks, merchant banks and investment promotion bodies interested in acting as financial intermediaries for the scheme.

14. Further Information:

Mr T Roe – Head of Sector
EC International Investment Partners
European Commission
DG I – External Relations
Rue de la Loi 200
B-1049 Brussels
Tel: (010 32 2) 299 2299
Fax: (010 32 2) 299 0203/0204/0205

Mr Brzozowski
Business Development Adviser
Commonwealth Development Corporation (CDC) B-1049
1 Bessborough Gardens
London SW1V 2JQ
Tel: (071) 828 4488
Fax: (071) 828 6505

Mr Suratgar
Director
Morgan Grenfell
23 Winchester Street
London EC2P 2AX
Tel: (071) 588 4545
Fax: (071) 588 5598

VENTURE CONSORT PILOT SCHEME

1. Summary:

The Venture Consort Pilot Scheme aims to encourage the growth of European small and medium-sized firms through promoting the formation of cross-border syndicates of venture capitalists. The scheme provides repayable advances, to be converted into equity by the lead investor, to invest in the purchase of or subscription for equity share capital in an enterprise undertaking a project consisting of the start-up or expansion of an SME.

2. Awarding Body:

Commission of the European Communities.

3. Location Restrictions:

Available in any Member State of the European Community. Venture capital firms located in at least two EC Member States must participate in the syndicate.

4. Sectoral Restrictions:

Investors must be members of EVCA, the European Venture Capital Association. At least two venture capital firms must participate in an investment proposal.

5. Size Restrictions:

Projects should involve the start-up or expansion of SMEs.

6. Programme Duration:

There is no specified terminal date for this scheme.

7. Submission of Applications:

Deadlines for the submission of applications are set annually, usually in November.

8. Other Restrictions:

Approval of investment proposals by venture capital syndicates will depend on: the degree of innovation in the project (ie how innovative the product, production process or technology involved is); the extent to which the project involves expansion into more than one EC Member State; whether the project is financed by a transnational venture capital syndicate; the viability of the project and financial situation of the investor. If an investment has already been made by the Venture Consort Pilot Scheme in the project, no further contribution may be made.

9. Eligible Expenditure:

Eligible expenditure relates to the equity investment resulting in the purchase of or subscription for equity share capital in an enterprise undertaking a project consisting of the starting-up or expansion of an SME.

10. Rate of Award:

EC support for syndicate investments by full EVCA Members will be up to 30 percent of the total of the new equity share capital being invested in the project. The award will normally be between a minimum of 50,000 ECUs and a maximum of 200,000 ECUs.

11. Payment Procedure:
Payment is made to the lead investor within three months of EC approval of an investment proposal.

12. Points to Note:
None.

13. Application Procedure:
Applications should be submitted to the European Venture Capital Association by lead investors. The EVCA Secretariat will check the application, and forward it to the European Commission within one week. The European Commission will advise EVCA and the lead investor of its decision within one month, and contract and payment will be concluded within three months.

14. Further Information:
Mr Daniel van Avermaet
EVCA
Keibergpark
Minervastraat 6, Box 6
B-1930 Zaventem
Belgium
Tel: (010 32 2) 720 6010
Fax: (010 32 2) 725 3036

PART ONE

INVESTMENT SUPPORT

1.4 SUPPORT FOR EASTERN EUROPE

PHARE	85
JOPP	88
TEMPUS	90

European Investment Bank – *see* Problem Area Development (page 23)

1.4 SUPPORT FOR EASTERN EUROPE

PHARE

1. Summary:

The central objective of the PHARE programme is to support the economic reform process in the countries of Central and Eastern Europe. The programme supports privatisation and restructuring programmes, and specific operations developing the private sector undertaken by the governments of beneficiary countries. Annual 'indicative programmes' for each eligible country in Central/Eastern Europe set out the priority areas of funding, on the basis of which specific sectoral, regional or multilateral programmes are then identified.

The programme does not deal directly with individual business propositions, projects or ventures but provides funds from which the respective beneficiary governments finance their own reconstruction programmes. Individual projects may therefore benefit indirectly as part of such programmes. There are also opportunities for the provision of technical assistance and services, and supplies.

A call for expressions of interest from firms regarding preselection for the carrying out of technical assistance in the field of privatisations under PHARE was published in OJ C314; 1.12.92; the deadline was 18 January 1993.

2. Awarding Body:

PHARE coordinates aid from the Group of 24 (G-24) countries ie the 12 EC Member States, plus Australia, Austria, Canada, Finland, Iceland, Japan, New Zealand, Norway, Sweden, Switzerland, Turkey and the United States of America. The European Commission acts as administrator, and also takes the lead in framing PHARE policy and strategy.

3. Location Restrictions:

The programme was initially set up for Poland and Hungary, but has since been extended to cover Albania, Bulgaria, Croatia, the Czech and Slovak Republics, Estonia, Latvia, Lithuania, Romania and Slovenia.

Tenders are open to all EC Member States and the eligible Central/Eastern European countries.

4. Sectoral Restrictions:

Any industry restrictions are specified when individual calls for tender are published.

5. Size Restrictions:

No size restrictions have been specified.

6. Programme Duration:

No terminal date has been specified for PHARE.

7. Submission of Applications:

Deadlines for supplies contracts are specified when calls for tender are published in the Official Journal of the European Communities. For the provision of technical assistance or services, application to the Commission may be made at any time. Individual business projects may be submitted to the appropriate national authorities at any time (see 13 for further details).

A call for expressions of interest from firms regarding preselection for the carrying out of technical assistance in the field of privatisations under PHARE was published in OJ C314; 1.12.92; the deadline was 18 January 1993.

8. Other Restrictions:

The main aspects of the economic reform in Central and Eastern Europe supported by PHARE are as follows: abolition of state monopolies; restructuring and privatisation of public enterprises; modernisation of financial services; promotion of the private sector, particularly SMEs, including training; and development of the labour market and social sector. Related priority sectors are also supported – these include: energy, environmental protection, telecommunications, transport, health and agriculture.

9. Eligible Expenditure:

Eligible expenditure may cover works, supplies, technical cooperation and, if necessary, local costs. PHARE funds are not intended to finance the costs of acquisition, capital provision, modernisation or investment in commercial ventures, or to cover operating costs.

10. Rate of Award:

The rate of award may vary depending on the nature of the project.

11. Payment Procedure:

The implementation of projects and programmes is the responsibility of the recipient national authorities, including all legal and financial obligations to the contractors. The Commission provides a financial contribution under conditions specified in the programme and has the right to monitor physical progress, inspect accounts and to ensure that the terms of the agreement are being observed.

12. Points to Note:

Council Regulation (EEC) 3906/89 (OJ L375; 23.12.89) established PHARE in Poland and Hungary, and was amended by Regulations (EEC) 2698/90 (OJ L257; 21.9.90), (EEC) 3800/91 (OJ L357; 28.12.91) and (EEC) 2334/92 (OJ L227; 11.8.92) extending coverage to the other eligible countries. Among the reconstruction programmes supported by PHARE are: TEMPUS (to modernise higher education and improve vocational training) and JOPP (a joint-venture support scheme). These are available in all PHARE countries and are both covered by separate descriptions. A further subprogramme of PHARE is ACE, which is also available in all PHARE countries and supports cooperation in the field of economics between professional and academic economists in the EC and Central/Eastern Europe. ACE supports: scholarships and research grants; seminars; networks and research projects; and study visits.

13. Application Procedure:

The application procedure for each type of possible contract is as follows:

1. Consultants providing technical assistance and services: Contracts valued under 50,000 ECU may be awarded by direct agreement. All contracts in excess of this value are subject to restricted tendering

procedures. For its own operational purposes, PHARE Operational Service selects consultants on the basis of EC-wide invitations to tender. An invitation to tender for firms wishing to 'prequalify' was published in OJ C251; 5.10.90. The 'prequalification' tender allowed the EC to draw up a shortlist of firms specialising in the provision of advice and technical assistance for major privatisation projects. Shortlisted firms may be invited to take part in restricted invitations to tender issued by East European countries, or to conclude private contracts for EC-financed projects. This list has not closed – firms may still apply to be included following periodic reviews. For services in the field of privatisations and restructuring (other than contracts for major privatisations) there is no specific list – companies should express their interest in being considered to the PHARE Operational Service.

2. Procurement of supplies: major supplies contracts are subject to open tenders, and are published in the Official Journal of the European Communities.
3. Private investors: PHARE funds are not made available for individual projects but for broader sectoral or regional programmes, and only at the request of the beneficiary country. However, individual projects may indirectly benefit from PHARE funds as part of such public programmes. Investors/promoters should apply to the banks, financial institutions or national authorities within the beneficiary country responsible for the implementation of programmes and credit schemes financed from PHARE funds. If such proposals are accepted by recipient countries as part of a wider reconstruction programme, they may be presented to the EC for financing.

The World Aid Section (WAS) of the DTI maintains a database of project and investment opportunities in Central and Eastern Europe. The DTI's Market Desk will assist with trading and legislative information in preparation for visits to Central and Eastern Europe. It may also be helpful to contact the Commercial Section of the British Embassy in the country concerned.

14. Further Information:

Initial Enquiries:
Philip Sack
Room 036
DTI World Aid Section
Ashdown House
123 Victoria Street
London SW1E 6RB
Tel: (071) 215 4255

Dr P Kalbe
European Commission
PHARE Operational Service
(L-84, 2/10)
200 rue de la Loi
B-1049 Brussels
Tel: (010 32 2) 299 1356

For enquiries related to ACE:
M D Descouteres
European Commission
DGXII/H-1/ACE
200 rue de la Loi
B-1049 Brussels
Tel: (010 32 2) 235 6876
Fax: (010 32 2) 236 3307

JOPP

1. Summary:

The JOPP programme aims to encourage private sector investment in the countries of Central and Eastern Europe by supporting the creation and development of joint ventures between businesses in the EC (particularly SMEs) and local partners. The JOPP programme operates within the framework of PHARE, the European Commission's programme to assist the economic restructuring of the countries of Central and Eastern Europe. Four facilities are offered covering the whole process of joint venture investment: assistance with the preparatory phase of the creation or development of a joint venture; assistance with capital requirements of a new or existing joint venture; technical assistance; and general assistance (see 8 for further details).

2. Awarding Body:

Commission of the European Communities, through a selected network of financial intermediaries.

3. Location Restrictions:

Available to firms located in any Member State of the European Community and interested in establishing or developing a joint venture with enterprises in Central and Eastern European countries supported by the PHARE programme. Eligible Central and Eastern European countries are as follows: Albania, Bulgaria, the Czech and Slovak Republics, Estonia, Hungary, Latvia, Lithuania, Poland, Romania, Slovenia and Yugoslavia.

4. Sectoral Restrictions:

Firms from all sectors (except bank lending) are eligible to receive assistance from JOPP, as long as the intended joint venture involves a direct and productive investment. Priority is given to joint ventures involving SMEs.

5. Size Restrictions:

Priority will be given to joint ventures set up in a Central/Eastern European country with net fixed assets below 10 MECU.

6. Programme Duration:

There is no specified terminal date for this scheme.

7. Submission of Applications:

Application may be made at any time.

8. Other Restrictions:

JOPP offers the following facilities to assist with different phases of joint venture investment:

- (i) Preparatory Phase: financing is available for the preparatory phases of the creation or development of a joint venture eg feasibility studies, pilot projects;
- (ii) Co-financing: contributing to the capital requirements of the joint venture (which may be a new joint venture or an existing one being expanded/restructured);
- (iii) Technical Assistance: interest-free loans to help finance the strengthening of a joint venture's human and technical resources;

(iv) General Assistance: general assistance for the identification of investment opportunities and partners in Central and Eastern Europe (ie not focused on individual investment projects). This action will be implemented by the Commission in collaboration with the network of intermediaries.

9. Eligible Expenditure:

Eligible costs vary according to the facilities used, and will be outlined by the financial intermediary.

10. Rate of Award:

The rate of award varies according to the action undertaken as follows:

(i) Preparatory Phase: interest-free loans of up to 50 percent of eligible costs up to a maximum of 75,000 ECU. If the project succeeds, 100 percent of eligible costs may be reimbursed through a grant (up to a maximum of 150,000 ECU);

(ii) Co-financing: up to 20 percent of the total investment. A financial intermediary must also co-finance the joint venture (directly or indirectly);

(iii) Technical Assistance: interest-free loans of up to 50 percent of eligible costs, up to a maximum of 150,000 ECU.

The total EC contribution for all projects relating to a single joint venture may not exceed 1 MECU.

11. Payment Procedure:

Payment procedure will be outlined by the financial intermediary.

12. Points to Note:

None.

13. Application Procedure:

Application should be made to one of the financial intermediaries selected to operate the scheme. The network of financial institutions is responsible for: promoting the scheme; identifying potential investors; evaluating project proposals; and following up approved projects. Applications are assessed on a case-by-case basis.

14. Further Information:

Mr Andrew Brzozowski
Business Development Department
Commonwealth Development Corporation (CDC)
1 Bessborough Gardens
London SW1V 2JQ
Tel: (071) 828 4488
Fax: (071) 828 6505

Mr Richard MacGeorge
Morgan Grenfell & Co Ltd
23 Great Winchester Street
London EC2P 2AX
Tel: (071) 826 7156/7165
Fax: (071) 826 7130

Mr Johan Weijers/Mr Ullrich Kiermayr
European Bank for Reconstruction and Development (EBRD)
122 Leadenhall Street
London EC3V 4QL
Tel: (071) 338 6356/6204
Fax: (071) 638 2375

Mr Enrico Cioffi (Director General)
or Mr Jean Marie Magnette (Head of Unit)
European Commission
DG XVII – Credit & Investments
Wagner Building
L-2920 Luxembourg
Tel: (010 35 2) 4301 6261
Fax: (010 35 2) 436 322

JOPP Assistance Unit
Tel: (010 35 2) 467 096
Fax: (010 35 2) 467 097

TEMPUS

1. Summary:

The TEMPUS programme (Trans-European Mobility Programme for University Studies) aims to promote the development of higher education systems in the countries of Central/Eastern Europe through cooperation with partners in the European Community. TEMPUS forms part of the overall programme of EC aid for the economic restructuring of Central/Eastern Europe (PHARE). The main objectives of TEMPUS are to promote the quality and support the development of higher education systems in eligible countries, and to encourage links with partners in the EC through joint activities and mobility programmes. TEMPUS covers three Action Lines: 1. Joint European Projects (JEPs); 2. Mobility Grants; and 3. Complementary and Youth Activities (see 8 for further details). TEMPUS has been adopted to run for four years from July 1990. Each eligible Central/Eastern European country decides the budget to be made available for TEMPUS projects on an annual basis, from within the overall sum allocated through PHARE.

2. Awarding Body:

Commission of the European Communities.

3. Location Restrictions:

Available in any Member State of the European Community. In Central and Eastern Europe, eligible countries are those designated as eligible for economic aid under Regulation (EEC) 3906/89.

Currently Albania, Bulgaria, the Czech and Slovak Republics, Estonia, Hungary, Latvia, Lithuania, Poland, Romania and Slovenia are eligible. The proposed second phase of TEMPUS (1994–98) would extend the programme to the republics of the former Soviet Union. EFTA countries, the USA, Canada, Japan, Australia, New Zealand and Turkey may also participate in TEMPUS, but are not eligible to receive EC funding.

Joint European Projects (see 8) must include at least one university (ie all types of post-secondary vocational training establishment) per eligible country involved; one Member State University; and one partner organisation (university, enterprise or organisation) from another EC Member State.

4. Sectoral Restrictions:

TEMPUS is open to all categories of higher education establishment and industry, including public and local authorities, private firms, chambers of commerce and industry, professional bodies, associations and employer or employee organisations.

5. Size Restrictions:

None.

6. Programme Duration:

TEMPUS has been adopted to run for an initial pilot phase of four years from 1 July 1990. A second phase (TEMPUS II) has been proposed to run from 1994 to 1998.

7. Submission of Applications:

Applications are assessed as they are received, and decisions taken on a continuous basis.

The final application deadlines for projects due to start in the academic year 1993/94 are: 31 January 1993 for Joint European Projects (JEPs); and 15 December 1992 and 15 June 1993 for mobility grants and complementary measures.

8. Other Restrictions:

TEMPUS covers three Action Lines:

1. Joint European Projects (JEPs): linking universities and/or enterprises in Central/Eastern Europe with EC partners. Grants may be awarded for: cooperative education and training actions; structural development of higher education; development of universities' capacities to cooperate with industry; student and teacher mobility; and regional activities. JEP projects may cover a range of activities, not including research. Priority areas for the current academic year are outlined in the Guide for Applicants available from the TEMPUS Office;
2. Mobility Grants: grants for staff (higher education teachers, administrative staff, and training staff) to prepare JEPs, to prepare teaching materials; to collect and disseminate information; to exchange know-how; or to participate in conferences/seminars in a priority subject area;
3. Complementary and Youth Activities: support for European associations in higher education; publications and information activities; surveys and studies; and youth activities.

9. Eligible Expenditure:

Eligible expenditure relates to the type of project being undertaken and is outlined in the Guide for Applicants.

10. Rate of Award:
The rate of award varies depending on the type of project undertaken, full details are outlined in the Guide for Applicants.

11. Payment Procedure:
Payment procedure varies depending on the nature of the project.

12. Points to Note:
Council Decision (EEC) 233/90 adopting TEMPUS was published in OJ L131; 23.5.90.

TEMPUS is intended to complement other EC education and training programmes such as ERASMUS, COMETT and LINGUA, all described in Part Two.

A call for expressions of interest in the evaluation of TEMPUS was published in OJ C68; 16.3.91; the deadline was 22 April 1991.

13. Application Procedure:
The TEMPUS Guide for Applicants outlines the application procedure for each type of project and is available from the TEMPUS Office in Brussels (see 14).

14. Further Information:

TEMPUS Office
Rue Montoyer 14
B-1040 Brussels
Tel: (010 32 2) 504 0711
Fax: (010 32 2) 504 0700

Europe Unit
Education & Science Division
The British Council
10 Spring Gardens
London SW1A 2BN
Tel: (071) 389 4545/4291
Fax: (071) 389 4948

PART ONE

INVESTMENT SUPPORT

1.5 ENVIRONMENTAL/ENERGY PROJECTS

ENVIREG – *see* Problem Area Development (page 31)
LIFE (Financial Instrument for the Environment) 95
Regional and Urban Energy Planning Programme 97

1.5 ENVIRONMENTAL/ENERGY PROJECTS

LIFE (FINANCIAL INSTRUMENT FOR THE ENVIRONMENT)

1. Summary:

The financial instrument for the environment (LIFE) promotes the development and implementation of Community environmental policy by financing: a) priority environmental actions in the Community, and b) technical assistance actions with third countries from the Mediterranean region or bordering on the Baltic Sea. In exceptional circumstances, actions concerning regional or global environmental problems provided for in international agreements may also be supported.

LIFE incorporates several EC environmental programmes (ACE, MEDSPA, ACNAT and NORSPA), and is implemented through the part-financing of programmes and projects, preparatory measures, demonstration schemes, awareness campaigns and actions providing incentives or technical assistance.

Specific priorities for assistance are set annually, as is the LIFE budget. A budget of 400 MECU has been set for the first phase of the programme (up to 1995), with 68 MECU proposed for 1993.

2. Awarding Body:

Commission of the European Communities.

3. Location Restrictions:

Available in any Member State of the European Community. Participation of non-EC countries may also be considered, where this concerns the provision of technical and financial support for the implementation of international conventions and the resolution of common or global problems. Preference will be given to demonstration/technical assistance projects which involve an association between at least two partners from within the Community, and to projects using an international network.

4. Sectoral Restrictions:

No industry restrictions have been specified.

5. Size Restrictions:

No size restrictions have been specified. However, it is anticipated that the Commission will prefer to support a small number of large-scale projects. As a general rule, only proposals for demonstration/technical assistance projects with a total cost of not less than ECU 600,000 will be considered by the Commission.

6. Programme Duration:

The first phase of the programme runs until 31 December 1995.

7. Submission of Applications:

Applications are invited by the Department of the Environment in the UK. The most recent deadline for the receipt of projects by the DoE was 15 February 1993, to meet the European Commission's deadline of 31 March 1993. In relation to measures of particular EC interest, the Commission may invite applications in the Official Journal of the European Communities. A call for proposals for demonstration projects and technical assistance schemes relating to new clean technologies was published in the OJ C300; 17.11.92. The deadline was 31 March 1993.

8. Other Restrictions:

Priorities for 1992–93 fall within the following broad areas: A. Within the EC: 1. Promotion of sustainable development and the quality of the environment; 2. protection of habitats and of nature; 3. administrative structures and environment services; 4. education, training and information; and B. Actions outside the EC. Further detailed priorities are available from the Department of Environment (see 14). Approximately 85 percent of resources are expected to be allocated to areas A1 and A2.

9. Eligible Expenditure:

Eligible expenditure varies according to the nature of the project undertaken.

10. Rate of Award:

The Commission's contribution to a project varies according to: the seriousness of the problems to be tackled; Community interest in the project; and the capacity of the country or beneficiary concerned to contribute.

The rate of award is up to 30 percent of total costs for income generating investments, up to 100 percent of total costs for the acquisition of information required to be able to carry out an action, and up to 50 percent of the cost of other actions.

11. Payment Procedure:

Payment procedure is outlined in the contract or agreement concluded with the beneficiaries. Commission payments are made in ECUs.

12. Points to Note:

Council Regulation (EEC) 1973/92 establishing LIFE was published in OJ L206; 22.7.92.

Projects receiving assistance under the Structural Funds (the European Regional Development Fund, the European Social Fund and the European Agricultural Guidance and Guarantee Fund), or under other Community financial instruments will not qualify for assistance under LIFE. A call for expressions of interest in providing technical support for the programme was published in OJ C181; 17.7.92; the deadline was 1 September 1992.

13. Application Procedure:

Applications for funding are invited by the designated national, regional or local authorities within each Member State (the DoE in the UK) and submitted to the European Commission for approval.

However, in relation to measures of particular EC interest, the Commission may also publish calls for expressions of interest in the Official Journal.

14. Further Information:

In England:
Richard Longman
Environmental Protection Division
Department of Environment
Romney House, Room A132
43 Marsham Street
London SW1P 3PY
Tel: (071) 276 8146
Fax: (071) 276 8626

Nature Conservation:
Mrs Hilary Neal
Directorate of Rural Affairs
Room 9/14
Tollgate House
Houlton Street
Bristol BS2 8PS
Tel: (0272) 218567

In Northern Ireland:
Graham Seymour
Environment Service
(Countryside and Wildlife)
Calvert House
23 Castle Place
Belfast BT1 1FY
Tel: (0232) 230560

In Scotland:
Neil Ingram
Scottish Office Environment Dept.
Room 266
27 Perth Street
Edinburgh EH3 5RA
Tel: (031) 244 5990

Nature Conservation:
John Gilmour
Scottish Office Environment Dept.
Room 6/62
New St Andrew's House
Edinburgh EH1 3SZ
Tel: (031) 244 4072

In Wales:
Derek Beames
Economic and Regional Policy Division 3
Welsh Office
Cathays Park
Cardiff CF1 3NQ
Tel: (0222) 825374

Mr C Pleinevaux
European Commission
DGXI
200 rue de la Loi
B-1049 Brussels
Tel: (010 32 2) 235 3960
Fax: (010 32 2) 236 9561

REGIONAL AND URBAN ENERGY PLANNING PROGRAMME

1. Summary:

The European Commission action in the field of regional and urban energy planning supports projects and studies which aim to improve energy management, particularly by making the most of local resources, improving energy efficiency and seeking optimum energy supply conditions for regions and urban areas, contributing to their economic and social development.

Applications are submitted in response to calls for proposals published annually in the Official Journal.

2. Awarding Body:

Commission of the European Communities.

3. Location Restrictions:
Available throughout the European Community.

4. Sectoral Restrictions:
Proposals must be submitted by one or more public or semi-public bodies including industrial or commercial public undertakings (in particular those covering a region, or urban or local administrative area).

5. Size Restrictions:
None.

6. Programme Duration:
The scheme runs on an annual basis.

7. Submission of Applications:
Applications are submitted in response to calls for proposals published annually in the Official Journal. The 1993 call for proposals was published in OJ C31; 4.2.93; the deadline was 30 April 1993.

8. Other Restrictions:
The following activities are eligible for support in 1993:

1. Regional energy planning studies;
2. Urban energy planning studies;
3. Feasibility studies on practical projects covering the technical, economic, financial, legal and other matters to be dealt with prior to energy investment;
4. Assistance in the setting-up and launching of local and regional developmental and advisory teams.

9. Eligible Expenditure:
Eligible expenditure relates to the total costs of the project.

10. Rate of Award:
The rate of award is up to 40 percent of total costs, up to a maximum of 100,000 ECUs. Support above this maximum is possible only in the case of joint projects submitted by two or more regions, towns or cities in different Member States.

11. Payment Procedure:
Payment procedure will be outlined in the agreed contract.

12. Points to Note:
None.

13. Application Procedure:
Application procedure is outlined when a call for proposals is published.

14. Further Information:
European Commission
DG XVII – Energy
Flanking Measures Unit
226–236 Avenue de Tervuren
B-1150 Brussels
Tel: (010 32 2) 236 3034

PART ONE

INVESTMENT SUPPORT

1.6 SUPPORT FOR THE ARTS AND HERITAGE

KALEIDOSCOPE	101
MEDIA	103
Pilot Conservation Projects (Architectural Heritage)	106

1.6 SUPPORT FOR THE ARTS AND HERITAGE

KALEIDOSCOPE

1. Summary:

The Kaleidoscope programme is a scheme of awards supporting innovative cultural events with a European dimension, related exchanges and cooperation networks.

The programme covers three Action Lines: 1. Cultural Events; 2. Mobility and Training; and 3. Networks (see 8 for further details).

2. Awarding Body:

Commission of the European Communities.

3. Location Restrictions:

Available in any Member State of the European Communities.

Eligible events/activities under Action 1 must involve partners from at least three Member States of the European Community. Events involving partners from Central/Eastern Europe are also eligible. Projects under Actions 2 and 3 must also have a European dimension.

4. Sectoral Restrictions:

Under Action 1, applications may be submitted by organisers of eligible events, including artists themselves. Under Action 2, entries may be submitted by cultural organisations (institutes, associations, foundations, residential centres, colleges, academies etc) that run workshops and training courses for creative and performing artists and others professionally active in the cultural field. Under Action 3, entries may be submitted by cultural networks combining either non-profit making organisations or professionals working on the development of shared cultural activities.

5. Size Restrictions:

None.

6. Programme Duration:

The programme is open to application annually.

7. Submission of Applications:

Applications must be submitted within deadlines set annually for the programme. In 1992, the programme opened to applications in September (OJ C237; 16.9.92), with a deadline of 31 December 1992.

8. Other Restrictions:

Events/activities must fall within one of the following Action Lines:

1. Cultural Events: Events should be of high quality and innovative or exemplary in nature, and concern either: contemporary artistic and cultural events (including theatre, dance, music, literature, visual arts and multimedia art forms); or appreciation and awareness of the cultural heritage. In 1993, priority will be given to the promotion of theatre projects.

2. Encouragement of artistic and cultural creation through training and mobility of creative and performing artists: Support for workshops and training courses (taking place in 1993) for creative and performing artists and others professionally active in the cultural world. Priority is given to high quality events that give young creative and performing artists the chance to boost their training and launch their professional career. Priority areas include: cultural heritage; literary translation; visual arts; music; theatre; the audiovisual field; and arts and cultural administration.
3. Cultural cooperation in the form of Networks including: cultural activities and projects developed by existing networks as part of their specific objectives (joint research, exchanges of experience, directories, guides, reference works, pilot projects etc); the extension of existing networks to enable them to work with other Member States; and the establishment of new networks in limited cases where required to develop cooperation in particular cultural areas. All cultural fields are included, as are arts sponsorship and administration and infrastructure (museums, libraries, archives etc). The following are excluded from the programme: under Action 1: events of a purely regional, national or bilateral nature; conservation and restoration of the architectural heritage; materials and publications not forming an integral part of the event; and recipients of an award under the programme in the previous three years; under both Actions 1 and 2: feasibility studies; investment or operation costs of cultural organisations; under Action 2 only: individual requests for admission to workshops or training courses; and under Actions 1, 2 and 3: projects to take place in 1994.

9. Eligible Expenditure:

Eligible expenditure includes the total costs of an eligible project. The financing, investment or operating costs of cultural organisations are not eligible.

10. Rate of Award:

The rate of award for Action 1 projects is up to 25 percent of total project costs, up to a maximum of 30,000 ECU. The rate of award for Action 2 projects is: from 750 ECU to 3,000 ECU per participant for projects lasting between three weeks and three months, or projects involving a series of shorter courses (one week) spread over the year; and from 2,500 ECU to 5,000 ECU per participant for longer projects (three months to one year). The actual award will vary depending on the nature of the project (duration, content, number of participants). A limited lump sum contribution (up to a maximum of 10,000 ECU) may also be made towards the cost of organising the project.

The rate of award for Action 3 projects is up to 30 percent of the full cost of the activity, up to a maximum of 50,000 ECU. Support may consist of a lump sum towards setting up new networks or extending existing networks, or support for joint projects. The amount will vary according to the nature of the project.

11. Payment Procedure:

Payment procedure is outlined when an award is made.

12. Points to Note:

Successful entries will be publicised and will acquire the right to use the 'Kaleidoscope Programme' logo in their publicity material. An acknowledgement of Commission support must feature prominently. The Kaleidoscope programme is a successor to the 'Platform Europe' award scheme.

13. Application Procedure:

Application forms are available between October and December from EC Offices.

14. Further Information:

European Commission
DG X/C-1 – Culture Unit
Kaleidoscope
120 rue de Treves
B-1049 Brussels
Tel: (010 32 2) 299 1111

European Commission
Jean Monnet House
8, Storey's Gate
London SW1P 3AT
Tel: (071) 973 1992

European Commission
4 Cathedral Road
Cardiff CF1 9SG
Tel: (0222) 371 631

European Commission
7 Alva Street
Edinburgh EH2 4PH
Tel: (031) 225 2058

European Commission
Windsor House
9/15 Bedford Street
Belfast BT2 7EG
Tel: (0232) 240 708

MEDIA

1. Summary:

The MEDIA programme (Measures to Encourage the Development of the Industry of Audiovisual Production) is intended to assist the promotion of the European audiovisual industry through a set of incentive measures, acting both upstream and downstream of production. The incentive measures cover the following areas: distribution mechanisms; improvement of production conditions; stimulation of financial investment; improving the economic and commercial management abilities of professionals in the industry; developing potential in countries with small audiovisual production capacities and/or a limited geographical/linguistic area; and participation in Audiovisual EUREKA projects. The current phase of the programme is set to run for five years from 1 January 1991, with a budget of 200 MECU.

2. Awarding Body:

Commission of the European Communities.

3. Location Restrictions:
Available throughout the European Community, non-Member States (including Central and Eastern European countries) may also participate.

4. Sectoral Restrictions:
MEDIA is open to individuals and organisations in the audiovisual industry.

5. Size Restrictions:
The European Film Distribution Office (EFDO) (see 12) provides loans to assist with the distribution costs of low-budget films (ie with production costs of up to 4.5 MECU).
No size restrictions are specified under other sectors of the programme.

6. Programme Duration:
MEDIA is set to run for five years from 1 January 1991.

7. Submission of Applications:
Deadlines for applications to the European Film Distribution Office (EFDO) will be announced in professional international film publications. Further information on application submission for the other MEDIA schemes can be obtained from the Commission. A call for expressions of interest in undertaking an audit of the first two years of the MEDIA programme was published in OJ C181; 17.7.92. The deadline was 24 August 1992.

8. Other Restrictions:
MEDIA covers the following areas (budget allocation in brackets):

1. Distribution Mechanisms: distribution of films in cinemas (40 MECU); distribution on video cassette (10 MECU); support for multilingualism in television programmes (10 MECU); and development of markets and support for the dissemination of the work of independent producers (25 MECU);
2. Improvement of Production Conditions: development of pre-production (23 MECU); restructuring of the animated cartoon industry (23 MECU); use of new technologies (in particular European ones) in the production of programmes (20 MECU); and contribution to the establishment of a 'second market', in particular using archive material (9 MECU);
3. Stimulation of financial investment (10 MECU);
4. Training measures improving the economic and commercial management abilities of professionals (14 MECU);
5. Developing potential in countries with small audiovisual production capacities and/or with a limited geographical and linguistic area (15 MECU);
6. Participation in Audiovisual EUREKA projects. Audiovisual EUREKA provides a framework for transnational projects in the production field (see 12 for further details).

The programme also supports: the Media Business School, which organises courses throughout the EC for those working in the audiovisual industry; GRECO – promoting the showing on television of films and serials presented by independent European producers; IVENS – to encourage the production and distribution of documentaries; and MAP-TV, to stimulate the use of audiovisual archives in film production.

9. Eligible Expenditure:
Eligible expenditure relates to the type of project undertaken.

10. Rate of Award:
Support may be for up to 50 percent of total project costs.

11. Payment Procedure:
Payment procedure varies depending on the project undertaken.

12. Points to Note:
Support for the pilot schemes initiated under the first phase of MEDIA will be continued under the current phase: the European Film Distribution Office (EFDO), Broadcasting Across Barriers of European Language (BABEL), the European Organisation for an Audio-Visual Independent Market (EURO-AIM), and the European Video Area (EVE) (Area 1 – Distribution Mechanisms); the European Script Fund, the European Centre for Animation Films (CARTOON) and the MEDIA Investment Club (Area 2 – Production Conditions); and European Audiovisual Entrepreneurs (EAVE) (Area 4 – Management Abilities). Participation in Audiovisual EUREKA projects is designed to: increase the coherence of various initiatives under the action programme by means of participation in projects which build on the measures already undertaken; generating synergies between projects; stimulating the independent production sector; helping to create a second market for the distribution of European works; providing projects with the extra finance they need to use and benefit from the new European technologies applied to programmes (eg HDTV); supporting projects developing the potential of countries with a 'lesser audiovisual capacity'; and in general boosting Europe's audiovisual capacity.

13. Application Procedure:
Details of the application procedure for all schemes can be obtained from the European Commission and the British Film Institute.

14. Further Information:

Holde Lhoest
(Head of Programme)
European Commission
DG X – MEDIA Programme
120 Rue de Treves
B-1049 Brussels
Tel: (010 32 2) 299 9436
Fax: (010 32 2) 299 9214
Telex: 21877 COMEU B

Louise Casey
UK Media Desk
c/o The British Film Institute
21 Stephen Street
London W1P 1PL
Tel: (071) 255 1444
Fax: (071) 436 7950

PILOT CONSERVATION PROJECTS (ARCHITECTURAL HERITAGE)

1. Summary:

Assistance is available for pilot projects to conserve and promote the European Community's architectural heritage. Support is given to projects concerned with the conservation of monuments/sites in rural or urban areas illustrating some aspects of the national, regional or local architectural heritage of the Community by reason of their artistic value, historic interest and socio-economic influence in bearing witness to the living and working conditions of a given section of the population. Emphasis is given each year to a particular theme. For 1993 the theme is the conservation and restoration of historic gardens.

Calls for proposals in relation to the programme are published annually in the Official Journal of the European Communities. The 1993 call was published in OJ C261; 10.10.92; the deadline for applications was 29 January 1993.

2. Awarding Body:

Commission of the European Communities.

3. Location Restrictions:

Available in any Member State of the European Community. The Commission is considering extending the programme to cover projects in Central and Eastern Europe.

4. Sectoral Restrictions:

Available to any individual or body in possession of, or responsible for a monument or site of European renown which illustrates some aspects of the national or regional architectural heritage of the Community.

5. Size Restrictions:

The maximum project cost eligible for grant is 5 MECU.

6. Programme Duration:

There is no specified terminal date for this scheme.

7. Submission of Applications:

Application must be made within the deadlines specified in each of the Commission's invitations for proposals to be submitted, published in the Official Journal. The call for proposals relating to the 1993 round of projects was published in OJ C261; 10.10.92. The deadline was 29 January 1993.

Application must normally be made and grant approved before work on the project is begun as no grant will be paid in respect of expenditure incurred prior to approval.

8. Other Restrictions:

The following theme will be highlighted in 1993: the conservation and restoration of historic gardens. The garden concerned must be open to the public. Small-scale gardens and larger, formally or naturally landscaped parks, botanical gardens, monastery gardens, orchard and green areas in historic centres are all included.

The provision of financial support is conditional on the following: the applicant must allow the conservation/restoration work to be inspected; the grant must be used entirely for the conservation/restoration work; the applicant must ensure that the Commission's financial contribution to the project is made known to the general public; and applications must not be submitted for projects which have already received Community financial support in previous years.

9. Eligible Expenditure:

Eligible expenditure covers the total approved conservation costs of the project. Modernisation work, technical improvements and new construction work are not eligible.

10. Rate of Award:

The rate of award varies according to the size of the project as follows: up to 25 percent for projects with a total investment of up to 750,000 ECU (maximum grant 130,000 ECU); up to 10 percent for projects costing between 750,000 ECU and 2.5 MECU (maximum grant 150,000 ECU); and up to 5 percent for projects costing between 2.5 and 5 MECU (maximum grant 125,000 ECU).

11. Payment Procedure:

Payment procedure will be arranged by individual contracts with successful applicants. The Commission grant will not be definitively paid until such time as the relevant regional or national organisation has accepted the conservation works.

12. Points to Note:

A total of 44 projects received grants totalling 3 MECU under this programme in 1992, when the theme was the upgrading of public spaces in historic centres as part of a restoration project. In the UK grants were awarded to: The Slopes/The Crescent, Buxton; Bristol Cathedral; Square Chapel/Piece Hall, Halifax; Hastings Pier; and Sheldonian Theatre, Oxford.

13. Application Procedure:

Application is made direct to the European Commission on a standard form, available from the Commission or the relevant regional address below, and must include descriptions of the monument and the project. Adequate documentation providing a clear explanation of the monument or site and the work to be carried out must be enclosed. A copy of the application must be sent at the same time to the relevant UK national organisation.

14. Further Information:

In England:
English Heritage
Historic Buildings & Monuments Commission for England
Fortress House
23–25 Savile Row
London W1X 1AB
Tel: (071) 734 6010

In Scotland:
Scottish Office Environment Department
Historic Scotland
20 Brandon Street
Edinburgh EH3 5RA
Tel: (031) 244 2946/2906

In Wales:
CADW Welsh Historic Monuments
Brunel House
2 Fitzalan Place
Cardiff CF2 1UY
Tel: (0222) 465511

European Commission
Cultural Action Division
(Office 0/16, 70 rue Joseph II)
Rue de la Loi 200
B-1049 Brussels
Tel: (010 32 2) 235 3844

In Northern Ireland:
Historic Monuments and Buildings Branch
5–33 Hill Street
Belfast BT1 2LA
Tel: (0232) 230560

PART TWO

EMPLOYMENT AND TRAINING

2.0	OVERVIEW	111
2.1	EMPLOYMENT AND TRAINING	113
2.2	SCIENTIFIC TRAINING	147

2.0 OVERVIEW

Employment and training link the economic and social policies of the European Community and, accordingly, constitute an important aspect of Commission activities. The Commission's principal instrument for tackling employment and training-related problems is the European Social Fund – one of the three Structural Funds. Since it was established in 1957, the Social Fund has made financial assistance available to public authorities, private firms and voluntary bodies to support the cost of vocational training and job-creation schemes. Although the scale of European Social Fund support is relatively modest when compared to national public expenditure on employment and training, it is interesting to note that the UK has been one of the chief beneficiaries of Social Fund assistance, receiving between 15 and 20 percent of the total Social Fund budget allocation in recent years. In 1991, for example, approximately £400 million of Social Fund money was allocated to 12,500 British projects. European Social Fund support thus plays an important role in funding training programmes in the UK. For the majority of firms in the UK, support comes indirectly through jointly funded Government programmes such as Employment Training and Youth Training.

The European Social Fund contributes to the achievement of all five Objectives of the Single Act legislation , but is primarily concerned with the achievement of Objectives 3 and 4. These apply across the whole Community and are aimed at combating long-term unemployment and the occupational integration of young people. A total of 7,450 million ECU has been allocated from the Fund for the period 1989–93 for expenditure on Objectives 3 and 4.

The European Social Fund supports two principal types of activities: vocational training projects (accompanied where necessary by vocational guidance); and subsidies toward recruitment into newly created stable jobs and self-employment activities. Roughly 80 percent of Social Fund expenditure is devoted to training activities.

In line with the other Structural Funds, Social Fund projects must be wholly or partly financed from public funds in the beneficiary state. In other words, projects submitted by non-public sector organisations must attract support from a national public-sector authority to qualify for support from the Social Fund. In the UK, public authorities most commonly associated with projects assisted by the Social Fund include local authorities, Training and Enterprise Councils (TECs) in England and Wales and Local Enterprise Companies (LECs) in Scotland.

As is the case with the other Structural Funds, recent reforms have shifted the operation of the Social Fund from a project-based to a programme-based approach, with operational programmes running for a three-year period within the context of agreed Community Support Frameworks (CSFs). In the UK, operational programmes are administered by a number of intermediary organisations. In Objective 2 regions, applications are channelled through a series of regional working groups and/or operational programme committees, set up to coordinate and administer measures funded by all of the Structural Funds. Applications covered by Objective 3 and Objective 4 operational programmes are coordinated by local authorities, TECs, LECs, voluntary organisations operating through the National Council for Voluntary Organisations, Industrial Common Ownership Movement, Women's Training Network, Industry Training Boards and the higher education sector.

Again, as with the other Structural Funds, the Regulation governing the operation of the European Social Fund expires at the end of 1993. A new implementing Regulation is due to be approved during the course of 1993. Following the new Treaty on European Union agreed at Maastricht, several new areas of responsibility were entrusted to the Social Fund. Whilst the current priorities (the long-term unemployed and young people) will still be relevant, the Fund may also cover people excluded from the labour market for various reasons, as well as vocational training and retraining to help workers adapt to industrial change and changing production systems. Furthermore, although Objectives 3 and 4 are still likely to be 'horizontal' ie not regionally restricted, the focus in non-assisted areas is likely to be on demonstration and innovative training measures.

A further indication of the direction in which the Social Fund may develop in the future are the priorities targeted by three Community Initiatives launched in 1991. Funded from the budget of the European Social Fund, EUROFORM, HORIZON and NOW support vocational training and employment measures with a European dimension, notably for women, and disabled and disadvantaged people.

While the European Social Fund is the Community's main instrument for addressing employment-related problems, a number of other employment and training-related programmes exist at the Community level. These promote a range of objectives such as: cooperation between universities and industries to develop training (COMETT II); the mobility of university students and staff (ERASMUS); the adaptation of training to changing technology (EUROTECNET); vocational training (FORCE and PETRA); foreign language training (LINGUA); improving the competitiveness of European industry (Executive Training Programme in Japan); local employment creation (SPEC) and women's employment initiatives.

A final group of programmes focus on a more specific aspect of employment and training, the mobility and training of the Community's scientific research staff. These are discussed in Section 2.2. It should be noted that four of the programme descriptions outlined in this Section make up the Commission's Human Capital and Mobility Programme, which is part of the Third Framework Programme for Research and Development.

PART TWO

EMPLOYMENT AND TRAINING

2.1 EMPLOYMENT AND TRAINING

European Social Fund	115
Community Initiatives:	
EUROFORM	118
HORIZON	120
NOW	122
COMETT II	124
ERASMUS	128
EUROTECNET	130
FORCE	131
LINGUA	134
PETRA II	137
TEMPUS – *see* Support for Eastern Europe (page 90)	
Executive Training in Japan	139
Support Programme for Employment Creation (SPEC)	141
Women's Local Employment Initiatives	143

2.1 EMPLOYMENT AND TRAINING

EUROPEAN SOCIAL FUND

1. Summary:

The European Social Fund (ESF), one of the three Community Structural Funds, aims to improve employment opportunities within the Community by funding vocational training and employment creation measures contributing to the attainment of the five objectives agreed in the Single Act, namely: the development and structural adjustment of underdeveloped regions (Objective 1); converting regions seriously affected by industrial decline (Objective 2); combatting long-term unemployment (Objective 3); facilitating the occupational integration of young people (Objective 4); promoting the development of rural areas (Objective 5b). Priority use of ESF assistance is directed towards Objectives 3 and 4. With respect to Objectives 1, 2 and 5(b), the ESF can act in concert with the European Regional Development Fund and the European Agricultural Guidance and Guarantee Fund: Guidance Section, as appropriate, to support approved employment and training measures.

The ESF co-finances measures within the context of operational programmes undertaken by various intermediary organisations (see 2). The following types of activity are eligible for support: vocational training operations; subsidies in relation to recruitment to new permanent jobs and for the creation of self-employed activities. Up to 5 percent of the total ESF budget can be directed towards relevant innovatory training and employment operations, studies and technical assistance, information exchange in relation to technology transfer and guidance counselling for the long-term unemployed.

2. Awarding Body:

European Social Fund. Applications in the UK must be channelled through the relevant intermediary organisation/sector (see 14). The intermediary organisations are responsible for selecting projects for support and recommending them to the Employment Department for formal approval.

3. Location Restrictions:

Assistance granted in respect of Objectives 3 and 4 (see 1) is available throughout the European Community. ESF assistance granted in respect of a plan which includes European Regional Development Fund and/or European Agricultural Guidance and Guarantee Fund: Guidance Section support under Objectives 1, 2 or 5(b) is restricted to regions designated under each of these, respectively (for a full list of qualifying regions see European Regional Development Fund).

4. Sectoral Restrictions:

None.

5. Size Restrictions:

Applications by, or in respect of, individuals are not eligible for support.

6. Programme Duration:

There is no specified terminal date for the activities of the ESF.

Current Community Support Frameworks (CSFs), outlining how Social Fund Assistance will be implemented, cover the period 1990–93. Within these CSFs, operational programmes outline groups of individual projects or measures to be supported throughout the lifetime of the agreed CSF. The CSFs and operational programmes may be revised annually if there are changes in the labour market. Progress of individual projects will be reviewed yearly, and funding adjusted if necessary.

7. Submission of Applications:

Individual projects will receive support within the context of agreed operational programmes which outline groups of projects or measures to be assisted throughout the period of a Community Support Framework (CSF). (CSFs outline the broad measures which will receive Social Fund assistance over a three to five year period.)

Individual projects are channelled through intermediate organisations, which submit selected projects to the Employment Department for formal approval (see 13).

8. Other Restrictions:

European Social Fund assistance is implemented in the form of operational programmes, outlining a series of projects or measures to be supported. These may cover Objective 2 regions, Objective 3 measures (for the long-term unemployed) or Objective 4 measures (the occupational integration of young people). The Objective 3 and 4 (nationwide) operational programmes cover the following:

For the long-term unemployed (Objective 3 – budget allocation in brackets):

(1) Training (327 MECU): to be carried out by local authorities, the higher education sector, industry training boards, the voluntary sector, and through the Employment Training scheme;

(2) Job-creation measures (68 MECU): to be carried out by local authorities, by offering premiums for new permanent jobs. The creation of self-employment opportunities will be undertaken through the Enterprise Allowance scheme, and the local authorities promoting Local Enterprise Agency schemes.

(3) Special assistance for women, migrants, and handicapped people (118 MECU): providing good quality vocational training, job creation, and innovatory transnational projects, to be implemented by the Employment Department.

For the young unemployed:

(1) Vocational training (308 MECU): mainly through the Employment Training scheme.

(2) Higher skills training (96 MECU): to be provided by the Employment Department, the higher education sector, local authorities, industry training boards and the voluntary sector.

(3) Women, migrants and handicapped young people (64 MECU): the provision of good quality vocational training, the creation of stable jobs and innovatory projects, to be run mainly through the local authorities and the Employment Department.

9. Eligible Expenditure:

Eligible expenditure for ESF part-financing includes:

(a) the income of persons receiving vocational training;

(b) the costs of preparing, operating, managing and assessing training operations including vocational guidance, costs of training teaching staff and subsistence and travel costs of those covered by vocational training operations;

(c) the cost of granting recruitment subsidies for a maximum period of 12 months and costs associated with the creation of self-employed activities; the cost of recruitment subsidies of at least six months' duration per person associated with non-productive projects which fulfil a public need and are located in Objective 1 regions;

(d) the cost of technical assistance and studies related to the implementation of the ESF Regulation; the cost of transnational exchange of information between undertakings related to the modernisation of production technology; the cost of guidance counselling for the reintegration of the long-term unemployed.

10. Rate of Award:

The rate of award in respect of the various Objectives (see 1) is subject to the following ceilings:

- in Objective 1 regions (in the UK – Northern Ireland), a maximum of 75 percent of total costs and, as a general rule, at least 50 percent of public expenditure on qualifying activities;
- elsewhere, a maximum of 50 percent of total costs and, as a general rule, at least 25 percent of public expenditure on qualifying activities.

Rates of award for individual measures forming part of operational programmes are differentiated in accordance with agreements concluded in the relevant Community Support Framework. With respect to recruitment subsidies, the maximum eligible amount per person and per week is determined each year at a rate equal to 30 percent of the average gross earnings of individual workers in the relevant Member State. Preparatory studies and technical assistance measures undertaken on the initiative of the Commission may be financed at 100 percent of total costs in exceptional cases.

11. Payment Procedure:

Payment is normally made over to the Employment Department as a partial reimbursement for its contribution to the project. The Department of Employment will make payments through the relevant intermediary organisation/sector.

12. Points to Note:

Measures covered by the agreed operational programmes include many of the existing employment and training schemes, such as Youth Training, Employment Training, Enterprise Allowance etc.

13. Application Procedure:

Individual organisations wishing to apply for Social Fund support should contact the appropriate coordinating body. In Objective 2 regions, applications will be coordinated by a series of regional working groups and/or operational programme committees. Applications for support under Objectives 3 and 4 (nationwide) should be made to the relevant organisation/sector: the Training and Enterprise Councils (TECs) and Local Enterprise Companies (LECs); National Council for Voluntary Organisations (NCVO); local authorities; Industrial Common Ownership Movement; Women's Training Network; Industry Training Boards; or higher education sector. Any organisation uncertain as to which coordinating body covers their interests should contact the Employment Department. The European Social Fund Unit of the Department has produced guidance notes on application procedures, available from the address below.

14. Further Information:

In Great Britain:
Employment Department
European Social Fund Unit
236 Gray's Inn Road
London WC1X 8HL
Tel: (071) 211 4740/4741

In Northern Ireland:
Dept. of Economic Development
European Communities Branch
The Arches Centre
11–13 Bloomfield Avenue
Belfast BT5 5HD
Tel: (0232) 732411

EUROFORM

1. Summary:

The EUROFORM initiative aims to provide a Community dimension to vocational training and employment promotion projects, and to promote the convergence of occupational skills, particularly between Objective 1 (underdeveloped) and other regions, and the occupational and geographic mobility of workers. The initiative funds two types of project: vocational training projects supplemented, if necessary, by vocational guidance projects; and support measures for employment in newly created stable jobs and for setting-up as a self-employed worker. (Within this framework, the European Social Fund will finance preparatory supporting and management activities, and guidance and advisory activities for the re-integration of the long term unemployed). The initiative is financed from the EC's Structural Fund budget, with a total budget allocation of 330 MECU. The UK has been allocated 35.4 MECU over the period 1991–93. (Approximately 31.3 MECU was allocated under the first two rounds of awards.)

2. Awarding Body:

Commission of the European Communities.

3. Location Restrictions:

Projects must be carried out in the form of a transnational partnership between two or more Member States, at least one partner must be from an Objective 1 region.

4. Sectoral Restrictions:

None.

5. Size Restrictions:
None.

6. Programme Duration:
The initiative is set to run from 1991 to 1993.

7. Submission of Applications:
The deadline for the third round of awards was 11 December 1992.

8. Other Restrictions:
All projects must show links with vocational training or employment subsidy projects, and must concern: the long-term unemployed (over 12 months) and young people (under 25) throughout the EC, or persons employed in small and medium-sized enterprises, the unemployed or those threatened by unemployment in areas eligible under Objectives 2 and 5(b) of the European Regional Development Fund.

The primary aim of EUROFORM is the promotion of new skills, qualifications and employment opportunities arising from the completion of the Single Market and technological change. The following areas will be a priority: the promotion of vocational skills and qualifications, especially in sectors particularly affected by the completion of the Single Market programme and technological developments; the promotion of mutual recognition and comparability of qualifications and vocational skills; support for innovation in basic and continuing vocational training; development of continuing vocational training in Objective 2 and 5(b) regions; local development initiatives to encourage job creation, taking account of local economic and natural resource conditions, promote job creation for the unemployed or socially disadvantaged groups or to exchange experience in the field of local employment development; and activities aimed at the long-term unemployed to promote transnational projects in the field of employment or labour market re-entry which combine assistance with re-entry with support for social problems, or are adapted to the needs and capabilities of the unemployed and the local labour market.

Projects must be innovative and have a multiplier effect at Community level.

The ESF Unit of the Employment Department has drawn up a detailed list of priorities which should also be met.

9. Eligible Expenditure:
Eligible expenditure includes: preparatory, operating and management costs of vocational training projects; wages and allowances of persons involved in vocational training projects; employment aid or wage subsidy costs; studies and setting-up costs.

10. Rate of Award:
EUROFORM will contribute up to 45 percent of the total costs of the project. The remaining 55 percent must normally be found through public authority support.

11. Payment Procedure:
Payment procedure will be outlined by the Employment Department.

12. Points to Note:
None.

13. Application Procedure:
Applications are coordinated by the ESF Unit of the Employment Department.

14. Further Information:

Lorraine Huggins
Employment Department
236 Gray's Inn Road
London WC1X 8HL
Tel: (071) 211 4710/11

Ms Barbara Nolan
European Commission
DG V
200 rue de la Loi
B-1049 Brussels
Tel: (010 32 2) 236 0755

Mr Fabio Marchetti
Technical Assistance Unit
MIDA
Rue Franklin 136
B-1040 Brussels
Tel: (010 32 2) 735 9601

HORIZON

1. Summary:
The HORIZON initiative aims to improve labour market entry opportunities for people with disabilities and certain other disadvantaged groups (eg refugees and people in inner city areas).

The initiative funds two types of projects: vocational training projects supplemented, if necessary, by vocational guidance projects; and support measures for employment in newly created stable jobs and for setting up as a self-employed worker. (Within this framework the European Social Fund will fund preparatory, supporting and management activities, and guidance and advisory activities for the re-integration of the long-term unemployed.)

The initiative is financed from the EC's Structural Fund budget, with a total budget allocation of 291 MECU. The UK has been allocated 28.9 MECU over the period 1991 to 1993. (Approximately 14.9 MECU of this budget was allocated under the first round of awards.)

2. Awarding Body:
Commission of the European Communities.

3. Location Restrictions:
Projects for the disabled must be carried out in the form of a transnational partnership between two or more Member States, and must include at least one partner from an Objective 1 region. Projects aimed at disadvantaged groups must also be carried out as a transnational partnership, with the exception of measures applied to refugees facing a new socio-economic situation.

Projects for the disadvantaged must cover one or more of the following geographical areas which have been identified as potentially being of strategic significance to city-wide regeneration and relieving inner city disadvantage: England: Newcastle; Middlesbrough; Bradford; Doncaster/Barnsley/Rotherham (Deane Valley); Liverpool; Manchester; Wirral; Wolverhampton; Nottingham; Lewisham; Tower Hamlets; Scotland: Westerhailes, Ferguslie, Castlemilk, Whitfield (these areas are covered by the New Life for Urban Scotland Initiative); Wales: no geographical restriction on projects, but they are expected to be in or clearly benefit those wards which show the highest incidence of urban deprivation.

4. Sectoral Restrictions:

Participants should be public and private organisations specifically responsible for the disabled, the disadvantaged, and for those faced with a socio-economic situation new to them.

5. Size Restrictions:

None.

6. Programme Duration:

The initiative is set to run from 1991 to 1993.

7. Submission of Applications:

The deadline for 1992 applications was 15 October 1992.

8. Other Restrictions:

Only projects aimed at groups eligible under European Social Fund regulations will qualify for support, ie the long-term unemployed (aged over 25 and unemployed for over 12 months), young people (under 25, regardless of length of unemployment), and those located in Objective 2 and 5(b) regions.

Projects for the disabled should involve: vocational training for qualifications, skills and the use of technologies for physically disabled people (a particular emphasis is placed on modular distance learning); vocational training and employment in suitable economic sectors or jobs for mentally handicapped people; training of trainers, care assistants, therapists, psychologists etc using techniques to improve the transition of people with disabilities from a sheltered environment towards the open labour market; the creation of SMEs and cooperatives, provided that these are capable eventually of being integrated into the market economy; creation of information networks; and exchanges of experience and specialists.

Projects for disadvantaged people may include: guidance and counselling measures; vocational training; exchange of specialist agencies at an EC level; preparatory studies and the setting-up of projects. In addition, and in particular in Objective 1 regions, measures may be supported for refugees who are obliged to adapt themselves to an entirely new socio-economic situation.

All projects must show links with vocational training or employment subsidy projects. Projects must be innovative and have a multiplier effect at Community level.

9. Eligible Expenditure:

Eligible expenditure includes: preparatory, operating and management costs of vocational training projects; wages and allowances of persons involved in vocational training projects; employment aid or wage subsidy costs; studies and setting-up costs.

10. Rate of Award:
HORIZON will contribute up to 45 percent of the total costs of the project. The remaining 55 percent must normally be found through public authority support.

11. Payment Procedure:
Payment procedure will be outlined by the Employment Department.

12. Points to Note:
None.

13. Application Procedure:
Applications should be submitted to the Employment Department.

14. Further Information:

Lorraine Huggins
Department of Employment
236 Gray's Inn Road
London WC1X 8HL
Tel: (071) 211 4710/11

G Katzourakis
European Commission
Arch 1 1/23
B-1049 Brussels
Tel: (010 32 2) 235 9044

Mr Fabio Marchetti
Technical Assistance Unit
MIDA
Rue Franklin 136
B-1040 Brussels
Tel: (010 32 2) 735 9601

NOW

1. Summary:
The NOW (New Opportunities for Women) initiative aims to: 1. contribute to upgrading and developing women's qualifications and improve the business environment, to help them establish their own enterprises or cooperatives; and 2. to contribute to the re-entry of women into the labour market. To help achieve objective 1, NOW funds vocational training measures (including pre-training) and assists with the creation of self-employed activities and employee recruitment; to achieve objective 2, NOW funds guidance, advisory, and vocational training measures. The initiative is financed from the European Commission's Structural Fund budget, with a budget allocation of 165 MECU for the period 1991 to 1993. The UK budget allocation for the period is 9.2 MECU (of which approximately 5.8 MECU was allocated under the first round of awards).

2. Awarding Body:
Commission of the European Communities.

3. Location Restrictions:

Projects must be carried out in the form of transnational partnerships between two or more Member States, preferably including an Objective 1 region.

4. Sectoral Restrictions:

Participants should be national, regional or local authorities, public or private vocational training agents, socio-economic partners, and public and private research and information centres for women.

5. Size Restrictions:

None.

6. Programme Duration:

The initiative is set to run from 1991 to 1993.

7. Submission of Applications:

The deadline for 1992 applications was 15 October 1992.

8. Other Restrictions:

Projects must be directed at: 1. Women who are long-term unemployed (over 12 months), regardless of their age (women seeking to re-enter the labour market after a long interruption are included in this category); or 2. Women employed in small and medium-sized enterprises, unemployed women or those threatened by unemployment in Objective 2 and 5(b) regions. (For a full list of Objective 2 and 5(b) regions, *see* European Regional Development Fund.)

Measures concerning the operating costs of day nurseries attached to vocational training centres, and vocational training for persons working professionally with young children will be eligible, provided they are linked to the NOW funding objectives (see 1).

All projects must show links with vocational training or employment subsidy projects, and must comply with UK legislation under the Sex Discrimination Acts of 1975 and 1986. Furthermore the projects must be innovative, and have a multiplier effect at Community level.

9. Eligible Expenditure:

Eligible expenditure includes: preparatory, operating and management costs of vocational training projects; wages and allowances of persons involved in vocational training projects; employment aid or wage subsidy costs; preparatory studies and assistance for setting-up projects.

10. Rate of Award:

NOW will contribute up to 45 percent of the total costs of the project. The remaining 55 percent must normally be found through public authority support.

11. Payment Procedure:

Payment procedure will be outlined by the Employment Department.

12. Points to Note:

None.

13. Application Procedure:
Applications should be submitted to the Employment Department.

14. Further Information:

Lorraine Huggins
Department of Employment
236 Gray's Inn Road
London WC1X 8HL
Tel: (071) 211 4710/11

Ms Celia Alexopolou
European Commission
DG V
200 rue de la Loi
B-1049 Brussels
Tel: (010 32 2) 235 4295

Mr Fabio Marchetti
Technical Assistance Unit
MIDA
Rue Franklin 136
B-1040 Brussels
Tel: (010 32 2) 735 9601

COMETT II

1. Summary:
The second phase of the COMETT action programme in Education and Training for Technology provides grants for a range of transnational measures designed to strengthen and encourage cooperation between universities and industry in developing training programmes within the European framework. COMETT covers both initial and continuing training programmes, in particular advanced technology areas which, in the context of the completion of the Single European Market, will strengthen economic and social cohesion in the Community. In the course of COMETT II, measures will be implemented under the following broad headings (see 8 for further details): A. European Network; B. Transnational Exchanges; C. Joint projects for continuing training in advanced technology and for multi-media distance training; D. Complementary promotion and back-up measures.

COMETT II is set to run from 1 January 1990 to 31 December 1994, with a budget allocation of 200 MECU.

2. Awarding Body:
Commission of the European Communities.

3. Location Restrictions:
Available in any Member State of the European Community. EFTA countries may also participate in COMETT II. Universities and undertakings in EFTA countries may cooperate with each other on COMETT II projects, provided that similar bodies from at least two Community Member States are also involved.

4. Sectoral Restrictions:
COMETT II is designed to stimulate cooperation between universities and

industries. For the purposes of the programme, 'university' is used as a general term covering all types of post-secondary education and training establishments which offer, within the framework of initial and/or continuing training, qualifications or diplomas of that level. The term 'industries' covers all types of economic activity, including large and small and medium-sized businesses, whatever their legal status and manner of applying new technologies. It also covers independent economic organisations, in particular Chambers of Commerce and Industry and/or their equivalents, professional associations and organisations representing employers or employees.

Measures to be implemented under COMETT II are directed at trainees, including those who have completed their initial training, and at persons in active employment, including employers' and workers' representatives and the training officers concerned.

5. Size Restrictions:

None.

Within the overall budget allocation, Strand A activities (see 8) will be allocated up to 12 percent, Strand B up to 40 percent, Strand C up to 40 percent, and Strand D up to 8 percent.

6. Programme Duration:

COMETT II is set to run from 1 January 1990 to 31 December 1994.

7. Submission of Applications:

Application is made within the deadlines specified in each of the Commission's invitations for proposals to be submitted, published in the Official Journal.

An open call under strands A and C, and a restricted call under B and C were published in OJ C238; 13.9.91; the deadline was 15 January 1992. A call for tenders for the evaluation of COMETT II was published in OJ C143; 5.6.92. The deadline was 15 July 1992.

8. Other Restrictions:

The following measures will be implemented in the course of COMETT II:

A. The development and reinforcement of university-industry training partnerships (UETPs) and the extension of the regional and sectoral European network, to further transnational cooperation, particularly through the: identification and resolution of technology training needs; the development and exploitation of projects within the other strands of COMETT II; strengthening of cooperation and inter-regional transfer in the development of training for the needs of technology, their application and transfer; and the development of transnational sectoral networks.

B. Transnational exchanges through the allocation of grants for: students undergoing 3 to 12 months training in industry in another Member State; industrial placements from 6 months to two years to undertake an industrial development project following completion of initial training; personnel seconded from universities and industry to industry or a university respectively in another Member State to bring their skills to the industry or university in question for the improvement of the training activities and professional practices of the host organisations.

C. Joint projects for continuing training, in particular in advanced technology and for multi-media distance training – ie, briefly, training courses designed for rapid dissemination of the results of R & D in the field of new technologies and their application, and the transfer of technological innovation to new sectors; devising, developing and testing joint training projects; multilateral agreements for training aimed at establishing systems for distance learning utilising new training technologies and/or resulting in transferable training products; and operations (as above) initiated by employers' and workers' organisations.

D. Complementary promotion and back-up measures covering support for preparatory activities particularly for the less developed regions; structured exchanges of information and experience; setting up a data bank on COMETT II projects, and electronic mail facilities between project partners; a programme of conferences, seminars, exhibitions etc; analysis and monitoring of skills needed by industry and consequent training needs; identification of obstacles to transnational cooperation; and evaluation of COMETT II.

Priority is given to training geared towards new skills, both in the growth technology industries and in more traditional sectors, and as regards technology transfer and administration.

9. Eligible Expenditure:

Eligible expenditure under each strand of the programme relates to the following:

A. European Networks: support for activities with a European dimension and towards the functioning of the UETPs.

B. Transnational Exchanges: support for direct and indirect mobility costs, the costs of organising and monitoring activities implemented and, where necessary, of foreign language preparation for grant recipients.

C. The costs of joint projects for continuing training, especially in advanced technologies, and for multi-media distance training.

D. The costs of complementary promotion and back-up measures.

10. Rate of Award:

The rates of award under each strand of COMETT II are as follows:

A. European Networks: up to 50 percent of eligible expenditure, reducing progressively with a ceiling per UETP of 70,000 ECU, 60,000 ECU and 50,000 ECU respectively for the first 3 years (however, in certain exceptional cases, the contribution may exceed 3 years).

B. Transnational Exchanges: up to 6,000 ECU for 12 months for students undergoing 3 to 12 months' training in another Member State; up to 25,000 ECU for 24 months for placements of new graduates of between 6 to 24 months; up to 15,000 ECU for 3 months for personnel seconded to other Member States. Shorter contracts will receive pro rata awards.

C. Joint projects: up to 50 percent of total expenditure, generally up to a maximum of 30,000 ECU for crash training courses, and 50,000 ECU per project for devising, developing and testing joint training projects and for multilateral agreements for training.

D. Complementary promotion and back-up measures: up to 100 percent of the annual expenditure committed for these initiatives.

11. Payment Procedure:

Payment varies according to the nature of the project and is decided on a case by case basis.

12. Points to Note:

COMETT II aims to reinforce training, in particular in advanced technology, the development of highly skilled human resources and the competitiveness of European industry. It is centred on the changing skill requirements of industry and its personnel requirements which necessitate complementary action both in the Member States and at Community level. COMETT II will contribute to the utilisation and exploitation of the results, methods and tools of technology developed by EC policy for R & D, and is intended to facilitate innovation and technology transfer as well as the balanced economic and social development of the Community. Council Decision (EEC) 27/89 adopting COMETT II was published in Official Journal No L13; 17.1.89. A call for proposals relating to student placements and staff secondments was issued under the 1987–89 operational phase of the first COMETT programme with a deadline for submissions of 28 February 1989. A call relating to all headings of COMETT II was published in OJ L299; 28.11.89. An invitation to tender for assistance with the evaluation of COMETT was published in OJ C191; 31.7.90.

13. Application Procedure:

All the information necessary for the submission of applications is given in the Guide for Applicants which can be requested by writing to the COMETT Technical Assistance Unit. The Guide contains application forms, a description of the Programme, conditions of eligibility, and criteria and principles governing the award of Community support.

14. Further Information:

The Guide for Applicants is available from:
COMETT Technical Assistance Office
14 rue Montoyer
B-1040 Brussels
Tel: (010 32 2) 513 8959
Fax: (010 32 2) 513 9346

Mr David O'Sullivan
European Commission
DG V
Task Force Human Resources Education, Training & Youth
Rue Joseph II 37
B-1040 Brussels
Tel: (010 32 2) 236 0948
Fax: (010 32 2) 235 9129/6507
Telex: 21877 COMEU B

The UK contact is:
Mr A G Dunne
UK COMETT Liaison Office
Department of Education and Science
Sanctuary Buildings
Great Smith Street
London SW1P 3BT
Tel: (071) 925 5254
Fax: (071) 925 6985

ERASMUS

1. Summary:

The ERASMUS programme (European Community Action Scheme for the Mobility of University Students) promotes and supports the mobility of university students and staff in the European Community, and greater cooperation between universities in the field of vocational training. The programme includes the following four types of action (see 8 for further details): establishment and operation of a European University Network of inter-university cooperation programmes (ICPs); student grant scheme; measures to promote mobility through the academic recognition of diplomas and periods of study; complementary measures to promote student mobility in the Community.

The current phase of ERASMUS is set to run until 1994/95. A budget of 192 MECU has been allocated to cover the three years from 1990 to 1992.

2. Awarding Body:

Commission of the European Communities. Student grants in the UK are administered through the UK ERASMUS Student Grants Council.

3. Location Restrictions:

Available in any Member State of the European Community. The EFTA countries (Austria, Finland, Iceland, Norway, Sweden and Switzerland) and Liechtenstein may also participate in the programme with effect from the 1992/93 academic year.

4. Sectoral Restrictions:

ERASMUS is open to any post-secondary education and training establishment (and staff and students at such establishments) which offers, where appropriate within the framework of advanced training, qualifications or diplomas at that level. ERASMUS covers all subject areas taught at university level, including language and teacher training. Research and technological development activities are not covered.

5. Size Restrictions:

None.

6. Programme Duration:

The current phase of ERASMUS runs until 1994/95.

7. Submission of Applications:

For inter-university cooperation programmes, the deadline for applications is 31 October of the calendar year preceding the academic year to which the application relates (eg October 31, 1992 for 1993/94). For visits and complementary measures, applications may be submitted at any time, but must be made at least six months before any visit or project is due to take place.

8. Other Restrictions:

ERASMUS covers four Action Lines:

1. Establishment and operation of a European University Network designed to stimulate Community-wide exchange of students and to allow students of one university to undertake a fully recognised period

of study in at least one other Member State, as an integral part of their academic qualification. Universities receive support for each inter-university cooperation programme (ICP) in which they participate. Support is also available for: ICPs allowing teaching staff to carry out integrated teaching assignments in another Member State; joint curriculum development projects; the organisation of short, intensive teaching programmes for students from several Member States; visits for higher education staff for the preparation of integrated study programmes; for giving a series of specialised lectures; or for finding out more about aspects of higher education in the country visited.

2. Student Grants scheme: supports students (up and including to doctorate level) who carry out a recognised part of their higher education in another Member State. Priority is given to student mobility organised within the European University Network.
3. Measures to promote mobility through the academic recognition of diplomas and periods of study: supports the pilot European Community Course Credit Transfer System (ECTS) and centres facilitating the exchange of information on the academic recognition of diplomas from other Member States (particularly where the information exchange is computerised).
4. Complementary measures: support for associations and consortia of universities, staff and students; publications; other initiatives promoting inter-university cooperation in the field of vocational training; dissemination of information on ERASMUS: EC ERASMUS prizes have also been awarded for outstanding contributions to the development of EC inter-university cooperation.

9. Eligible Expenditure:

Eligible expenditure relates to the costs of the action being undertaken.

10. Rate of Award:

The rate of award varies depending on the measure undertaken; further details are available from the ERASMUS Bureau (see 14).

11. Payment Procedure:

Payment procedures vary with the type of action being undertaken; further details are available from the ERASMUS Bureau (see 14).

12. Points to Note:

Council Decision (EEC) 327/87 adopting the ERASMUS programme was published in OJ L166; 25.6.87. The programme was extended to run until 1994/95 by Council Decision (EEC) 663/89, published in OJ L395; 30.12.89. An invitation to tender was published in OJ C199; 8.8.90, concerning the undertaking of an evaluation study of ERASMUS. A further invitation to tender for the evaluation of the programme was published in OJ C54; 1.3.91.

A call for expressions of interest from universities willing to participate in the extension of the ECTS (European Community Course Credit Transfer System) was published in OJ C116; 30.4.91. A call for proposals relating to evaluation of ECTS was published in OJ C36; 14.2.92.

13. Application Procedure:

Application for inter-university cooperation programmes and visits is by form, available as part of the Programme Guidelines for Applicants from the ERASMUS Bureau (see 14). Application for support for complementary measures and visits is by writing to the ERASMUS Bureau. The procedure for applications for ERASMUS student grants varies according to the country of the outgoing eligible student grantholders.

14. Further Information:

ERASMUS Bureau
70 Rue Montoyer
B-1040 Brussels
Tel: (010 32 2) 233 0111
Fax: (010 32 2) 233 0150

UK ERASMUS Student Grants Council
The University
Canterbury
Kent
Tel: (0227) 762712
Fax: (0227) 762711

EUROTECNET

1. Summary:

The EUROTECNET programme aims to promote innovation in relation to basic and continuing vocational training, with particular regard to current and future technological change and its impact on employment, work, qualifications and skills. The programme is implemented through a European network of national and transnational innovative projects designed to develop and improve vocational training policies and technology-related training policies. The programme also supports a set of supplementary measures such as exchanges, publications, conferences and seminars. Funding is not available for individual training projects, only for promoting the networking process. Applications are currently particularly welcome for networks concerned with the financial services sector and women returners to the workforce.

The programme is set to run from 1990 to 1994 with a budget of 7.5 MECU (£5.5 million) for the first three years.

2. Awarding Body:

Commission of the European Communities.

3. Location Restrictions:

Available in any Member State of the European Community.

4. Sectoral Restrictions:

None.

5. Size Restrictions:

None.

6. Programme Duration:

The programme is set to run from 1990 to 1994.

7. Submission of Applications:

Application can be made at any time.

8. Other Restrictions:

While EUROTECNET is not itself a funding programme, participation may lead to increased opportunities for support and funding under other EC initiatives, particularly FORCE and EUROFORM. EUROTECNET also offers opportunities to identify potential partners in other Member States.

9. Eligible Expenditure:

Eligible expenditure relates to the costs involved in forming or extending a network of vocational training projects.

10. Rate of Award:

Funding is not available for individual training projects, only for promoting the networking process.

11. Payment Procedure:

Not applicable.

12. Points to Note:

Council Decision (EEC) 657/89 adopting the programme was published in OJ L393; 30.12.89.

An invitation to tender for technical assistance with the operation of the programme was published in OJ C34; 14.2.90.

13. Application Procedure:

The Employment Department will advise on application procedure.

14. Further Information:

Mr Jack Horgan
EUROTECNET
Technical Assistance Office
37, Rue des Deux Eglises
B-1049 Brussels
Tel: (010 32 2) 230 5378
Fax: (010 32 2) 230 0254

Ms Diane Faichney
TEED
Employment Department
Moorfoot, Room E315
Sheffield S1 4PQ
Tel: (0742) 594266
Fax: (0742) 594103

FORCE

1. Summary:

FORCE is an action programme supporting the development of continuing vocational training in the European Community ie vocational training undertaken by employees in all types of company in the EC throughout their working life.

The programme's five main objectives are: to encourage a greater investment effort in continuing vocational training, the demonstration and dissemination of examples of good practice; and innovations in the management of continuing vocational training, methodology and equipment; to take better account of the consequences of a completed Single European Market; and to help continuing vocational training mechanisms become more effective.

The programme is implemented through two action lines: 1. a common framework of guidelines to support and complement policies and measures adopted by Member States; and 2. a number of transnational measures including: a transnational network; an exchange scheme for instructors and specialists; pilot schemes; cooperation in forecasting trends in skills and qualifications; sectoral surveys; the exchange of comparable data; and the analysis of contractual policy (see 8 for further details). The programme is set to run from 1 January 1991 to 31 December 1994, with a budget of 30.4 MECU for the first two years.

2. Awarding Body:
Commission of the European Communities.

3. Location Restrictions:
Available in any Member State of the European Community. Priority is given to projects involving at least three Member States.

4. Sectoral Restrictions:
No industry restrictions have been specified, although priority is given to small and medium-sized firms. Priority is also given to projects involving social partners such as employers' associations and trade unions.

5. Size Restrictions:
No size restrictions have been specified.

6. Programme Duration:
The programme is set to run from 1 January 1991 to 31 December 1994.

7. Submission of Applications:
An invitation to tender for the evaluation of the FORCE programme was published in OJ C297; 13.11.92. The deadline was 15 January 1993. The 1993 call for proposals was published in OJ C92; 2.4.93; the deadlines are 9 September and 31 October 1993.

8. Other Restrictions:
The programme supports a number of transnational measures implemented at Community level. These include the following action lines:

I. Support for innovation in continuing vocational training, including the setting-up of a network of transnational operations aimed at improving vocational training and encouraging the transfer of knowledge:

   A. Achieving synergy in innovation: assistance for an exchange scheme to promote the rapid dissemination of innovations in continuing vocational training and a significant improvement in access to it. Grants will be provided for full-time instructors, personnel staff, staff representatives and training specialists in regional consortia, to undertake training courses in another Member State;

   B. Preparatory work on the design and development of transnational or cross-frontier pilot schemes by undertakings, groups of undertakings or training bodies in various Member States.

C. Grants for exchanges encouraging the dissemination of innovatory contractual agreements and forecasting trends in skills and qualifications.

II. Analysis, monitoring, assessment and forecasting: exchange of comparable data on continuing vocational training; European sectoral surveys of continuing vocational training plans.

III. Accompanying measures, including technical assistance, evaluation of the programme and result dissemination activities.

Area I is subject to open calls for application published by the Commission; Areas II and III are subject to restricted selection procedures.

9. Eligible Expenditure:

Eligible expenditure will vary depending on the nature of the project undertaken.

10. Rate of Award:

With respect to preparatory work designing and elaborating transnational pilot projects, the Commission's financial contribution will be up to 50 percent of expenditure on the preparatory work, with a ceiling of 100,000 ECU per year per project, for projects of a maximum duration of two years. With respect to grants for exchanges, the Commission's financial contribution will be limited to the direct costs of mobility, and must not exceed 7,500 ECU per grant per beneficiary, for exchanges of up to three months. Forecasts concerning demands for skills and qualifications and accompanying measures will be eligible for a rate of award of up to 100 percent of total costs, up to a maximum of 75,000 ECU. The Commission will bear up to 100 percent of the total costs of administering the network, cooperation activities (conferences, seminars and workshops), result dissemination activities and the costs of planning, implementation and assessment of sectoral surveys, with a 500,000 ECU ceiling per survey in total.

The rate of award for statistical surveys and for models for analysing collective agreements will be up to 80 percent of total costs.

11. Payment Procedure:

Payment procedure will vary depending on the nature of the project.

12. Points to Note:

Council Decision (EEC) 267/90 adopting FORCE was published in OJ L156; 21.6.90.

An invitation to tender for the coordination and technical administration of FORCE was published in OJ C173; 14.7.90.

The first call for applications was published in OJ C111; 26.4.91; the deadline was 31 July 1991.

13. Application Procedure:

The FORCE Vade-mecum is available from the Employment Department.

14. Further Information:

Mr W Thompson
Employment Department
Room E315
Moorfoot
Sheffield S1 4PQ
Tel: (0742) 594 819
Fax: (0742) 758316/594724

FORCE Technical Assistance Bureau
Rue du Nord 34
B-1000 Brussels
Tel: (010 32 2) 209 1311
Fax: (010 32 2) 209 1320

LINGUA

1. Summary:

The LINGUA programme aims to promote an improvement in EC foreign language training, and ensure the necessary levels of foreign language expertise in the workforce.

Five main action areas have been identified: I. In-service training of teachers and trainers; II. Measures to promote the learning of foreign languages; III. The development of foreign language teaching in the business community; IV. Educational exchanges for young people; V. Support for transnational organisations and bodies, and the development and exchange of teaching materials.

This description focuses on Action III; brief details of the other action areas can be found in 12 below. Eligible projects under Action III include: development and dissemination of techniques for the diagnosis and analysis of linguistic needs (linguistic audit); development of curricula and certification systems; promotion of transnational recognition of certification; and development of innovative teaching materials (including distance learning, multimedia projects and self learning materials) specific to a sector of economic life. Preparatory visits to discuss projects are also eligible, as are study visits for representatives of SMEs, relevant professional organisations and foreign language trainers. It should be noted that LINGUA does not fund language courses in individual firms. LINGUA is set to run from 1st January 1990 to 31 December 1994 with a budget allocation of 200 MECU. The bulk of the LINGUA budget is allocated to Actions I, II and IV.

2. Awarding Body:

Commission of the European Community.

3. Location Restrictions:

Available in any Member State of the European Community. Applications must be based on cooperation between participants established in two different Member States, one participant must be established in the Member State in which the chosen language is spoken. Priority will be given to the less-used Community languages.

4. Sectoral Restrictions:

Applications will be considered from: small and medium-sized firms; employers or employees' organisations, professional associations, Chambers of Commerce; and vocational training organisations (provided relevant foreign language expertise is involved in the partnership). Applications will also be considered from universities and language research centres provided there is a clear representation of SMEs in the partnership. Representatives from SMEs, and professional and workers' organisations, and foreign language trainers are the only applicants eligible for study visits. Priority will be given to applications involving partners with a particular interest in and capacity for dissemination eg publishers, software companies.

5. Size Restrictions:
None, although projects must address the needs of SMEs.

6. Programme Duration:
LINGUA is set to run from 1 January 1990 to 31 December 1994.

7. Submission of Applications:
Applications should be submitted to the designated UK national authority responsible for the administration and implementation of LINGUA. Applications are accepted on a continuous basis, with annual deadlines of 15 March and 15 September. The deadlines for study visits are 1 February (for visits after 1 May); 1 May (for visits after 1 August); 1 August (for visits after 1 November); and 1 November (for visits after 1 February).

8. Other Restrictions:
Languages covered are: Spanish, Danish, German, Greek, English, French, Irish, Italian, Letzeburgesch, Dutch and Portuguese, when taught as foreign languages. Priority will be given to applications involving the least widely used and least taught languages. Priority will also be given to projects involving the development and adaptation of new technologies in foreign language teaching, in particular self and distance-learning.

Action III of the LINGUA programme is designed to promote the development of foreign language teaching and learning in the business community. It provides for a series of measures which cover the essential stages in the setting-up of appropriate language training strategies and the design of relevant training curricula and materials. There is also provision for a preparatory and study visit scheme. It is not designed to provide financial support to individual firms for giving foreign language training to their workforces.

9. Eligible Expenditure:
Eligible expenditure varies according to the measures being undertaken.

10. Rate of Award:
The rate of award for Action III projects is up to 50,000 ECUs per year for three years, except in the case of projects involving the development of teaching materials/self learning materials, where the rate of award is up to a maximum of 200,000 ECUs per year for up to three years. Grants will not exceed 50 percent of actual project costs. The rate of award for visits is up to 1,500 ECUs per visit per person.

11. Payment Procedure:
Payment procedure varies according to measures undertaken.

12. Points to Note:

Council Decision (EEC) 489/89 adopting LINGUA was published in OJ L239; 16.8.89. LINGUA also covers the following Actions:

- I. In-service training of teachers and trainers. Grants are available for individuals or groups to enable them to take part in in-service training in another Member State, and for European Cooperation Programmes (ECPs) involving institutions in two or more Member States;
- II. Measures to promote the learning of foreign languages in universities and other higher education institutions, and develop the initial training of foreign language teachers;
- IV. Exchanges of young people (16–25) involved in professional, vocational or technical education. Grants are available for setting up Joint Education Projects (JEPs) with institutions in other Member States and for exchanges;
- V. Support for transnational organisations and bodies, and for the development and exchange of teaching materials. The Commission published a call for tenders for an organisation to provide assistance with the animation, coordination and technical administration of the programme (OJ No C207; 12.8.89).

13. Application Procedure:

Applications should be submitted to the LINGUA Bureau, with copies sent to the relevant UK LINGUA Unit.

14. Further Information:

In England & Wales:
UK LINGUA Unit
Seymour Mews House
Seymour Mews
London W1H 9PE
Tel: (071) 224 1477
Fax: (071) 224 1906

In Scotland:
Judith Cantley
The LINGUA Office
The Central Bureau
3 Bruntsfield Crescent
Edinburgh EH10 4HD
Tel: (031) 447 8024
Fax: (031) 452 8569

In Northern Ireland:
Bernadette McAllister
The LINGUA Office
Central Bureau
16 Malone Road
Belfast BT9 5BN
Tel: (0232) 664418
Fax: (0232) 661275

LINGUA Bureau
10, rue du Commerce
B-1040 Brussels
Tel: (010 32 2) 511 4218
Fax: (010 32 2) 511 4376

PETRA II

1. Summary:

PETRA II is the second stage of a European Commission action programme for the vocational training of young people (aged between 16 and 27). PETRA supports: vocational training or work experience in another Member State for young people in initial vocational training, young workers, young job-seekers and young people in 'advanced' vocational training; joint training of trainers; the joint development of training modules leading to recognised vocational qualifications (which comply with national training systems); and projects giving a European dimension to vocational information and guidance. The programme covers four Actions: I. Training and work experience placements in another Member State; II. European network of training partnerships; III. Youth Initiative Projects; and IV. Vocational Information and Guidance (see 8 for further details). PETRA II is set to run for three years from 1 January 1992, with a budget of 177.4 MECU.

2. Awarding Body:

Commission of the European Communities.

3. Location Restrictions:

Available in any Member State of the European Community.

4. Sectoral Restrictions:

Target groups for each of the Actions are as follows:

I. Training/Work Experience Placements: applications may be submitted by any organisation on behalf of young people in initial vocational training (short-term placements). (Initial vocational training is deemed to be training leading to a recognised vocational qualification below university level.) Individual young workers or job seekers and young people on advanced vocational training courses may apply for long term placements.

II. European Network of Training Partnerships: any organisation or body (public, private or voluntary) which provides young people with vocational training leading to a recognised vocational qualification.

III. Youth Initiative Projects: groups of young people aged 16–27 inclusive.

IV. Vocational Information and Guidance: further details of eligible groups are available from the NCU (see 14).

5. Size Restrictions:

None.

6. Programme Duration:

The programme is set to run for three years from 1 January 1992.

7. Submission of Applications:

The deadlines for project applications under Action I (see 8) were 30 April 1992 and 31 October 1992. Anticipated deadlines for 1993 were 31 January 1993 and 30 June 1993. For Action II, projects are selected annually. For Action III and IV, potential applicants should contact the NCU for further information.

8. Other Restrictions:

Four main Action Lines are covered by PETRA:

I. Training and work experience placements in another Member State for young people in initial vocational training (placements cover on average a three-week period, with a maximum of 12 weeks), or in advanced training (placements cover on average a three-month period, up to a maximum of 1 year). Funding is also available for preparatory visits, but only for the initial contact between partner organisations.

II. European Network of Training Partnerships: each year Member States select a small number of vocational education and training projects according to agreed criteria based on themes and occupational sectors, innovation and a multiplier effect. The projects are matched with similar ones in other Member States. The resulting partnerships cooperate on joint development of training modules and/or the joint training of trainers. Projects may be of up to three years' duration.

III. Youth Initiative Projects: assistance is provided for projects conceived and managed by young people, which aim to promote creativity, initiative and enterprise. Projects may be of up to one year's duration.

IV. Vocational Information and Guidance: the programme supports national systems for the exchange of vocational guidance data, information about good practice and effective vocational guidance methods. Support is available for additional training of guidance counsellors and specialists on European aspects of guidance.

9. Eligible Expenditure:

For training and work placements, the grant covers up to 75 percent of travel costs to and from the host country, accommodation, insurance, pocket money and linguistic and cultural preparation. For the European Network of Training Partnerships, the grant covers the costs of transnational cooperation. For Youth Initiative Projects and Vocational Guidance Projects, eligible expenditure relates to total project costs.

10. Rate of Award:

The rate of award for each Action Line is as follows:

I. For short-term placements, the average grant is 718 ECU for a three week placement; for long-term placements the average contribution is 2769 ECU for a three month placement.

II. For the European Network of Training Partnerships, the rate of award is as follows: up to 10,000 ECU in year 1 and up to 25,000 ECU in both years 2 and 3.

III. For Youth Initiative Projects, the rate of award is up to a maximum of 10,000 ECU which must represent not more than 50 percent of total costs.

IV. For Vocational Information and Guidance projects, the rate of award is up to 50,000 ECU per project, representing not more than 50 percent of total project costs.

11. Payment Procedure:

Payment procedure will be outlined in the agreed contract. Normally, 80 percent is awarded on signature of the contract, and 20 percent on completion and submission of adequate reports and financial records, indicating that the total amount of the EC advance has been spent.

12. Points to Note:

Council Decision (EEC) 387/91 amending Decision (EEC) 569/87 and extending PETRA was published in OJ L214; 2.8.91. PETRA II incorporated the Young Worker Exchange programme which terminated on 31 December 1991.

A call for tenders relating to the provision of technical assistance was published in OJ C237; 12.9.91.

13. Application Procedure:

Copies of the Vade-mecum are available from the UK's National Coordination Units.

14. Further Information:

Mr Jason Forsythe
Central Bureau
Seymour Mews House
Seymour Mews
London W1H 9PE
Tel: (071) 486 5101
Fax: (071) 935 5741

Liz Carter
Employment Department
ETPI, Room 513
Steel House
Tothill Street
London SW1H 9NF
Tel: (071) 273 5399
Fax: (071) 273 5475

PETRA Office
IFAPLAN Technical
Assistance Bureau
Square Ambiorix, 32
B-1040 Brussels
Tel: (010 32 2) 230 7106
Fax: (010 32 2) 230 7167

EXECUTIVE TRAINING IN JAPAN

1. Summary:

Grants are available from the European Commission to sponsor executives from export-oriented firms in Europe on an eighteen month training course in Japan. The executives undertake a twelve month full-time intensive course in business Japanese followed by a six month attachment to one or perhaps two Japanese companies normally operating in a related field. There is also a parallel programme of seminars, conferences, visits to firms and professional contacts.

2. Awarding Body:

Commission of the European Communities. The scheme is administered in the UK by PA Consulting Group.

3. Location Restrictions:

Applicants must be EC nationals. Sponsoring companies will normally be EC-based.

4. Sectoral Restrictions:

None, although the applicant's firm must either be doing business with Japan or be planning to do so. Bodies such as Chambers of Commerce which are responsible for promoting exports to Japan by small and medium-sized firms on a sectoral or regional basis may also submit applications.

5. Size Restrictions:

There is no restriction on the size of an applicant's firm; applications from small and medium-sized firms are particularly welcome. Only one individual per group of companies is eligible for full assistance; for subsequent placements, the firm must put forward 50 percent of the costs at the start of the scheme.

6. Programme Duration:

There is no specified terminal date for this scheme.

7. Submission of Applications:

The programme is open to applications on an annual basis. Applications may be submitted at around the same time each year; the 1992 programme deadline was 31 July 1992. Successful 1992 applicants will undertake their training programme from May 1993 to November 1994.

8. Other Restrictions:

Applicants should be of graduate calibre, aged 25 to 37, with a minimum of two years' business experience. They must have a linguistic ability of 'better than A-level standard', international exposure (ie show an ability to live in different environments), and demonstrate an interest in international business.

Applicants will normally be working in (or be intended to occupy) an export-related or international capacity. The programme aims to extend to as many areas as possible and therefore the candidates' business backgrounds will vary from marketing to technical and even scientific fields.

9. Eligible Expenditure:

The assistance is available towards a monthly living and rent allowance, language tuition costs and allowances towards installation and resettlement at the commencement and completion of the Programme. The cost of travel to and from Japan at the start and end of the secondment is not eligible and must be paid by the applicant's firm.

10. Rate of Award:

The level of assistance is approximately 90,000 ECU per participant, however firms are expected to contribute to the participants' upkeep.

Firms sponsoring a second or subsequent participant must pay approximately 50 percent of the total costs, and 100 percent of total costs for every additional candidate.

11. Payment Procedure:

Successful applicants receive a monthly allowance, as well as one-off payments for installation and resettlement.

12. Points to Note:

None.

13. Application Procedure:

Application should be made by the sponsoring company, application forms are available from the addresses below.

Applications are reviewed and, where necessary, supplementary information is elicited from both the applicants and their sponsoring firms. Nominations are then forwarded to the European Commission for shortlisting.

14. Further Information:

Mr John Patrick
PA Consulting Group
123 Buckingham Palace Road
London SW1W 9WR
Tel: (071) 730 9000
Fax: (071) 333 5050

PA Consulting Group
Ulster Bank House
Shaftsbury Square
Belfast BT2 7DL
Tel: (0232) 327467
Fax: (0232) 242292

Mr Rudie Filon
European Commission
DG I – F-I
200 rue de la Loi
B-1049 Brussels
Tel: (010 32 2) 299 0662
Fax: (010 32 2) 299 0204

SUPPORT PROGRAMME FOR EMPLOYMENT CREATION (SPEC)

1. Summary:

The SPEC programme provides financial and technical support for employment creation projects, in particular those linked to the completion of the Single Market. SPEC support is targeted at local employment development projects which try to tackle the problems or use the opportunities arising from the processes of European economic and social integration. Priority is given to: small, local initiatives which are innovative or provide demonstration effects; transnational cooperation; and support for less-favoured regions (see 8 for further details). The SPEC programme had a budget of 920,000 ECU for 1992.

2. Awarding Body:

Commission of the European Communities. SPEC is managed by a Programme Secretariat provided by the Council of European Municipalities and Regions (CEMR).

3. Location Restrictions:
Available in any Member State of the European Community. Priority is given to small, local initiatives. Furthermore, approximately 70 percent of the SPEC budget is targeted at transnational cooperation and support for the least developed regions of the Community. Transnational cooperation projects must involve at least two organisations in different Member States. Cooperation with non EC countries will only be eligible in exceptional circumstances. In support of less-developed regions, preference will be given to projects from Objective 1 regions and the new German Lander.

4. Sectoral Restrictions:
SPEC is open to firms, local government, Chambers of Commerce, trade unions, development agencies, training institutions, non-profit organisations and other local bodies.

5. Size Restrictions:
Priority is given to small, local projects. Support is generally awarded for a period not usually exceeding one year.

6. Programme Duration:
There is no specified terminal date for this scheme.

7. Submission of Applications:
Application deadlines are announced annually; the 1992 deadline was 10 October.

8. Other Restrictions:
Projects should promote local employment development. This could concern: development of new industrial activities or improvement of existing ones (eg diversification of activities in areas affected by restructuring); new employment opportunities in urban problem areas; development support in rural areas; or improvement of the functioning of the labour market. The following are examples of possible project actions: direct employment creation eg start-up support; support schemes for SMEs; training schemes; innovative methods to match demand and supply in the labour market; or transfer of know-how and experience to other parts of the Community. Conferences, seminars and studies are eligible for support, but should preferably be undertaken in conjunction with one of the above-mentioned actions. Small, local initiatives should be innovative, (either in terms of technical innovation or employment creation) or have demonstration effects eg pilot projects improving awareness of employment problems and opportunities. Preference will be given to projects which cannot be supported under other EC funding programmes.

The start-up phase of a new activity can be regarded as a project.

9. Eligible Expenditure:
Eligible expenditure relates to total project costs.

10. Rate of Award:
The rate of award will be up to a maximum of 70 percent of total project costs for a project located in an Objective 1 region or the new German Lander, and up to a maximum of 50 percent for projects located in other areas. The

grant will generally be in the range of 4,000 and 20,000 ECU per project. For projects involving mainly information and advice (seminars, publicity activities, research studies) an upper limit of 10,000 ECU applies.

The remaining proportion of total costs must be met from the participants' own (or other non-EC) resources. Such own resources need not be financial but can also be provided in kind (staff hours, services). The upper limit for support can only be exceeded in exceptional cases.

11. Payment Procedure:

The grant awarded will be paid in two equal instalments: 50 percent after signature of a statement of acceptance by the project leader; and the remainder on receipt of a final report, including a signed financial statement. An audited report may be requested.

12. Points to Note:

Only a limited number of projects will be selected for financial support and technical assistance under the programme. Applicants are requested to submit one project only; projects selected in previous years are not generally eligible for support. Selected projects may benefit from technical assistance, including documentation, guidelines and workshops.

13. Application Procedure:

Applications should be submitted to the Programme Secretariat at CEMR (see 14).

14. Further Information:

Programme Secretariat:
Council of European
Municipalities and Regions
(CEMR)
23 Boulevard Charlemagne
B-1040 Brussels
Tel: (010 32 2) 230 4927
Fax: (010 32 2) 230 7456

Technical Assistance Unit:
Local and Regional Development
Planning (LRDP)
106 Rue Franklin
B-1040 Brussels
Tel: (010 32 2) 732 4250
Fax: (010 32 2) 732 4973

European Commission
DGV/B-1
Rue de la Loi 200
B-1049 Brussels
Tel: (010 32 2) 299 1111

WOMEN'S LOCAL EMPLOYMENT INITIATIVES

1. Summary:

The Women's Local Employment Initiatives (LEIs) Programme provides small start-up grants to businesses and other employment initiatives which create jobs for women, and technical advice and information on the creation and planning of LEIs.

The Women's LEI Programme is part of the Commission's Third Medium-Term Action Programme (1991–1995) for Equal Opportunities for Women, and has an annual budget of at least 1.5 MECU.

2. Awarding Body:
Commission of the European Communities.

3. Location Restrictions:
Available throughout the European Communities.

4. Sectoral Restrictions:
The programme is open to any woman or group of women who plan to start new businesses, cooperatives and local employment initiatives where management positions and the majority of jobs are held by women. An LEI can either be a commercial company or a non-profit initiative with social or environmental goals.

There is no restriction on legal form; the programme is open to conventional firms, workers' cooperatives, partnerships and non-profit organisations.

5. Size Restrictions:
None. The maximum grant available is 7,500 ECU, the minimum is 3,000 ECU (relating to two full-time jobs).

6. Programme Duration:
The programme is set to run from 1991 to 1995.

7. Submission of Applications:
There are three annual deadlines for applications – 1 February, 1 June and 1 October. Application should normally be made before commencement of the initiative/business.

8. Other Restrictions:
The financial viability of the business/project is taken into account, and priority is given to applications from LEIs where jobs are being created for women from marginalised groups: women returners; single parents; disabled women; ethnic minorities; migrant and immigrant women; and the long-term unemployed.

Where proposed LEIs are innovative, and match local development plans and needs, applications will be looked on particularly favourably .

9. Eligible Expenditure:
Eligible expenditure will vary according to the nature of the project.

10. Rate of Award:
The rate of award is 1,500 ECU per full-time job (or its equivalent in part-time jobs). The maximum grant available is 7,500 ECU; the minimum is 3,000 ECU (creating at least two full-time jobs).

11. Payment Procedure:
Successful applicants must sign a contract and complete two reports. An interim report must be completed before payment of the first tranche of the grant (80 percent). The final report must be completed prior to the second and

final payment (20 percent). In the contract, a time limit is laid down stating when the project/business must commence operation.

12. Points to Note:

Although the grants awarded are small, the Commission hopes that they will act as a 'lever', encouraging banks and other funding institutions to give loans or other forms of support.

13. Application Procedure:

Application forms are available from Women's LEI Grants Management. It is strongly advised that prospective applicants contact the National Network Expert for advice and assistance in completing the application forms. The completed form should be returned to Grants Management, and a copy should be sent to the national Network Expert.

Following each deadline, selection of successful applicants is undertaken by the European Commission and Grants Management, on the advice of the national Network Expert.

14. Further Information:

UK Network Expert:
Patricia Richardson
Women's Enterprise Unit
Scottish Enterprise Foundation
University of Stirling
Stirling FK9 4LA
Tel: (0786) 67353/67348
Fax: (0786) 50201

Coordinator of EC LEI
Caroline Turner
BREAKTHROUGH
Consultants
36, Vas-Georgiou Street
GR-54640 Thessaloniki
Greece
Tel: (010 30 31) 250907
Fax: (010 30 31) 537375

Equal Opportunities Unit
DG V/B-4
200 Rue de la Loi
B-1049 Brussels
Tel: (010 32 2) 299 1111

Women's LEI Grants Management
Gerda van Biervliet/Simonetta Risaio
Comitato Impresa Donna – CNA
1, Avenue de la Joyeuse Entree
B-1040 Brussels
Tel: (010 32 2) 280 0054/280 0992
Fax: (010 32 2) 280 0901

PART TWO

EMPLOYMENT AND TRAINING

2.2 SCIENTIFIC TRAINING

Human Capital and Mobility Programme:
- Access to Large-Scale Facilities 149
- R & D Euroconferences 151
- Research Training Fellowships 152
- Scientific and Technical Research Networks 154

STA Fellowship in Japan 156
S & T Fellowships in Japan 158

2.2 SCIENTIFIC TRAINING

HUMAN CAPITAL AND MOBILITY: ACCESS TO LARGE-SCALE FACILITIES

1. Summary:

Support encouraging access to large-scale research facilities in the Community is available from the European Commission within the context of the Human Capital and Mobility Programme, which aims to increase the quality and quantity of human resources in research and development within the European Community.

Support is available both to researchers wishing to have access to the facilities and organisations with such facilities at their disposal.

The programme is set to run from 16 March 1992 to 31 December 1994, with a budget allocation of 488.07 MECU (55 MECU has been allocated for access promotion).

2. Awarding Body:

Commission of the European Communities.

3. Location Restrictions:

Available in any Member State of the European Community. Participation is also open to EFTA countries and Central and Eastern European countries with which the Community has concluded cooperation agreements.

4. Sectoral Restrictions:

A 'large-scale facility' is understood as being an establishment which requires a high initial investment, or a group of smaller establishments which have complementary capacities. All scientific and technological sectors are covered by the programme.

5. Size Restrictions:

None.

6. Programme Duration:

The programme is set to run from 16 March 1992 to 31 December 1994.

7. Submission of Applications:

A second call for proposals was published in OJ C346;30.12.92, addressed to centres with large-scale scientific and technical facilities at their disposal. The deadline was 20 February 1993. Proposals received in response to this call must be accompanied by expressions of interest from potential users. A second (and final) call will be published with the list of selected organisations, and will aim to obtain joint equipment–user proposals.

8. Other Restrictions:

None.

9. Eligible Expenditure:

Eligible expenditure relates to the costs arising from granting access to new scientists (travel, subsistence expenses and user fees). As a general rule, this aid will not be granted to purchase basic durable equipment or contribute to infrastructural costs; however, special contributions to adapt and upgrade large installations to favour the access of guest researchers can be considered. Management costs are also eligible.

10. Rate of Award:

The rate of award will be based on the quality and unique features of the facility, interest shown by potential users, the cost/benefit ratio of EC support, and value for the Community in terms of the importance of the facility. Forty percent of the total EC contribution will cover expenses related to the researchers themselves, while the remaining 60 percent will cover expenses related to the use of equipment and its adaptation or improvement, as well as management costs.

11. Payment Procedure:

Payment will be made in accordance with the agreed contract.

12. Points to Note:

Council Decision (EEC) 217/92 adopting the programme was published in OJ L107; 24.4.92. A call for proposals was published in OJ C139; 2.6.92, addressed to centres with large-scale scientific and technical facilities at their disposal. A further call for proposals was published in OJ C212; 18.8.92, with a list of pre-selected organisations, to obtain joint proposals from organisations and potential users. A second list was published in OJ C261; 10.10.92.

13. Application Procedure:

Application procedure is outlined in the Information Package available from the European Commission.

14. Further Information:

Marco Malacarne
European Commission
DG XII-H-I
Square de Meeus 8
B-1049 Brussels
Tel: (010 32 2) 235 5277
Fax: (010 32 2) 236 3307

For Information Packages:
Tel: (010 32 2) 236 0254
Fax: (010 32 2) 236 3307

For General Information:
Paul de Lusignan
Tel: (010 32 2) 236 6189

Mr C de Grouchy
Department of Education & Science
Sanctuary Buildings
Great Smith Street
London SW1
Tel: (071) 925 5945
Fax: (071) 925 6989

HUMAN CAPITAL AND MOBILITY: R & D EUROCONFERENCES

1. Summary:

Support for the organisation of Research and Development 'Euroconferences' is available from the European Commission within the context of the Human Capital and Mobility Programme, which aims to increase the quality and quantity of human resources in research and development within the European Community. The assistance is for the organisation of a series of meetings providing high-level specialists with an opportunity to present and discuss their ideas and latest scientific or technical results, and for young researchers to hold discussions and interact with experts during the presentation of their work. The programme is set to run from 16 March 1992 to 31 December 1994, with a budget allocation of 488.07 MECU (13.07 MECU has been allocated for Euroconferences).

2. Awarding Body:

Commission of the European Communities. Participation is also open to EFTA countries and Central and Eastern European countries with which the Community has concluded cooperation agreements.

3. Location Restrictions:

Available in any Member State of the European Community.

4. Sectoral Restrictions:

All scientific and technological sectors are covered by the programme. Participants may be organisations, scientific associations or learned societies.

5. Size Restrictions:

None.

6. Programme Duration:

The programme is set to run from 16 March 1992 to 31 December 1994.

7. Submission of Applications:

A call for proposals was published in OJ C139; 2.6.92. The call is open on a continuous basis.

8. Other Restrictions:

The R & D Euroconferences should be a series of high-level meetings for debating the latest work undertaken in advanced scientific or technical areas.

9. Eligible Expenditure:

Eligible expenditure includes: participation expenses (registration, travel and subsistence) of young scientists attending the conferences, with priority being given to those from less-favoured regions; and some administrative costs (comprising up to a maximum of 15 percent of the total grant).

10. Rate of Award:

The rate of award is up to 100 percent of eligible expenditure.

11. Payment Procedure:

Payment will be made in accordance with the agreed contract.

12. Points to Note:
Council Decision (EEC) 217/92 adopting the programme was published in OJ L107; 24.4.92.

13. Application Procedure:
Application procedure is outlined in the Information Package available from the European Commission.

14. Further Information:

Jane Shiel
European Commission
DG XII-H-I
Rue Montoyer 75
B-1040 Brussels
Tel: (010 32 2) 236 2984
Fax: (010 32 2) 236 3307

Mr C de Grouchy
Department of Education & Science
Sanctuary Buildings
Great Smith Street
London SW1
Tel: (071) 925 5945
Fax: (071) 925 6989

For Information Packages:
Tel: (010 32 2) 236 0254
Fax: (010 32 2) 236 3307

For General Information:
Paul de Lusignan
Tel: (010 32 2) 236 6189

HUMAN CAPITAL AND MOBILITY: RESEARCH TRAINING FELLOWSHIPS

1. Summary:
Support for research training fellowships is available from the European Commission within the context of the Human Capital and Mobility Programme which aims to increase the quality and quantity of human resources in research and development within the European Community.

Support is available both to individual recipients of training fellowships and laboratories or research teams receiving recipients of fellowships. The programme is set to run from 16 March 1992 to 31 December 1994, with a budget allocation of 488.07 MECU (220 MECU will be allocated for research training fellowships).

2. Awarding Body:
Commission of the European Communities.

3. Location Restrictions:
Recipients of fellowships must be nationals of an EC Member State, or resident in the EC, while laboratories or research teams must be based within the Community. Certain non-EC countries may participate subject to negotiation.

4. Sectoral Restrictions:

The programme covers all scientific and technological sectors. Fellowships are available for young researchers at doctoral or post-doctoral level. Scientists shall be considered at post-doctoral level if they have had at least six years higher education and hold a doctorate or equivalent degree, or, if not, have had two years research experience following a post-graduate course. Support may also be given to established researchers who need specific training in a field other than their own, in the context of retraining, or to apply their scientific knowledge in new areas where their participation is required. Participating laboratories or research teams may be based within research centres, academic institutions, scientific foundations or industrial firms.

5. Size Restrictions:

Fellowships may be for a period of between six months to two years, or in certain cases, three years for researchers from disadvantaged regions.

6. Programme Duration:

The programme is set to run from 16 March 1992 to 31 December 1994.

7. Submission of Applications:

Applicant researchers will be matched with host organisations following annual calls for proposals published in the Official Journal of the European Communities. The second call was published in OJ C346; 30.12.92 and was addressed to three categories of host organisation: individual research teams or laboratories; networks of research teams or laboratories; and institutions with large-scale facilities. The deadline was 20 February 1993.

Researchers may also apply to the Commission for a fellowship together with a host centre of their own choice. The call to individual researchers is also open on a continuous basis (OJ C139; 2.6.92). From 1993 onwards, three selection rounds per year are foreseen.

8. Other Restrictions:

The training of researchers should consist of their active participation in advanced research projects carried out in teams or research laboratories. Support may also be granted to experienced researchers to enable them to carry out R & D projects in a centre located in a disadvantaged region, to assist the training of a number of young scientists locally. These fellowships will generally be for up to one year.

9. Eligible Expenditure:

Expenditure related to researchers covers subsistence and mobility-related expenses, and special expenses for publication of the findings. Administrative and research costs of host organisations are also covered.

10. Rate of Award:

The rate of award is generally 100 percent of the marginal costs of the action (including full fellowship costs). Research and administrative costs should not exceed 15 percent of the EC grant for each individual case.

11. Payment Procedure:

Payment will be made in accordance with the agreed contract.

12. Points to Note:

Council Decision (EEC) 217/92 adopting the programme was published in OJ L107; 24.4.92.

The first call for proposals was published in OJ C346; 30.12.92. A list of selected centres was published in OJ C212; 18.8.92, and researchers were invited to apply directly to the host institutes listed. The call for applications is open on a continuous basis. A second call, with a further list of centres, was published in OJ C261; 10.10.92.

13. Application Procedure:

Application procedure is outlined in the Information Package available from the European Commission.

14. Further Information:

Irmela Branch
European Commission
DG XII-H-I
Square de Meeus 8
B-1040 Brussels
Tel: (010 32 2) 236 6316
Fax: (010 32 2) 236 3307

For Information Packages:
Tel: (010 32 2) 236 0254
Fax: (010 32 2) 236 3307

For General Information:
Paul de Lusignan
Tel: (010 32 2) 236 6189

Mr C de Grouchy
Department of Education & Science
Sanctuary Buildings
Great Smith Street
London SW1
Tel: (071) 925 5945
Fax: (071) 925 6989

HUMAN CAPITAL AND MOBILITY: SCIENTIFIC AND TECHNICAL RESEARCH NETWORKS

1. Summary:

Support for the creation and development of research networks for scientific and technical cooperation is available from the European Commission within the context of the Human Capital and Mobility Programme which aims to increase the quality and quantity of human resources in research and development within the European Community.

Research teams or laboratories are encouraged to form intra-European networks, linked for a scientific and technical project or theme. The programme is set to run from 16 March 1992 to 31 December 1994, with a budget allocation of 488.07 MECU (a total of 200 MECU has been allocated for research networks).

2. Awarding Body:

Commission of the European Communities.

3. Location Restrictions:

The number of Member States taking part in each network should be as high as possible. As a general rule, five research laboratories/teams, in at least three EC countries should take part, working jointly on at least one or more R&D project. The association of recognised high-quality laboratories and promising laboratories in less-favoured EC regions is particularly encouraged. Twinnings and networks of fewer than five centres involving research teams in different Member States may be supported in certain circumstances. Participation is also open to EFTA countries and Central and Eastern European countries with which the Community has concluded cooperation agreements.

4. Sectoral Restrictions:

Networks may consist of public and/or private research laboratories and/or teams.

All scientific and technological sectors are covered by the programme.

5. Size Restrictions:

None.

6. Programme Duration:

The programme is set to run from 16 March 1992 to 31 December 1994.

7. Submission of Applications:

A call for proposals was published in OJ C139; 2.6.92. This call is open on a continuous basis.

8. Other Restrictions:

Networks will be chosen on the basis of the originality of their approach, scientific excellence, appropriateness of topics and demonstrable added benefit to European science deriving from their linkage. They should encourage the interaction of different disciplines, the combining of various technologies and the application of techniques from one field to another. Where an innovative or complex scientific area is covered, encouragement may be given to the setting-up of new networks consisting of research teams or laboratories with additional capacity.

9. Eligible Expenditure:

Eligible expenditure includes: expenses incurred in engaging researchers outside the network needed to complete the research project; incidental costs arising from international cooperation (travel, accommodation and joint meetings); a contribution to research expenditure (experimental products, special purchases and the use of large-scale facilities if required) and administrative costs. If a researcher trained under this programme sets up a new research team in a disadvantaged region, EC assistance may include funds to equip the team, if it joins an EC-supported network.

10. Rate of Award:

The rate of award is generally 100 percent of the marginal costs of the action. Expenses related to the researchers themselves will amount to 60 percent of the total amount granted, and certain expenses related to research and administration will be covered by the remaining 40 percent.

11. Payment Procedure:

Payment will be made in accordance with the agreed contract.

12. Points to Note:
Council Decision (EEC) 217/92 adopting the programme was published in OJ L107; 24.4.92.

13. Application Procedure:
Application procedure is outlined in the Information Package available from the European Commission.

14. Further Information:

Manuela Soares
European Commission
DG XII-H-I
Rue Montoyer 75
B-1040 Brussels
Tel: (010 32 2) 236 2148
Fax: (010 32 2) 236 3307

For Information Packages:
Tel: (010 32 2) 236 0254
Fax: (010 32 2) 236 3307

For General Information:
Paul de Lusignan
Tel: (010 32 2) 236 6189

Mr C de Grouchy
Department of Education & Science
Sanctuary Buildings
Great Smith Street
London SW1
Tel: (071) 925 5945
Fax: (071) 925 6989

STA FELLOWSHIP PROGRAMME IN JAPAN

1. Summary:
The STA (Science and Technology Agency, Tokyo) Fellowship programme offers promising young researchers in the fields of science and technology the opportunity to undertake research at Japan's national laboratories and public research corporations. To promote the programme and to organise the selection of potential candidates, the STA has established contacts with the European Commission, which may nominate a limited number of candidates for STA fellowships.

2. Awarding Body:
Science and Technology Agency (STA), Tokyo. The European Commission has the opportunity of nominating a limited number of candidates to the programme.

3. Location Restrictions:
Available in any Member State of the European Community.

4. Sectoral Restrictions:
Applicants must be researchers in a scientific or engineering field.

5. Size Restrictions:
None.

6. Programme Duration:
There is no specified terminal date for this scheme.

7. Submission of Applications:
The programme is open annually for applications. The 1992 deadline was 1 June 1992, candidates for this round were to receive interviews in July. The programme is normally run in parallel with the EC's S&T Fellowship Programme in Japan, and the same deadlines apply. However, in exceptional cases, *ad hoc* interviews for the STA Fellowship programme can be organised up to the end of October each year.

8. Other Restrictions:
STA Fellowship applicants must: possess a doctorate degree in a scientific or engineering field, or an equivalent qualification; be aged under 35 (in principle); have sufficient language ability to pursue research in Japan; be a researcher in a scientific or engineering field; be in good health. Tenure is between six months and two years, to be negotiated between the candidate and the host institute. The field of research must be agreed by the candidate and the host institute. The results of research work produced during the tenure will be subject to the regulations of the host institute. Potential host institutes include Japan's national laboratories and public research corporations (excluding universities and university-affiliated institutes).

9. Eligible Expenditure:
Eligible expenditure relates to: travel costs; subsistence expenses; relocation expenses; housing costs; family allowance; and language tuition costs (see 10 for further details).

10. Rate of Award:
Recipients of STA Fellowships will be awarded the following: a round-trip (economy class) airline ticket to Japan; a living allowance of 270,000 yen per month; a family allowance of 50,000 yen per month; a single international relocation allowance of 200,000 yen; a travel allowance (within Japan for research activities) up to a maximum of 115,000 yen per year; and either free accommodation or a housing allowance of up to 100,000 yen per month. STA Fellowship award recipients resident in the Tsukuba area of Japan will receive free Japanese language lessons; those resident elsewhere will be reimbursed up to a specified amount for their Japanese language school tuition.

11. Payment Procedure:
Payment procedure is outlined when the fellowship is awarded.

12. Points to Note:
None.

13. Application Procedure:
Applicants must obtain an official invitation letter from a host institute in Japan, and then submit an application to the Commission. A list of potential host institutes is outlined in the STA Fellowship brochure, available from the Commission.

14. Further Information:

M Merla
European Commission
DG XII – S & T Cooperation with Non-Member Countries
200 rue de la Loi
B-1049 Brussels
Tel: (010 32 2) 235 3990/6509
Fax: (010 32 2) 236 3308

S & T FELLOWSHIP PROGRAMME IN JAPAN

1. Summary:

Grants are available from the European Commission to sponsor young research scientists on a 15 to 21 month placement in Japan. Participants undertake a three-month full-time language course in Japan, followed by 12 to 18 months full-time in a Japanese host laboratory.

The aim of the programme is to improve European research scientists' personal contacts with Japan, allowing Europe to benefit from advances in Japanese research. Researchers will concentrate on fields in which Community programmes exist or are being explored, and in which Japanese work is currently or potentially interesting.

2. Awarding Body:

Commission of the European Communities.

3. Location Restrictions:

Applicants must be EC nationals.

4. Sectoral Restrictions:

None.

5. Size Restrictions:

None.

6. Programme Duration:

There is no specified terminal date for this programme. It is, however, subject to annual review.

7. Submission of Applications:

The annual deadline for applications is 1 June.

8. Other Restrictions:

Applicants should normally be between the ages of 25 and 35, have a reasonable command of English and have completed their doctorate degree or acquired equivalent professional experience. Participants are required to submit regular reports and return to work in Europe immediately after participation in the programme. When selecting candidates, the Commission will consider: (a) the relevance of the research theme to current Community research programmes, or to fields which might be developed in the future; (b) the interest to Europe of current or planned Japanese work in the field; (c) the agreement of the prospective host institute to the applicant's proposed work programme and the mutual scientific interest shown; (d) the existing contacts, if any, between European and Japanese research in the field; and (e) the interest of the candidate's European research institute (if applicable) in their participation in the programme and their willingness to create follow-up links. On application, candidates should submit a proposed work programme and give evidence of having initiated contact with a potential host institute in Japan where it would be worth carrying out the proposed work. Candidates should also be able to show how their proposed research work and stay in Japan would fit into the R & D strategy of their present institutions, if appropriate, and their future professional career.

9. Eligible Expenditure:

The assistance is available towards a monthly living allowance, travel expenses between Europe and Japan, an installation allowance and language course costs.

10. Rate of Award:

Participants are paid a fixed monthly allowance of 435,000 yen as well as travel costs, an installation allowance and fees for language courses.

11. Payment Procedure:

The living allowance is paid monthly. All other eligible expenses are covered by one-off payments.

12. Points to Note:

Participants may be placed in any national research laboratory supervised by the Japanese Science and Technology Agency, Ministry for International Trade and Industry, Ministry for Agriculture, Forestry and Fisheries, other Ministries, university laboratories or research institutes attached to national universities. Private sector research institutes may be considered on an individual case basis.

13. Application Procedure:

Application is by form available from the Commission. Applications are reviewed and selected candidates invited to Brussels for an interview. A shortlist is drawn up and reviewed in conjunction with the Japanese authorities.

14. Further Information:

M. Merla
European Commission
DG XII/S & T Cooperation with Non-Member Countries
Rue de la Loi 200
B-1049 Brussels
Tel: (010 32 2) 235 3990/6509
Fax: (010 32 2) 236 3308

PART THREE

RESEARCH AND DEVELOPMENT/INNOVATION

3.0	OVERVIEW	163
3.1	INNOVATION/RESEARCH DISSEMINATION AND EVALUATION	169
3.2	INFORMATION TECHNOLOGY/COMMUNICATIONS	177
3.3	INDUSTRIAL AND MATERIALS TECHNOLOGIES/MEASUREMENT AND TESTING	195
3.4	ENERGY	207
3.4.1	NUCLEAR ENERGY	207
3.4.2	NON-NUCLEAR ENERGY	217
3.5	ENVIRONMENTAL RESEARCH	227
3.6	BIOTECHNOLOGY/HEALTHCARE	233
3.7	AGRICULTURE AND FISHERIES RESEARCH	241
3.8	PROGRAMMES WITH FULLY ALLOCATED BUDGETS	253

3.0 OVERVIEW

In 1987, the Single European Act established research and technological development (RTD) as a formal area of Commission responsibility, according it, for the first time, equal status with the Commission's traditional remit covering economic and social policy. Previously, EC research funding had been restricted to areas directly associated with economic policy concerns, eg coal, steel, energy. The policy shift to extend RTD support beyond these traditional areas was intended to enhance the competitiveness of European industry by funding pre-competitive research – specifically, research which could be carried out more rationally, cost effectively and efficiently at the European level.

When compared with public sector science and technology expenditure within individual Member States the current level of EC research funding is generally considered to be fairly low. However, the absolute amounts of funding allocated at EC level to certain priority fields have been sufficiently large that, within these targeted areas, the main source of public funding has been shifting from national to EC level.

In addition, and reflecting the increasing importance given to research, Community expenditure on RTD programmes has increased considerably in recent years. The total amount of funding available over the period 1990–94 is 5.7 billion ECU, accounting for 3.8 percent of the total Community budget. This represents an increase of about one-third over average annual EC expenditure on RTD in the previous five-year period.

To maximise the effectiveness of its relatively limited RTD budget, the Commission awards research grants on a competitive basis. Apart from promoting specific research goals, projects are expected to contribute to broader European objectives. Thus, projects are expected to involve transnational collaboration and coordination, and mobility between science and industry. A further objective associated with many of the programmes is the integration of research and technology into the context of completing the Single Market, for example, agreeing European-wide standards in scientific disciplines, promoting access to expertise and equipment irrespective of location etc.

The Framework Programmes

Priority research areas for EC RTD programmes are agreed in 'Framework Programmes for Research and Development'. Each Framework Programme sets out the objectives, priorities and scope of Commission support for RTD in the medium term. The First Framework Programme ran from 1984 to 1987. It was followed by the Second Framework Programme (1987–91) which consisted of eight high priority areas comprising 32 specific programmes. The Third Framework Programme was agreed in April 1990 and overlapped the Second Framework Programme by two years, running from 1990–94.

Table 2 lists the main priority areas and budget assigned to the Third Framework Programme. Under this Programme a number of shifts of

TABLE 2

Third Framework Programme 1990–1994			
Focal areas	**Sums in million ECU**		**Proportion of total budget (%)**
I. Enabling technologies			
1. Information and communications technologies		2,221	38.9
— Information technologies	1,352		
— Telecommunications	489		
— Development of technological systems of general interest	380		
2. Industrial and materials technologies		888	15.6
— Industrial and materials technologies	748		
— Measurement and testing	140		
II. Management of natural resources			
3. Environment		518	9.1
— Environment	414		
— Marine science and technology	104		
4. Life sciences and technologies		741	13.0
— Biotechnology	164		
— Agricultural and agro-industrial research (incl. fisheries)	333		
— Biomedical and health research	133		
— Life sciences and technologies for developing countries	111		
5. Energy		814	14.3
— Non/nuclear energies	157		
— Nuclear fission safety	199		
— Controlled thermonuclear fusion	458		
III. Management of intellectual resources			
6. Human capital and mobility		518	9.1
Total[1]		**5,700**	**100.0**

[1] including ECU 57 million for the centralised management of the dissemination and exploitation of research results, and ECU 550 million for the Joint Research Centre (JRC)

Source: Commission of the European Communities (DG XII)

emphasis were made. In particular, the proportion of funds targeted on Environmental Research, Biotechnology and the Mobility of Research Personnel increased appreciably, while the level of support for Energy Research (a top priority in the mid-1970s) fell. Information and Communications Technologies and Materials Technologies remained the main focus of Community-funded research, accounting for over 50 percent of the total 5.7 billion ECU budget.

To concentrate the resources available under the Third Framework Programme, the 32 research programmes which had previously been highlighted under the Second Framework Programme were streamlined into fifteen, falling within a more limited set of six strategic sectors. At the beginning of 1993, the Commission's proposals for the next and Fourth Framework Programme covering the period 1994–98 had not yet been approved.

The proposals presented by the Commission for the Fourth Framework Programme envisage continued support for some of the major RTD programmes currently underway. However, the proposed structure is somewhat different, and involves a greater concentration of research effort on a number of generic technologies with a broad range of applications.

The proposed budget of 14.7 billion ECU represents a very significant increase from the current programme's budget of 5.7 billion ECU. This reflects the Commission's concern that the level of expenditure on RTD within the Community, although increasing, is still inadequate when compared to its main competitors, and that a strengthening of research policy and a redirection of strategy is required. Table 3 lists the main activities and budget proposed for the Fourth Framework Programme.

TABLE 3

Proposed Fourth Framework Programme 1994–98

Activities	**Sums in million ECU**
First Activity: Cooperative RTD & demonstration programmes	11,600
Second Activity: Cooperative RTD with third (non-EC) countries and international organisations	1,400
Third Activity: Dissemination and optimisation of RTD results	700
Fourth Activity: Training and mobility of researchers	1,000
Total	**14,700**

Source: Commission of the European Communities

The programme is divided into four thematic Activities, under which specific areas for research are set out:

1. *First Activity:* Cooperative RTD and demonstration programmes, involving firms, research centres and universities. Research under this heading falls into two major categories: science and technology to promote industrial innovation (including IT research, image technologies and advanced manufacturing technologies) and science and technology to promote social and European integration (including telematic systems in the field of health care, environment and energy). In addition, a number of 'technological priority projects' directly linked to key generic technologies will be supported.
2. *Second Activity:* promotion of RTD cooperation with non-EC countries and international organisations, including non-European industrialised countries, Central and Eastern Europe and developing countries.
3. *Third Activity:* Dissemination and optimisation of the results of Community RTD activities. Included under this heading is a proposed new support mechanism for small and medium-sized firms (SMEs) providing them with additional support to enable them to optimise/apply research results.
4. *Fourth Activity:* Training and mobility for researchers, involving mobility grants mainly at a postgraduate level and the setting-up of scientific and technical cooperation networks, including networks linking laboratories, universities and business.

In the meantime, until the Fourth Framework Programme comes into effect, the Commission has proposed a supplementary budget for the Third Framework Programme, to avoid any detrimental effects of funding decreases due to possible delays in the adoption of the Fourth Framework Programme. The Treaty on European Union agreed at Maastricht at the end of 1991 introduced more complex decision-making procedures as regards research, and as the Maastricht Treaty amends the Single European Act, this changes the legal basis of the Framework Programmes. Delays in the adoption of the Fourth Framework Programme are therefore quite likely. An extra 1,600 million ECU funding has been proposed for the years 1993 and 1994 (400 million ECU for 1993 and 1,200 million ECU for 1994). If agreed, this will increase the total budget for the Third Framework Programme to 7.3 billion ECU.

Characteristics of Community Research Programmes

Although there have been changes of emphasis under the different Framework Programmes, the specific research programmes supported have retained certain common characteristics. These are as follows:

1. Research programmes run for a four or five year period with most funding allocated within the first two years.
2. Research must be innovative and pre-competitive (ie somewhere between basic fundamental research and commercial application, and at least five years from the market place).

3. Applications are judged on a competitive basis in relation to the perceived importance of the proposed work, and the extent to which the project satisfies Community objectives.
4. Transnational collaboration is usually required although in cases where projects are assigned high priority by the Commission, or where collaboration cannot be justified on economic grounds (eg because of their small scale), this condition may be waived. Generally, at least two independent industrial partners from different countries must be involved in each project. Small company participation in collaborative projects is looked on particularly favourably.
5. Special funding arrangements exist to encourage partnerships between industry and higher education institutes (HEIs). Funding is referred to as 'shared cost', with the Commission contributing 50 percent of industrial partner project costs and 100 percent of direct marginal costs incurred by HEIs.
6. Applications must generally be made in response to a call for proposals published in the Official Journal. Each call sets a strict deadline by which proposals must be submitted, usually some 10 or 12 weeks from the publication date. To help firms prepare for a formal call for proposals, many new programmes invite 'expressions of interest' prior to publication of the actual call. Firms which indicate an interest in participating in an RTD programme will then receive guidance on the scope of the programme and expected timing, before committing substantial resources in the preparation of a formal proposal. They are also kept informed directly about any developments in a particular research programme and receive notice of the formal calls for proposals as they are issued. Expressions of interest are also used as a feedback mechanism to assess the interest of industry in the particular area of research, and to help establish priorities in relation to specific research topics.
7. Application is made direct to the Commission, though nationally based representatives in the relevant Government Departments may assist with proposal preparation and provide up-to-date information on programme progress, expected call dates etc.
8. In addition to funding research directly through 'shared-cost contracts', the Commission also: undertakes 'concerted actions' in which it coordinates research undertaken in different countries; provides training and mobility grants to promote scientific interchange; and funds research carried out at its own wholly funded Joint Research Centre (JRC) based at four sites – Ispra (Italy); Geel (Belgium); Petten (Netherlands); and Karlsruhe (Germany).

Participation in EC Research Programmes

The obstacles to participating in EC research programmes are considerable – not only in terms of identifying suitable projects and partners, but also in working to the unpredictable time-scale created by delays in the procedure for adopting new programmes, and dealing with the highly competitive proposal selection procedure. Fortunately, much progress has been made within the past few years to minimise the difficulties faced by participating firms.

To ease the task of finding partners from other countries, the Commission will try to provide a match-making service for firms who register a need. This is of particular benefit to smaller firms and can obviously bring with it new commercial opportunities quite separate from the actual research involvement.

Putting together a suitable project proposal involving transnational collaboration requires a significant resource commitment and represents a considerable challenge. However, for those firms that do succeed, the advantages of participating in an EC RTD programme go far beyond the financial contribution offered by the Commission. Participating in a multinational collaborative research programme gives firms access to specialists throughout Europe, access to results of research carried out by others and the acquisition of know-how. At a more indirect level it introduces firms in related areas of business to each other, providing valuable links and information for future commercial opportunities. Furthermore, for those firms willing to take the first difficult steps necessary for participation in an EC RTD programme, there is a sharp learning curve and a greater likelihood that they will be in a position to take advantage of opportunities presented in other EC programmes. In some cases, further assistance to exploit the results of Community-funded RTD (ie nearer to the market place research) may be available under a nationally funded research programme. In brief, although initial entry costs of participation may be high, the benefits of doing so may accrue over many years.

The programme descriptions which follow describe the Commission's research and development/innovation activities under eight broad headings. Section 3.1 focuses on Innovation, and Research Dissemination and Evaluation. Section 3.2 covers Information Technology and Communications Research. Section 3.3 deals with Industrial and Materials Technologies, and Measurement and Testing Research. Energy Research is considered in Section 3.4, which is divided into two parts: 3.4.1 focuses on Nuclear Energy, while 3.4.2 concentrates on Non-Nuclear Energies. Section 3.5 covers Environmental Research, Section 3.6 Biotechnology/Healthcare and Section 3.7 Agriculture and Fisheries Research. Finally, Section 3.8 deals with five programmes whose budgets have been fully allocated, effectively closing the programmes to any new participants. It should be noted, however, that in most cases new programmes have been adopted which continue similar research.

One aspect of the Commission's Third Framework Programme not discussed in this chapter is the Human Capital and Mobility Programme. While falling within the RTD framework, the programme's emphasis on scientific training has led to its inclusion in Chapter 2 (Section 2.2).

PART THREE

RESEARCH AND DEVELOPMENT/INNOVATION

3.1 INNOVATION/RESEARCH DISSEMINATION AND EVALUATION

SPRINT 171
VALUE II 173

3.1 INNOVATION/RESEARCH DISSEMINATION AND EVALUATION

SPRINT

1. Summary:
SPRINT (Strategic Programme for Innovation and Technology Transfer) provides financial assistance for the following broad actions (see 8 for further details). (A) Strengthening of the innovation services infrastructure in Europe; (B) Supporting intra-Community pilot projects for information transfer; (C) Improving the innovation environment. One current pilot project operating under SPRINT is the Technology Performance Financing Scheme, which is designed to assist traditional industries to buy high technology processes, services and equipment (see 8 for further details). SPRINT has been adopted to run from 1 January 1989 to 31 December 1993 with a budget of 90 MECU.

2. Awarding Body:
Commission of the European Communities.

3. Location Restrictions:
Available in any Member State of the European Community. A significant part of the budget will be targeted to benefit regions designated under Objective 1 (lagging in development) or Objective 2 (in industrial decline) of the EC's Structural Funds.

4. Sectoral Restrictions:
Projects, other than studies and services, must involve the participation of organisations from at least two different Member States.

5. Size Restrictions:
None.

6. Programme Duration:
SPRINT has been adopted to run from 1 January 1989 to 31 December 1993.

7. Submission of Applications:
Application is made within the deadlines specified in each of the Commission's invitations for proposals to be submitted, published in the Official Journal. A call for proposals for participation in a science park consultancy scheme was published in OJ C185 and three calls relating to network support measures were published in OJ C205; 13.8.92. The deadline for applications was 30 October 1992.

8. Other Restrictions:
Priority action lines under SPRINT are as follows:

- A. Strengthening the European infrastructure for innovation through intra-Community networks, in particular: (1) consolidation of existing networks, formation of new networks, strengthening intra-Community cooperation, and introduction of linkage mechanisms; (2) network support measures – actions of information, awareness, promotion and the transfer of know-how in innovation management and related measures, specific instruments to enhance the effectiveness of networks, and the launching of innovations emerging from networks by improving the dialogue between sources of funding, technical experts and innovators.

- B. Supporting specific technology transfer projects, particularly by means of transnational projects, accompanying measures to heighten awareness of new technologies and to train companies adopting them, the provision of technical support for potential users and support for the effective execution of projects, particularly by mobilising public and private sector funding.
- C. Improving the innovation environment through a European Innovation Monitoring System and evaluation measures, and strengthening concertation actions and the exchange of experience in the field of innovation policy and technology transfer.

Technology Performance Financing (TPF) is a pilot scheme under SPRINT designed to assist traditional industries to buy high technology processes, services and equipment. The scheme links payment for the purchase of high technology to its performance – the user initially only pays a small fraction for the equipment. Both supplier and buyer agree to a set of performance related milestones that the technology must meet before payments are made. If the technology does not measure up, the buyer need not pay the full price; however, if the technology exceeds expectations then the supplier receives extra payment. Suppliers are supported by a financial institution which advances them a substantial proportion of the equipment after it has been delivered to the user. The institution profits from the users' performance payments which they share with the supplier after receiving the initial advance.

9. Eligible Expenditure:

Eligible expenditure covers the cost of the specific project.

10. Rate of Award:

The rate of award is generally up to 50 percent of eligible project costs although, in exceptional cases, a higher contribution is possible, in particular for the purposes of taking account of the specific difficulties encountered by Objective 1 and 2 regions in taking part in transnational activities.

The Community's financial contribution will be adapted to the characteristics of each specific project. It may take the form of a direct or indirect subsidy, an advance on own capital, or any other appropriate form. As a percentage of total costs, this contribution will be lower the greater the proximity of the action or project is to the market.

11. Payment Procedure:

Payment procedure varies according to the type of project being undertaken.

12. Points to Note:

The 1990 series of calls for proposals covered the following fields: transnational technology transfer networks; the development of a European Innovation Monitoring System (EIMS); a science park consultancy scheme;

organising transnational seminars for innovation support service (ISS) suppliers; network support measures; and the definition phase of technology transfer projects. A call for proposals and expressions of interest for the implementation of the technology performance financing scheme was published in OJ C65; 13.3.91. A further call for proposals relating to technology diffusion through networks of research and technology organisations was published in OJ C122; 8.5.91. A call for proposals to take part in a science park consultancy scheme was published in OJ C198; 27.7.91; the deadline was 31 October 1991. The Council Decision (EEC) 286/89 adopting SPRINT was published in Official Journal L112; 25.4.89.

13. Application Procedure:
Application procedure is outlined in each call for proposals.

14. Further Information:

Mr Robin Miege
European Commission
DG XIII/D/4
Batiment Jean Monnet
Rue Alcide de Gasperi
L-2920 Luxembourg
Tel: (010 35 2) 4301 4180
Fax: (010 35 2) 4301 4544
Telex: 2752 EURDOC LU

Ms Linda O'Connor
Department of Trade and Industry
Research & Technology Policy Division
3/189 Green Zone
151 Buckingham Palace Road
London SW1W 9SS
Tel: (071) 215 1656
Fax: (071) 215 2909
Telex: 88 13148 DIHQ G

VALUE II

1. Summary:
The VALUE II programme offers financial support for the dissemination and exploitation of the results from Community research and technological development activities. VALUE II is implemented through shared-cost projects and concerted actions, forging closer links and disseminating results in three main fields: the research–industry interface; the interface between research and the scientific community; and the interface between research and society (see 8 for further details). VALUE II is set to run from 29 April 1992 to 31 December 1994, with a budget of 57 MECU.

2. Awarding Body:
Commission of the European Communities.

3. Location Restrictions:
As a general rule, participants in shared-cost projects must be established in the European Community. Projects should be transnational and should preferably include two independent contractors in two different Member States.

4. Sectoral Restrictions:

Participants may include universities, research organisations and industrial firms, including small and medium-sized firms. Projects concerning the utilisation of research results may only be submitted by research contractors who are or have been participants in EC research projects, or by their licensees and/or exploitation partners.

5. Size Restrictions:

None.

6. Programme Duration:

VALUE II is set to run from 29 April 1992 to 31 December 1994.

7. Submission of Applications:

Application is made within the deadlines specified in a call for proposals published in the Official Journal. A call for project proposals utilising research results was published in OJ C230; 8.9.92. Applications may be submitted at any time.

8. Other Restrictions:

The programme seeks to forge closer links in three main areas (budget allocation in brackets):

I. Research–Industry Interface (50 MECU):
   1. Setting up new channels of information including: a network of relay centres undertaking a range of activities to promote the dissemination and exploitation of EC R&D results; and updating and expansion of the CORDIS computerized information service;
   2. Utilisation of Results: utilising R&D results which are the property of the EC, and helping utilisation of results of shared-cost projects;
   3. Protection of Results: provision of patenting expertise, financial support for searches for prior claims to novelty and first patent applications; public awareness campaigns;
   4. Promotional Activities: financial support for organisations making an active contribution to the promotion of results or facilitating, promoting and coordinating access to EC programmes; organisation of seminars, conferences etc; attendance at trade fairs.

II. Research–Scientific Community Interface (4 MECU): covering four areas:
   1. General context of research: to study the constraints and/or opportunities for the dissemination and exploitation of R&D activities. Possible topics are: history and comparative analysis of public and private research structures; aspects of civil and public law, mainly in respect of intellectual property rights; and international rules on scientific and technological information;
   2. Communication of Research: improving the communication of research towards its various users by obtaining a better understanding of communication patterns;
   3. Economics of Research: use of macroeconomic instruments and business sciences to determine the optimum use of resources to be channelled into research as part of general economic development objectives and company objectives;

4. Management of Research: to promote knowledge of best practice in the management of R&D in order to contribute to a better exploitation of results, including management studies helping with the organisation of research and laboratory management, project management, administrative procedures and management methods.

III. Research–Society Interface (3 MECU): covering measures designed to identify and study the impact on society of new scientific and technological knowledge acquired as a result of EC activities. Three main areas will be covered:
1. Contribution to assessment of the social impact of science and technology, developing more general 'technology assessment' schemes and monitoring areas relating to the exploitation of new technologies affecting health, safety, the environment, and ethical and legal questions relating to the exploitation of results;
2. Communication and information provision to the public;
3. Analysing public demand and new requirements through studies and surveys.

9. Eligible Expenditure:

For organisations other than universities, eligible expenditure covers: labour (actual cost or at approved rates), travel and subsistence, consumables, equipment, computing costs, external work (sub-contracts or services), reasonable overheads. The following are not allowable: profits; marketing, distribution, advertising expenses; any interest or return on capital employed; taxes (except in limited circumstances); cost of proposal preparation; patent protection costs. Specific arrangements exist to recover non-reclaimable VAT.

Universities and higher education establishments may elect to have their support calculated according to the marginal costs of the project (ie the actual additional direct costs of the research not met by normal recurrent expenditure, other financial sources or other third parties), unless their costing and recording systems enable them to submit and justify full costs. Each university is normally expected to operate on the basis of either marginal costs or full costs for all Community R & D programmes, and not reach a decision on a project-by-project basis. Marginal costs may include all the items listed above, although labour costs only relate to temporary additional staff specifically engaged for the research; routine and minor computing costs may not be charged; and overheads may be fixed at a percentage, corresponding to a maximum of 20 percent of all expenditure except associated contracts and VAT.

10. Rate of Award:

The rate of award is normally up to 50 percent of the full economic costs of the R & D project. Universities and higher education establishments may, however, attract a contribution of up to 100 percent of the actual marginal costs of the research project. Concerted actions (where the EC coordinates rather than funds research) may receive funding of up to 100 percent of coordinating expenditure.

11. Payment Procedure:

Payment is made in accordance with the agreed contract and takes the form of an advance payment following signature of the contract by all partners and the Commission, followed by periodic instalments on approval of progress reports and cost statements submitted as work progresses. Ten percent of the total financial contribution is retained (or, in the case of larger contracts, 500,000 ECUs, whichever is lower) and is paid, along with any other sums due, on approval of final technical reports and cost statements. In all cases the Commission's contribution is made in ECUs and no liability is held for exchange losses incurred.

12. Points to Note:

Council Decision (EEC) 272/92 adopting the programme was published in OJ L141; 23.5.92.

The VALUE II programme continues measures carried out under VALUE (1989–1991), and introduces new topics concerned particularly with the repercussions of RTD activities and their results on society as a whole. Detailed rules relating to intellectual property rights and results dissemination is outlined in the Council Decision.

13. Application Procedure:

Application forms and background material are available from the European Commission.

14. Further Information:

Ms Christine Symes
Department of Trade and Industry
RTP, Third Floor
Buckingham Palace Road
London SW1W 9SS
Tel: (071) 215 1614
Fax: (071) 821 1298

European Commission
DG XIII C-2 – VALUE Programme
Batiment Jean Monnet
Rue Alcide de Gaspari
L-2920 Luxembourg
Tel: (010 35 2) 4301 3610/3453
Fax: (010 35 2) 4301 4129
Telex: 2752 EURDOC LU

PART THREE

RESEARCH AND DEVELOPMENT/ INNOVATION

3.2 INFORMATION TECHNOLOGY/ COMMUNICATIONS

ESPRIT III	179
IMPACT II	182
RACE II	184
TEDIS II	187
Telematic Systems Programme	189

3.2 INFORMATION TECHNOLOGY/ COMMUNICATIONS

ESPRIT III

1. Summary:

The Information Technology Programme (ESPRIT III) supports collaborative R & D in the following six fields: 1. Microelectronics; 2. Information Processing Systems and Software; 3. Advanced Business and Home Systems and Peripherals; 4. Computer Integrated Manufacturing and Engineering; 5. Basic Research; and 6. Open Microprocessor Initiative.

The third phase of ESPRIT (European Strategic Programme for R & D in Information Technology) will run from 1991 to 1994, with a budget allocation of 1,330 MECU.

2. Awarding Body:

Commission of the European Communities.

3. Location Restrictions:

Available in any Member State of the European Community. Organisations in non-Member States which have concluded cooperation agreements with the European Communities may participate in the programme, although they will not be eligible for Commission funding.

4. Sectoral Restrictions:

The programme is open to industry, universities, research institutes and individuals, or any combination or association thereof, in particular European Economic Interest Groupings (EEIGs). Projects must be carried out by at least two independent partners established in different Member States.

5. Size Restrictions:

None.

6. Programme Duration:

The programme is set to run from 8 July 1991 to 31 December 1994.

7. Submission of Applications:

Applications are invited within deadlines specified in each of the Commission's calls for proposals, published in the Official Journal. The first call was published in OJ C198; 27.7.91. The second call was published in OJ C67; 10.3.93; the deadline was 22 April 1993. It is also expected that the European Systems and Software Initiative (ESSI) will be launched during 1993.

8. Other Restrictions:

The programme covers the following technical areas:

1. Microelectronics. Within this area the aim is to strengthen the Community capability in the design and manufacture of leading edge Integrated Circuits (ICs) and to ensure their ready availability to a broad range of user companies in synergy with the Joint European Submicron Silicon Initiative (JESSI). Emphasis is placed on Application Specific ICs (ASICs) because they are widely recognised as offering the

means to realise worldwide competitive products in many application sectors.

2. Information Processing Systems and Software. The objectives are to apply software intensive systems design and engineering to user needs, to develop information servers and their interfaces appropriate to user tasks and level of expertise and to develop advanced architectures and their applications. The R & D tasks in this area take account of a major technology transfer initiative, the European Systems and Software Initiative (ESSI), which aims to improve the productivity and standard of software production in Europe.
3. Advanced Home and Business Systems and Peripherals. The work in this area aims to develop user friendly support for cooperative working, to promote the development and use of multimedia systems to develop loosely coupled distributed systems and promote the introduction of the intelligent home. The development of selected peripheral technologies also falls in this area.
4. Computer Integrated Manufacturing and Engineering. This area encompasses the whole range of computer integrated manufacturing activities including architectures and communications, the design of manufacturing systems and products, management and control, and robotics and shop-floor systems. The aim is to demonstrate how the manufacturing sectors may benefit from the development of advanced integration techniques and their application to products, processes and manufacturing management.
5. Basic Research Actions. The intention here is to enhance the potential for future technological breakthroughs in information technologies, to contribute to the programme's main objectives from an upstream position and to reinforce interdisciplinary links. Apart from projects in this area, there will be additional activities such as working groups which will help produce added value to research through cooperation at European level.
6. Open Microprocessor Initiative. This horizontal initiative will interact and build on the results of all the technological areas, as well as on standards and other developments world wide. The goal of OMI is to extend the concept of open systems and standards to the microprocessor systems environment by the provision of an open environment based on the macrocell approach and software portability.

9. Eligible Expenditure:

For organisations other than universities, eligible expenditure covers: labour (actual cost or at approved rates), travel and subsistence, consumables, equipment, computing costs, external work (sub-contracts or services), reasonable overheads. The following are not allowable: profits; marketing, distribution, advertising expenses; any interest or return on capital employed; taxes (except in limited circumstances); cost of proposal preparation; patent protection costs. Specific arrangements exist to recover non-reclaimable VAT.

Universities and higher education establishments may elect to have their support calculated according to the marginal costs of the project (ie the actual additional direct costs of the research not met by normal recurrent expenditure, other financial sources or other third parties).

Each university is normally expected to operate on the basis of either marginal costs or full costs for all Community R & D programmes, and not reach a decision on a project-by-project basis. Marginal costs may include all the items listed above, although labour costs only relate to temporary additional staff specifically engaged for the research; routine and minor computing costs may not be charged; overheads may be fixed at a percentage, corresponding to a maximum of 20 percent of all expenditure, except associated contracts and VAT.

10. Rate of Award:

The rate of award is normally up to 50 percent of the full economic costs of the R & D project (although cuts in the project are frequently sought before the contract is agreed).

Universities and higher education establishments may, however, attract a contribution of up to 100 percent of the actual marginal costs of the research project.

11. Payment Procedure:

Payment is made in accordance with the agreed contract and takes the form of an advance payment following signature of the contract by all partners and the Commission, followed by periodic instalments on approval of progress reports and cost statements submitted as work progresses. Ten percent of the total financial contribution is retained (or, in the case of larger contracts, 500,000 ECUs, whichever is lower) and is paid, along with any other sums due, on approval of final technical reports and cost statements.

In all cases the Commission's contribution is made in ECUs and no liability is held for exchange losses incurred.

12. Points to Note:

Council Decision (EEC) 394/91 adopting the programme was published in OJ L218; 6.8.91.

13. Application Procedure:

Application procedure is outlined in the work programme, available from the European Commission when a call for proposals is published.

14. Further Information:

European Commission
DG XIII
ESPRIT Operations
Rue de la Loi 200
B-1049 Brussels
Tel: (010 32 2) 236 8596
Fax: (010 32 2) 236 8597

ESPRIT Unit
Department of Trade and Industry
Fourth Floor Grey
151 Buckingham Palace Road
London SW1W 9SS
Tel: (071) 215 1378
Fax: (071) 215 1967

For enquiries from Universities/Academic Organisations:
Dr D Worsnip
SERC
Central Office
Polaris House
North Star Avenue
Swindon SN2 1ET
Tel: (0793) 411104

For enquiries specifically related to the CIME field:
B Brinkley
Information Technology Division
Department of Trade and Industry
151 Buckingham Palace Road
London SW1W 9SS
Tel: (071) 215 1501

IMPACT II

1. Summary:

The IMPACT II programme supports projects and activities which contribute to the aim of improving the accessibility of information at the European level.

A wide range of potential project areas are covered, under the following measures: improving the understanding of the information market; overcoming legal and administrative barriers; stimulating the application of norms and standards; awareness, user support and training; and supporting strategic information initiatives (see 8 for further details). IMPACT II is set to run for four years from 31 December 1991, and has been allocated a budget of 64 MECU.

2. Awarding Body:

Commission of the European Communities.

3. Location Restrictions:

Available throughout the European Community. Countries which have concluded cooperation agreements with the EC may also participate in the programme, although they will not benefit from EC funding.

4. Sectoral Restrictions:

None.

5. Size Restrictions:

None.

6. Programme Duration:

The programme is set to run for four years from 31 December 1991.

7. Submission of Applications:

Projects are generally submitted in response to a call for proposals published in the Official Journal. A call for proposals concerning the setting-up of pilot information services for standards in information encoding was published in OJ C310; 27.11.92. The deadline was 15 January 1993. A call for definition-phase projects for new electronic information services based on Geographic Information Systems (GIS) technology was published in OJ C308; 26.11.92. The deadline was 1 March 1993.

The Commission may also implement a more flexible funding scheme than calls for proposals to provide incentives for the creation of partnerships (in particular involving SMEs and underdeveloped regions), or for other exploratory activities. The Commission may, in exceptional cases, accept unsolicited project proposals involving a particularly promising and significant information market development, a highly innovative approach, or an exceptional technology or methodology, and which cannot be submitted within the normal call for proposals procedure.

8. Other Restrictions:

The programme covers four Action Lines:

1. Improving the understanding of the information market including: the collection and analysis of market data; the analysis of the competitive strengths and weaknesses of the European information industry; the analysis of the role of information in the economy and society; and enhancement of the dissemination of IMO results.
2. Overcoming legal and administrative barriers including: personal data protection; legal protection of databases; public/private sectors synergy in the information market; principles for a legal framework concerning electronic information services; awareness of legal problems affecting the information market; and strengthening the position of the LAB (Legal Advisory Board).
3. Stimulating the application of norms and standards; awareness, user support and training including: development of guidelines for the awareness of information standards; and creation and management of an 'awareness network' implementing general and sectoral awareness campaigns; support for users and providers of information services, information exchange with the marketplace; and training of trainers, intermediaries and end-users.
4. Supporting strategic information initiatives: focusing on the theme of stimulating the improvement of European-wide access to information (INFO EURO ACCESS), including work on Information Standards (OII); implementation of kiosk-type applications; stimulating cooperation between market actors; and increasing awareness of problems, opportunities and solutions.

Under each of these action lines, a wide range of activities and potential project areas are planned. Full details are outlined in the IMPACT II Workprogramme.

9. Eligible Expenditure:

Eligible expenditure relates to labour costs, travel costs, services such as printing, translation, dataprocessing or consultancy, materials and durable equipment and subcontracting. The following are not allowable: costs of obtaining patent or copyright protection for project results, financial charges; exchange losses; costs related to normal commercial operation of the products or services developed (including updating and running costs).

10. Rate of Award:

The rate of award for shared-cost projects is normally up to 50 percent of eligible costs.

11. Payment Procedure:

Payment procedure will be outlined in the agreed contract.

12. Points to Note:

Council Decision (EEC) 691/91 adopting IMPACT II was published in OJ L377; 21.12.91. A call for tenders relating to the preparation of information and discussion documents covering issues to be examined by the LAB (Legal Advisory Board) to be set up under IMPACT II was published in OJ C84; 4.4.92. A further call concerning the setting up of databases specialised in information law was published in OJ C140; 3.6.92. A call for proposals for the development of interactive multimedia information services was published in OJ C139; 2.6.92. A call for tenders for training in less-favoured regions was published in OJ C175; 11.7.92. The deadline was 15 September 1992. A call for tenders for the undertaking of a market study on European access points to information services was published in OJ C199; 6.8.92; the deadline was 25 September 1992.

13. Application Procedure:

Application procedure is outlined when a call for proposals is published.

14. Further Information:

IMPACT Central Office
European Commission
DG XIII/B
Batiment Jean Monnet
Plateau du Kirchberg
L-2920 Luxembourg
Tel: (010 35 2) 34 981 222
Fax: (010 35 2) 4301 2847

RACE II

1. Summary:

The Communications Technologies Programme (RACE II) will support RTD projects in the following fields: development and implementation strategies for Integrated Broadband Communications (IBC) systems, services and applications; advanced communications technologies; and validation of standards and common functional specifications for IBC. The programme will be implemented through shared-cost research contracts, accompanying measures and concerted actions in eight priority areas: Integrated Broadband Communications (IBC) R & D; Intelligence in Networks/Flexible Communications Resource Management; Mobile and Personal Communications; Image and Data Communications; Integrated Services Technologies; Information Security Technologies; Advanced Communications Experiments; and Test Infrastructures and Interworking. The programme will involve the use of experimental equipment and services to address generic applications.

The programme is set to run for five years from 1991 to 1994, with a budget allocation of 484 MECU.

2. Awarding Body:

Commission of the European Communities.

3. Location Restrictions:

Available in any Member State of the European Community. Organisations in non-Member States which have concluded co-operation agreements with the European Communities may participate in the programme, although they will not be eligible for Commission funding.

4. Sectoral Restrictions:

The programme is open to industrial firms, universities, research institutes and individuals, or any combination or association thereof, in particular European Economic Interest Groupings (EEIGs). Projects must be carried out by at least two independent partners established in different Member States. Projects will require the collaboration of two or more telecommunications sector organisations.

5. Size Restrictions:

None.

6. Programme Duration:

The programme is set to run for five years, from 7 June 1991 to 31 December 1994.

7. Submission of Applications:

Application is normally made within the deadlines specified within each of the Commission's calls for proposals, published in the Official Journal. The first call for proposals was published in OJ C154; 12.6.91; the initial deadline was 16 September 1991. The call was reopened for a small number of tasks and finally closed on 10 February 1992.

8. Other Restrictions:

The programme focuses on eight priority areas (budget allocation in brackets):

1. IBC (Integrated Broadband Communications) R & D (111 MECU) building on the work done under the RACE programme and covering: IBC systems design, architecture and operation; IBC transition strategies; common operational environment; techniques for basic IBC system functions; integration of IBC demonstrators; verification tools;
2. Intelligence in Networks/Flexible Communications Resource Management (43 MECU): research will be related to the use of new

techniques for information transfer, optical communications and, possibly, artificial intelligence with a view to enhancing flexibility in respect of both provision of new network services and network management.

3. Mobile and Personal Communications (53 MECU): development of third generation integrated mobile communication systems aimed at providing universal personal communications using audio, data and image;
4. Image and Data Communications (68 MECU): development of technologies for the introduction and exploitation of advanced low-cost and flexible image and data communication services, for both domestic and business needs;
5. Integrated Services Technologies (39 MECU): IBC modular standardisation; integrated service technologies; service technology verification. The objective is to contribute to the definition of common functional specifications for new communication services and multimedia systems.
6. Information Security Technologies (29 MECU): service quality, security and reliability; information security technologies; information security verification;
7. Advanced Communications Experiments (121 MECU): study of generic functions; technology and techniques for advanced communications experiments; application experiments;
8. Test Infrastructure and Interworking (20 MECU): provision of a test structure to connect those involved in the introduction of IBC services and to validate standards and functional specifications.

9. Eligible Expenditure:

For organisations other than universities, eligible expenditure covers: labour (actual cost or at approved rates), travel and subsistence, consumables, equipment, computing costs, external work (sub-contracts or services), reasonable overheads. The following are not allowable: profits; marketing, distribution, advertising expenses; any interest or return on capital employed; taxes (except in limited circumstances); cost of proposal preparation; patent protection costs. Specific arrangements exist to recover non-reclaimable VAT.

Universities and higher education establishments may elect to have their support calculated according to the marginal costs of the project (ie the actual additional direct costs of the research not met by normal recurrent expenditure, other financial sources or other third parties), unless their costing and recording systems enable them to submit and justify full costs. Each university is normally expected to operate on the basis of either marginal costs or full costs for all Community R & D programmes, and not reach a decision on a project-by-project basis. Marginal costs may include all the items listed above, although labour costs only relate to temporary additional staff specifically engaged for the research; routine and minor computing costs may not be charged; overheads may be fixed at a percentage, corresponding to a maximum of 20 percent of all expenditure, except associated contracts and VAT.

10. Rate of Award:

The rate of award may be up to 50 percent of the full economic costs of the R & D project. Universities and higher education establishments may, however, attract a contribution of up to 100 percent of the actual marginal costs of the research project.

11. Payment Procedure:

Payment is made in accordance with the agreed contract and takes the form of an advance payment following signature of the contract by all partners and the Commission, followed by periodic instalments on approval of progress reports and cost statements submitted as work progresses. Ten percent of the total financial contribution is retained (or, in the case of larger contracts, 500,000 ECUs, whichever is lower) and is paid, along with any other sums due, on approval of final technical reports and cost statements.

In all cases the Commission's contribution is made in ECUs and no liability is held for exchange losses incurred.

12. Points to Note:

Council Decision (EEC) 352/91 adopting the Communications Technologies programme was published in OJ L192; 16.7.91.

13. Application Procedure:

Application procedure is outlined in the documents available from the European Commission.

14. Further Information:

European Commission
DG XIII – RACE II
Rue de la Loi 200
B-1049 Brussels
Tel: (010 32 2) 236 3410
Fax: (010 32 2) 235 0654
Telex: COMEU B 21877

Mr T French
Department of Trade and Industry
151 Buckingham Palace Road
London SW1W 9SS
Tel: (071) 215 1795
Fax: (071) 931 7194

TEDIS II

1. Summary:

The second phase of the TEDIS programme (Trade Electronic Data Interchange Systems) has three main objectives: (1) the intersectoral integration of work carried out in Member States on defining and implementing EDI (electronic data interchange) systems; (2) analysing the impact of EDI on the management of public and private enterprises; and (3) making potential users aware of the systems, in particular SMEs, software and hardware manufacturers and service companies. The programme is set to run for three years from July 1991, with a budget of 25 MECU.

2. Awarding Body:

Commission of the European Communities.

3. Location Restrictions:

Available in any Member State of the European Community. EFTA countries may also participate in the programme, as may other countries which have concluded association agreements with the Commission.

4. Sectoral Restrictions:

None, contracts may be concluded with businesses (including SMEs), research establishments, national administrations and other bodies.

5. Size Restrictions:

None.

6. Programme Duration:

The programme is set to run for three years from July 1991.

7. Submission of Applications:

A call for proposals for EDI development projects was published in OJ C144; 6.6.92. The deadline was 2 September 1992.

8. Other Restrictions:

The programme covers the following action lines:

1. Standardisation of EDI messages;
2. Specific EDI needs as regards telecommunications;
3. Legal aspects of EDI;
4. Security of EDI messages;
5. Multi-sector and Europe-wide projects;
6. Analysis of the impact of EDI on company management;
7. Information campaigns.

9. Eligible Expenditure:

Eligible expenditure will be outlined when a call for proposals is published.

10. Rate of Award:

The rate of award will be outlined when a call for proposals is published.

11. Payment Procedure:

Payment procedure will be outlined in the contract agreement.

12. Points to Note:

Council Decision (EEC) 385/91 establishing the second phase of the TEDIS programme was published in OJ L208; 30.7.91. A preliminary call for tenders was published in OJ C217 on 20.8.91. A call for proposals was published in OJ C29; 6.2.92; the deadline was 10 April 1992.

13. Application Procedure:

Application details are available from the Commission when a call for proposals is published.

14. Further Information:

Robert Wakeling
European Commission
DG XIII/D-5 – TEDIS
200 rue de la Loi
B-1049 Brussels
Tel: (010 32 2) 299 0258
Fax: (010 32 2) 299 0286

TELEMATIC SYSTEMS PROGRAMME

1. Summary:

The Telematic Systems in Areas of General Interest programme aims to promote trans-European telematic services networks contributing to the successful completion of the Single European Market, concentrating on seven priority areas: 1. Administrations; 2. Transport Services; 3. Health Care Services; 4. Distance and Flexible Learning Services; 5. Libraries; 6. Linguistic Research and Engineering; and 7. Telematic Systems for Rural Areas. The programme will be implemented through shared-cost RTD contracts, concerted actions and accompanying measures.

The programme is set to run for five years, from 1991 to 1994, with a budget allocation of 376 MECU.

2. Awarding Body:

Commission of the European Communities.

3. Location Restrictions:

Available in any Member State of the European Community. Organisations in non-Member States which have concluded cooperation agreements with the European Communities may participate in the programme, although they will not be eligible for Commission funding.

4. Sectoral Restrictions:

The programme is open to industrial firms, universities, research institutes and individuals, or any combination or association thereof, in particular European Economic Interest Groupings (EEIGs). Projects must be carried out by at least two independent partners established in different Member States.

5. Size Restrictions:

None.

6. Programme Duration:

The programme is set to run for five years, from 7 June 1991 to 31 December 1994.

7. Submission of Applications:

Application is normally made within the deadlines specified in each of the Commission's calls for proposals, published in the Official Journal.

Two calls for proposals relating to Areas 5 (Libraries) and 6 (Linguistic Research and Engineering) were published in OJ C259; 8.10.92. The deadlines were 11 January 1993 (Area 6) and 15 February 1993 (Area 5).

8. Other Restrictions:

The programme covers the following areas (budget allocation in brackets):

1. Support for the Establishment of Trans European Networks Between Administrations (41 MECU): defining common requirements for electronic information exchange, examining the need for interoperability between electronic information networks within Member States, and carrying out studies and pre-normative research for the definition and establishment of trans-European telematic services networks required by national administrations for the completion of the Single Market. The priority sub-areas will initially be customs, social services, emergency services and statistics. Research will cover: identification of needs and implementation strategies; development of the technologies relating to telematic services and validation of common functional specifications.
2. Transport Services (124 MECU): developing integrated trans-European services using advanced IT and communications to improve the performance (security and efficiency) of passenger and goods transport services, and reducing the impact of transport on the environment. There will be close liaison with relevant EUREKA projects. Work will cover the following sub-areas: road transport, building on work done under the DRIVE programme; strategies for the use of technologies, telematic services and systems and the definition of common functional specifications; technologies and experimental development of systems; validation and pilot projects;
3. Healthcare (97 MECU): stimulating the development of harmonised applications of information and communications technologies in health care, and the development of a European health-care information infrastructure. Work will be carried out along three main lines (building on the exploratory work done under the AIM programme); strategies for the use of technologies, telematic systems and services and the definition of common functional specifications; development of telematic technology applied to medicine; and validation and integration.
4. Distance and Flexible Learning (55 MECU): continuing exploratory work done under the DELTA programme, and covering three themes: strategies for the use of technologies, telematic systems and services, and the definition of common functional specifications; technology and systems development; and experiments on the validation and integration of services.
5. Libraries (22 MECU): facilitating user access by development of equipment and telematic systems, while reducing handicaps caused by the present disparate Community infrastructures. Work will help develop modern library services throughout the Community by promoting faster, but orderly and cost-effective, penetration of new technologies into libraries.

6. Linguistic Research and Engineering (22 MECU): developing a basic linguistic technology which can be incorporated into a large number of computer applications. This requires the creation of linguistic resources for the nine official EC languages, and the definition of standards for these resources. The area is divided into three parts: research; development of resources; and pilot applications, and is based on the results and experience of the EUROTRA programme and certain ESPRIT projects.
7. Telematic Systems for Rural Areas (14 MECU): understanding the needs and opportunities for telematic services in rural areas, and the impact of such services of rural life; understanding network configuration requirements and options, and requirements for telematic services; and preparing the way for the planning and introduction of telematic service infrastructures in rural areas. Actions will involve: consensus development with industry and rural development agencies; identification of needs and opportunities for telematic services and assessment of their impacts; specification of service and technology requirements; development of telematic systems; pilot applications; and research on infrastructure planning and implementation strategies.

9. Eligible Expenditure:

For organisations other than universities, eligible expenditure covers: labour (actual cost or at approved rates), travel and subsistence, consumables, equipment, computing costs, external work (sub-contracts or services), reasonable overheads. The following are not allowable: profits; marketing, distribution, advertising expenses; any interest or return on capital employed; taxes (escept in limited circumstances); cost of proposal preparation; patent protection costs. Specific arrangements exist to recover non-reclaimable VAT.

Universities and higher education establishments may elect to have their support calculated according to the marginal costs of the project (ie the actual additional direct costs of the research not met by normal recurrent expenditure, other financial sources or other third parties), unless their costing and recording systems enable them to submit and justify full costs. Each university is normally expected to operate on the basis of either marginal costs or full costs for all Community R & D programmes, and not reach a decision on a project-by-project basis. Marginal costs may include all the items listed above, although labour costs only relate to temporary additional staff specifically engaged for the research; routine and minor computing costs may not be charged; overheads may be fixed at a percentage, corresponding to a maximum of 20 percent of all expenditure, except associated contracts and VAT.

10. Rate of Award:

The rate of award is up to 50 percent of the full economic costs of the R & D project. Universities and higher education establishments may, however, attract a contribution of up to 100 percent of the actual marginal costs of the research project.

11. Payment Procedure:

Payment is made in accordance with the agreed contract and takes the form of an advance payment following signature of the contract by all partners and the Commission, followed by periodic instalments on approval of progress reports and cost statements submitted as work progresses. Ten percent of the total financial contribution is retained (or, in the case of larger contracts, 500,000 ECUs, whichever is lower) and is paid, along with any other sums due, on approval of final technical reports and cost statements.

In all cases the Commission's contribution is made in ECUs and no liability is held for exchange losses incurred.

12. Points to Note:

Council Decision (EEC) 353/91 adopting the programme was published in OJ L192; 16.7.91. The first call for proposals was published in OJ C157; 15.6.91; the deadline was 16 September 1991. A further call under area 7 was published in OJ C211; 13.8.91; the deadline was 30 September 1991. Two calls were published in OJ C184; 16.7.91 and OJ C218; 21.8.91; the deadlines were 2 December 1991.

13. Application Procedure:

Application procedure is outlined in a work programme, available from the European Commission.

14. Further Information:

Mr Graham Jenkins
Department of Trade & Industry
Information Technology Division
Fourth Floor (Grey)
151 Buckingham Palace Road
London SW1W 9SS
Tel: (071) 215 1226
Fax: (071) 931 2909

European Commission
Telematic Systems
DG XIII-B
JMO B4/11
L-2920 Luxembourg
Tel: (010 35 2) 4301 2126/3006
Fax: (010 35 2) 4301 3530

Specialist Area Contacts:

Transport:
Mr A Waddams
Department of Transport
Room P2/040
2 Marsham Street
London SW1P 3EB
Tel: (071) 276 5878

Mr D Mason
Department of Trade & Industry
ITD1c, 4th Floor, Grey Core
151 Buckingham Palace Road
London SW1W 9SS
Tel: (071) 215 1243

Libraries:
Mr C C Leamy
Office of Arts & Libraries
Horse Guards Road
London SW1P 3AL
Tel: (071) 270 5860

Linguistics:
Mr T Denvir
Department of Trade & Industry
ITD4a, 4th Floor, Green Core
151 Buckingham Palace Road
London SW1W 9SS
Tel: (071) 215 1268

Healthcare:
Mr D Preston
Department of Health
Room 920
Market Towers
1 Nine Elms Lane
London WC2A 2LS
Tel: (071) 720 2188 Ext. 3544

Mr B Jones
Department of Trade & Industry
ITD1e, 4th Floor, Grey Core
151 Buckingham Palace Road
Tel: (071) 215 1225

Flexible & Distance Learning:
Ms R Gilfellon
Department of Employment
Room 340
Caxton House
London SW1H 9NF
Tel: (071) 273 5398

Rural Areas:
Ms G Hackman
Department of the Environment
Room N19/16
2 Marsham Street
London SW1P 3EB
Tel: (071) 276 3673

Mr K Miltiadou
Department of Trade & Industry
TP3b, 2nd Floor
151 Buckingham Palace Road
London SW1W 9SS
Tel: (071) 215 1809

PART THREE

RESEARCH AND DEVELOPMENT/ INNOVATION

3.3 INDUSTRIAL AND MATERIAL TECHNOLOGIES/ MEASUREMENT AND TESTING

BRITE/EURAM II	197
Steel Research Programme	200
Measurements and Testing Programme	203

3.3 INDUSTRIAL AND MATERIAL TECHNOLOGIES/ MEASUREMENT AND TESTING

INDUSTRIAL AND MATERIALS TECHNOLOGIES (BRITE/EURAM II)

1. Summary:

The Industrial and Materials Technologies programme (BRITE/EURAM II) supports collaborative research aiming to improve the performance of materials at a competitive cost over a broad range of applications, and to improve industry's capability to design and manufacture products which are both competitive and socially and environmentally acceptable. The programme covers the following fields: 1. Materials - Raw Materials: Recycling, New and Improved Materials; 2. Design and Manufacturing and 3. Aeronautics. It is implemented by shared-cost research projects (CRAFT), cooperative research projects, concerted actions, accompanying measures (eg result dissemination, coordination and training of participants) and direct research undertaken by the Joint Research Centre (JRC). Feasibility awards will also be available for small and medium-sized enterprises (SMEs) (see 12 for further details).

The programme is set to run from 1991 to 1994, with a budget allocation of 633.3 MECU.

2. Awarding Body:

Commission of the European Communities.

3. Location Restrictions:

Available in any Member State of the European Community. Organisations in non-Member States which have concluded cooperation agreements with the European Communities may participate in the programme, although they will not be eligible for Commission funding.

4. Sectoral Restrictions:

The programme is open to industrial firms, universities, research institutes and individuals, or any combination or association thereof, in particular European Economic Interest Groupings (EEIGs). Shared-cost projects must be carried out by at least two independent partners established in different Member States. These two partners will normally be industrial firms except in the case of projects in the field of basic research. Where basic research is undertaken by a group made up solely of research centres and universities, industrial support will be sought.

Cooperative research is intended for groups which do not have their own research facilities, and which appoint one or more outside bodies to carry out the research.

5. Size Restrictions:

None.

6. Programme Duration:

The programme is set to run from 9 September 1991 to 31 December 1994.

7. Submission of Applications:

Application is normally made within the deadlines specified in each of the Commission's calls for proposals, published in the Official Journal. The second call for proposals was published in OJ C268; 17.10.92; the deadline was 26 February 1993. An open call for applications for feasibility awards, cooperative research actions (CRAFT) and training activities was published in OJ C333; 24.12.91. The deadline is December 1993, subject to the availability of funds.

8. Other Restrictions:

The programme covers the following fields (budget allocation in brackets):

1. Materials (308.8 MECU): contributing to improving the performance of materials at a cost which permits competitive industrial exploitation over a broad range of applications not restricted to a few high performance items. The accent is on the innovative use of industrial minerals and natural stone for the construction industry, metals and industrial materials, including their exploration, exploitation, recovery, transformation, production and recycling. Subprogrammes cover Raw Materials; Recycling; New and Improved Materials and their Processing.
2. Design and Manufacturing (301.5 MECU): improving the capability of industry to design and manufacture products which are, at the same time: of high quality; easy to maintain; highly competitive; and environmentally and socially acceptable. Research is directed to the application of advanced enabling disciplines such as physics and chemistry, mathematical modelling, mechanics, optics, acoustics, fluid dynamics and process engineering, and their integration into new technological developments such as optomatronics, mechatronics, microtechnology and micro- and nanostructural engineering, including molecular engineering.
3. Aeronautics (53 MECU): contributing to strengthening the technology base of the European aeronautical industry; contributing to the knowledge base which supports actions to minimize environmental impact; enhancing the safety and efficiency of aircraft operations; and promoting further cooperation between large high-technology companies and smaller companies and research institutes/ universities. Subprogrammes cover: Environment Related Technologies; Technologies of Aircraft Operation; Aerodynamics and Aerothermodynamics; Technologies of Aeronautical Structures and Manufacturing Technologies; Avionic System Technologies; and Mechanical, Utility and Activation Technologies.

The second call for proposals (see 7) covers Areas 1 and 2 of the programme only.

9. Eligible Expenditure:

For organisations other than universities, eligible expenditure covers: labour (actual cost or at approved rates), travel and subsistence, consumables, equipment, computing costs, external work (sub-contracts or services), reasonable overheads. The following are not allowable: profits; marketing, distribution, advertising expenses; any interest or return on capital employed; taxes (except in limited circumstances); cost of proposal preparation; patent

protection costs. Specific arrangements exist to recover non-reclaimable VAT.

Universities and higher education establishments may elect to have their support calculated according to the marginal costs of the project (ie the actual additional direct costs of the research not met by normal recurrent expenditure, other financial sources or other third parties), unless their costing and recording systems enable them to submit and justify full costs. Each university is normally expected to operate on the basis of either marginal costs or full costs for all Community R & D programmes, and not reach a decision on a project-by-project basis. Marginal costs may include all the items listed above, although labour costs only relate to temporary additional staff specifically engaged for the research; routine and minor computing costs may not be charged; overheads may be fixed at a percentage, corresponding to a maximum of 20 percent of all expenditure, except associated contracts and VAT.

10. Rate of Award:

The rate of award for shared-cost projects is up to 50 percent of the full economic costs of the R & D project. Universities and higher education establishments may, however, attract a contribution of up to 100 percent of the actual marginal costs of the research project.

The rate of award for cooperative research projects is up to 50 percent of research costs (which are normally between 400,000 ECU and 1 MECU) for up to two years.

For feasibility awards for SMEs (see 12), support of up to 75 percent of the cost of research lasting up to nine months is available (up to a maximum of 30,000 ECU).

11. Payment Procedure:

Payment is made in accordance with the agreed contract and takes the form of an advance payment following signature of the contract by all partners and the Commission, followed by periodic instalments on approval of progress reports and cost statements submitted as work progresses. Ten percent of the total financial contribution is retained (or, in the case of larger contracts, 500,000 ECUs, whichever is lower) and is paid, along with any other sums due, on approval of final technical reports and cost statements.

In all cases the Commission's contribution is made in ECUs and no liability is held for exchange losses incurred.

12. Points to Note:

Council Decision (EEC) 506/91 adopting the Industrial and Materials Technologies Programme was published in OJ L269; 25.9.91.

Feasibility awards will be awarded on a highly competitive basis to assist SMEs establish the feasibility of a device, process or concept as a means of enhancing their potential to find a partner in a subsequent call for proposals under the shared-cost action.

Cooperative research (CRAFT) is a form of research in which companies, in particular SMEs, facing a technical problem common to one or more industrial sectors, join together and assign a third party (research association, university or firm) to carry out R & D in order to find a solution to the problem.

Three types of training action are covered by the programme: research fellowships in the context of ongoing research projects; subsidies for host organisations to cover expenses incurred; and grants and support for courses and conferences.

Calls for proposals relating to all areas of the programme were published in OJ C333; 24.12.91. The deadlines were: 6 March 1992 for Aeronautics projects; and 3 April 1992 for Raw Materials or Design and Manufacturing Projects.

13. Application Procedure:

Application procedure is outlined when a call for proposals is published.

14. Further Information:

Mr G A Gadge
Department of Trade & Industry
Manufacturing Technologies Division
1/037 Red Zone
151 Buckingham Palace Road
London SW1W 9SS
Tel: (071) 215 1554
Fax: (071) 215 2909

European Commission
DG XII/C-2 (BRITE/EURAM)
Rue Montoyer 75
B-1040 Brussels
Tel: (010 32 2) 235 2345
Fax: (010 32 2) 235 8046
Telex: COMEU B 21877

For information on Aeronautics:
Mr B K Glenister
Department of Trade and Industry
Business Task Force 2
1/168 Yellow Zone
151 Buckingham Palace Road
London SW1W 9SS
Tel: (071) 215 1158
Fax: (071) 215 2902

For information on CRAFT:
Dr Bob Keown
Beta Technology Ltd
Riverside House
Weedon Street
Sheffield S9 2FT
Tel: (0742) 422004

STEEL RESEARCH PROGRAMME

1. Summary:

Under Article 55 of the ECSC Treaty, the European Commission is empowered to provide financial support for collaborative steel process and product oriented research, concentrating on the priority technological needs of the steel industry.

Within the Steel Research Programme, specific project areas are outlined in medium-term guidelines, in order to direct support to projects of specific interest to the Community. Under the current guidelines covering the period 1991–95, the major objectives identified are: the achievement of improved steel quality and reduction of production costs; maintenance of traditional steel markets and the development of new markets; and adaption of production conditions to meet increasingly stringent environmental requirements (see 8 for further details).

2. Awarding Body:
Commission of the European Communities.

3. Location Restrictions:
Available in any Member State of the European Community.

4. Sectoral Restrictions:
Available to any enterprise, research institute or individual. Projects supported under this programme generally involve collaborative research. Applicants do not need to be directly connected with the iron and steel industry, but research projects must be of interest to a large number of undertakings in this sector.

5. Size Restrictions:
Where a project involves only one organisation, total project costs should not exceed 1 MECU over three years. Preference will be given to large scale transnational projects of major industrial importance, requiring budgets greater than 1 MECU.

6. Programme Duration:
There is no specified terminal date for this scheme. The current guidelines for steel research projects cover the period 1991–95.

7. Submission of Applications:
Applications should be submitted before 1 September each year to be considered for support in the following financial year.

8. Other Restrictions:
Priorities identified for the period 1991–95 are:

A. Production Processes: optimising existing production methods and developing new techniques which (a) reduce processing time, or improve processing plant reliability, output quality or processing line flexibility; (b) provide a more detailed knowledge of the physical and chemical phenomena of multiphase systems and develop processes giving new and improved properties; and (c) achieve economies in the consumption of raw materials, manpower and energy. Research will focus on: reducing the cost of energy consumed and its effect on the environment, developing treatments for the secondary refining of liquid metal; improving measuring and analysis techniques; modelling of production processes; developing control, automation and robotisation; improving the reliability of installation; developing new processes for making/shaping steel; improving environmental quality and up-grading the value of by-products;

B. Products: optimising properties of existing products and developing new products by (a) speeding-up production, improving promotion and information provision; (b) improving consistency of quality and reliability; and (c) developing new uses for steel and the use of new steel grades. Research will concentrate on the following sectors: transport; energy; civil, plant and mechanical engineering; household and packaging; and environment. Research priorities will be: the development of steel products by existing methods and new techniques (covering forming, weldability, joining and assembly, machinability, aptitude for thermal treatment, surface treatment and coatings); the development of user properties (eg fatigue, fracture and corrosion resistance) and the development of new categories of materials.

C. Environmental Protection: improving environmental control techniques for existing processes; developing new clean technologies for steel production and processing; and upgrading the value of by-products to reduce steelplant wastes.

9. Eligible Expenditure:

Eligible expenditure includes: depreciation on land and buildings used for the research work; the cost of equipment, apparatus and materials (the rate of depreciation charged to research costs is generally 20 percent of the purchase price per estimated year of use); gross salaries and statutory charges on all staff directly employed (both full and part-time) on the research; operational costs directly chargeable to the project; for research institutes, a fixed allowance of 30 percent of gross personnel costs for other expenditure not specified elsewhere (eg travel, administrative etc.) and overheads.

10. Rate of Award:

As a general rule, the Commission contributes approximately 60 percent of estimated project costs. However, in the case of steel undertakings operating on the competitive steel market, the rate of award may not exceed 35 percent (net grant equivalent) of eligible project costs for basic industrial research. In addition, in the case of such undertakings, financial support may not be authorised in combination with national aid if the financing ceiling set by the EC would be exceeded as a result. These restrictions have been made to apply the USA–ECSC/EEC consensus on steel (OJ C160; 20.6.91). As a general rule, these rates do not apply to the financing of independent research institutes (public or private, including universities) by means of public funds, unless the R & D activities are carried out on a contractual basis or in cooperation with certain ECSC undertakings.

11. Payment Procedure:

The Commission makes an advance payment, followed by half-yearly instalments, but normally not more than 90 percent of its total share until the closure of the contract.

12. Points to Note:

The guidelines for the programme for 1991–95 were published in Official Journal No. C252; 6.10.90.

13. Application Procedure:

The procedure applicable to the lodging and consideration of applications, the terms and conditions of aid, and the obligations of the beneficiary as regards protection and dissemination of research results are outlined in a communication published in Official Journal C159; 24.06.82.

14. Further Information:

P R V Evans
European Commission
DG XII C/4
Rue de la Loi 200
B-1049 Brussels
Tel: (010 32 2) 235 3707
Telex: COMEU B 21877

MEASUREMENTS AND TESTING PROGRAMME

1. Summary:

The research and development programme in the field of Measurements and Testing aims to improve measurements, testing techniques and chemical analyses where they are not sufficiently accurate (resulting in laboratories not being able to agree on results), and where measurement methods are insufficient to meet the needs of industry in the monitoring of the environment, food quality and health.

The programme is implemented through research projects, accompanying measures and concerted actions in the following fields: Support to Regulations and Directives; Sectoral Testing Problems; Common Means of Calibration for the Community; and Development of New Methods of Measurement.

The programme is set to run for five years until 31 December 1994, with a budget allocation of 47.52 MECU.

2. Awarding Body:

Commission of the European Communities.

3. Location Restrictions:

Available in any Member State of the European Community. Organisations in non-Member States which have concluded cooperation agreements with the European Communities may participate in the programme, although they will not be eligible for Commission funding.

4. Sectoral Restrictions:

The programme is open to industrial firms, universities, research institutes and individuals, or any combination or association thereof, in particular European Economic Interest Groupings (EEIGs). Projects must be carried out by at least two independent partners established in different Member States.

5. Size Restrictions:

None.

6. Programme Duration:

The programme is set to run for five years, until 31 December 1994.

7. Submission of Applications:

Application is normally made within the deadlines specified within each of the Commission's calls for proposals, published in the Official Journal. The first call for proposals was published in OJ C178;15.7.92; the deadlines were 11 September and 30 September 1992.

8. Other Restrictions:

The programme covers the following fields (budget allocation in brackets):

1. Support to Regulations and Directives (12 MECU): to improve methods of obtaining reliable and internationally accepted results for the application of Directives, in particular, on food products, industrial products, the environment and health. Work will consist of developing, improving and harmonising test methods required for preparation of new Regulations and Directives, and the implementation of existing Directives.
2. Sectoral Testing Problems (11.52 MECU): support for European standardisation, laboratory accreditation and mutual recognition; work will include collaborative projects for improving or developing new testing methods; to solve measurement and testing problems; and organisation of interlaboratory comparisons.
3. Common Means of Calibration for the Community (12 MECU): supporting projects to develop the calibration means required by testing laboratories in the Community, to ensure that measurements and tests are done on a common basis, and can be compared with measurements done outside the Community.
4. Development of New Methods of Measurement (12 MECU) as required by Community policies; work will include: R & D on measurement principles which could lead to new instrumentation; and new measurement methods in the specialist areas mentioned in 3 above.

9. Eligible Expenditure:

Areas 1, 2 and 3 of the programme (see 8) will normally be implemented as concerted actions, in which all research costs are borne by the participants themselves; the Community provides funding for coordination costs up to 100 percent (eg cost of meetings, preparation of samples, synthesis reports). Area 4 will be implemented by means of shared-cost projects.

For organisations other than universities, eligible expenditure covers: labour (actual cost or at approved rates), travel and subsistence, consumables, equipment, computing costs, external work (sub-contracts or services), reasonable overheads. The following are not allowable: profits; marketing, distribution, advertising expenses; any interest or return on capital employed; taxes (except in limited circumstances); cost of proposal preparation; patent protection costs.

Universities and higher education establishments may elect to have their support calculated according to the marginal costs of the project (ie the actual additional direct costs of the research not met by normal recurrent expenditure, other financial sources or other third parties), unless their costing and recording systems enable them to submit and justify full costs. Each university is normally expected to operate on the basis of either marginal costs or full costs for all Community R & D programmes, and not reach a decision on a project-by-project basis. Marginal costs may include all the items listed above, although labour costs only relate to temporary additional staff specifically engaged for the research; routine and minor computing costs may not be charged; overheads may be fixed at a percentage, corresponding to a maximum of 20 percent of all expenditure, except associated contracts and VAT.

10. Rate of Award:

The rate of award for shared-cost projects is up to 50 percent of the full economic costs of the R & D project. A substantial proportion of the programme will be conducted by means of concerted actions whereby participants pay the costs of their own work, but the EC pays the costs of coordination. Universities and higher education establishments may, however, attract a contribution of up to 100 percent of the actual marginal costs of the research project.

11. Payment Procedure:

Payment is made in accordance with the agreed contract and takes the form of an advance payment following signature of the contract by all partners and the Commission, followed by periodic instalments on approval of progress reports and cost statements submitted as work progresses. Ten percent of the total financial contribution is retained (or, in the case of larger contracts, 500,000 ECUs, whichever is lower) and is paid, along with any other sums due, on approval of final technical reports and cost statements.

In all cases the Commission's contribution is made in ECUs and no liability is held for exchange losses incurred.

12. Points to Note:

Council Decision (EEC) 247/92 adopting the programme was published in OJ L126; 12.5.92.

The programme builds on work done under the Applied Metrology and Chemical Analysis (BCR) programme.

13. Application Procedure:

Application procedure is outlined when a call for proposals is published.

14. Further Information:

Mr Matthew Clark
Department of Trade and Industry
Room 201, 2nd Floor
151 Buckingham Palace Road
London SW1W 9SF
Tel: (071) 215 1424
Fax: (071) 215 2909

Dr H Marchandise
European Commission
DG XII/C (MO75)
Programme Measurements and Testing (BCR), Room 3/51
Rue Montoyer 75
B-1040 Brussels
Tel: (010 32 2) 235 5014
Fax: (010 32 2) 235 8072
Telex: COMEU B 21877

Mr P J Wagstaffe (Analysis of Food and Agriculture)
Tel: (010 32 2) 235 7464

Mr B Griepink (Environmental Analysis)
Tel: (010 32 2) 235 8812

Mrs E Colinet (Biomedical Analysis)
Tel: (010 32 2) 235 7609

Mr D Gould (Metrology and Standardised Tests)
Tel: (010 32 2) 235 9313

PART THREE

RESEARCH AND DEVELOPMENT/ INNOVATION

3.4. ENERGY

3.4.1 NUCLEAR ENERGY

TELEMAN	209
Controlled Thermonuclear Fusion Programme	211
Nuclear Fission Safety Programme	213

3.4.1 NUCLEAR ENERGY

TELEMAN

1. Summary:

The TELEMAN programme offers support for research and training projects in the field of remote handling in nuclear hazardous and disordered environments. The objective of TELEMAN is to reinforce the scientific and technical base used for the design of nuclear remote handling equipment – tele-operators – especially mechanical arms to which a variety of tools and sensors can be attached, manipulators attached to moveable gantries and partially autonomous vehicles equipped for specialised jobs.

The technical content of the programme covers: I. Tele-operator component and subsystem development; II. Environmental tolerance; III. Research machine projects; IV. Product evaluation and studies.

The programme is implemented through research and development actions, concerted actions, studies and coordination activities. Training/mobility grants are included to facilitate the assembly of relevant skills at appropriate locations for the work of the projects, and to promote effective diffusion of knowledge. TELEMAN is set to run from 18 July 1989 until 31 December 1993 with a budget allocation of 19 MECU.

2. Awarding Body:

Commission of the European Communities.

3. Location Restrictions:

Available in any Member State of the European Community.

Once firmly established the programme may be extended to EFTA countries, although they will not be entitled to EC funding.

4. Sectoral Restrictions:

Preference is given to projects in which industry, universities and research organisations from Community countries collaborate, and where participants come from more than one Member State.

Help with choosing a partner is available from the Commission. The participation of small and medium-sized enterprises is particularly encouraged.

5. Size Restrictions:

None, although the recommended project size has a total cost of between 0.3 and 2 MECU.

6. Programme Duration:

The programme is set to run from 18 July 1989 to 31 December 1993.

7. Submission of Applications:

Application is made within the deadlines specified in each of the Commission's invitations to submit proposals, published in the Official Journal. The second call for proposals was published in OJ C255; 1.10.91; the deadline was 14 February 1992.

8. Other Restrictions:

TELEMAN covers the following areas (budget allocation in brackets):

I. Tele-operator component and subsystem development (8.8 MECU): R & D on the utilisation, modification and, where necessary, the development of sensors, perception and decision-making systems, information transmission and engineering for tele-operator mobility and dexterity in nuclear environments.

II. Environmental tolerance (2.5 MECU): research to be carried out throughout the life of the programme on the adaptation of sensors and electronic hardware to nuclear environments, the development of machine monitoring systems and design strategies that permit easy repair or recovery of stranded machines.

III. Research machine projects (6.4 MECU): products of research on components and subsystems will be demonstrated by incorporating them into existing or new research machines. Development will focus on tele-operators that typify nuclear industry requirements (eg intelligent manipulators for cranes for use in high radiation fields, and a mobile platform for information gathering).

IV. Product evaluation and studies (1.3 MECU): end-users of TELEMAN will be encouraged to test and evaluate the practicality and reliability of the products of the programme in realistic environments to guide the subsequent commercialisation of successful products by industry. Studies will cover the application of new technologies, new uses for computer-assisted tele-operators, the evolution of guidelines and standards and programme development. TELEMAN will, in particular, help the nuclear industry to comply with the requirements that workers be exposed to the minimum practicable amount of radiation without compromising inspection, maintenance and repair operations.

9. Eligible Expenditure:

Eligible expenditure relates to the total cost of the project.

10. Rate of Award:

The rate of award for research contracts is up to 50 percent of project costs.

11. Payment Procedure:

Payment procedure is outlined in the Information Pack available from the Commission.

12. Points to Note:

The first call for proposals was published in OJ C242; 22.9.89. This call covered areas I and II of the programme.

Council Decision (Euratom) 464/89 adopting TELEMAN was published in Official Journal No L226; 3.8.89.

13. Application Procedure:

Application procedure is outlined in the Information Pack available from the Commission.

14. Further Information:

Herman de Nordwall
European Commission
DG XII
Rue de la Loi 200
B-1049 Brussels
Tel: (010 32 2) 235 5355

Mr T Hayward
Department of Trade and Industry
1 Palace Street
London SW1E 5HE
Tel: (071) 238 3798

CONTROLLED THERMONUCLEAR FUSION PROGRAMME

1. Summary:

The research and training programme in the field of Controlled Thermonuclear fusion forms part of the European Commission's strategy to achieve the joint creation of safe, environmentally sound prototype reactors by the middle of the 21st century.

A step by step strategy towards a prototype commercial reactor is foreseen, including after JET (Joint European Torus), an experimental reactor (Next Step), and a demonstration reactor (Demo).

The programme has as its priority the establishment of the required scientific and technical base and the preparation of industry for the construction of a 'Next Step' experimental fusion reactor, producing self-sustaining and long-duration fusion reactions.

The programme is implemented mainly through the funding of government research organisations attached to the programme; however, some funding is available for related shared-cost research contracts.

The programme is set to run from 19 December 1991 to 31 December 1994, with a budget allocation of 411.8 MECU.

2. Awarding Body:

The European Atomic Energy Community (EAEC).

3. Location Restrictions:

Participants in the programme may be located in any Member State of the European Community. Sweden and Switzerland are also associated with the programme. Countries, other than Sweden or Switzerland, which have concluded scientific and technical research agreements with the Community may participate in the programme but will not receive EC funding and must contribute to the programme's administrative costs.

4. Sectoral Restrictions:

The work will mainly be carried out within the framework of: Contracts of Association with organisations in the Member States, the JET Joint Undertaking; the NET Agreement; the Long-Term Development Agreement (to be established); and other contracts of limited duration. Participants may be universities, research organisations or industrial firms, including small and medium-sized enterprises, or associations thereof, in particular European Economic Interest Groupings (EEIGs).

5. Size Restrictions:

None.

6. Programme Duration:

The programme is set to run from 19 December 1991 to 31 December 1994.

7. Submission of Applications:

Participation generally takes place within the framework of Contracts of Association between the EAEC and certain national research institutes.

8. Other Restrictions:

The programme covers the following research areas (budget allocation in brackets):

1. 'Next Step' Design (75 MECU): the major physics goal of 'Next Step' will be the achievement of self-sustained thermonuclear burn of deuterium-tritium plasma and its control during long pulse operation. 'Next Step' should demonstrate the safe operation of a device that integrates the important technologies of a fusion reactor and should test essential components and subsystems. The 'Next Step' must provide the basic data for building a future demonstration reactor ('DEMO') capable of producing electricity with a capacity comparable to that of future commercial plants, taking due account of environmental constraints. 'Next Step' conceptual design activities have been completed in the European-wide framework through NET (Next European Torus) and in the framework of international collaboration through ITER (International Thermonuclear Experimental Reactor).
2. Long-term Technical Developments (21 MECU): focusing on environmental and safety criteria. In particular, research will cover issues such as: the development of low-activation materials relevant to a reactor; the development of reactor blanket modules; and a reference design for a commercial fusion reactor.
3. JET (Joint European Torus) (210 MECU): establishing reliable methods of plasma purity control in conditions relevant for the 'Next Step' Tokamak. Where appropriate, JET equipment and expertise will be used for specific developments in support of 'Next Step'. A substantial contribution to the JET programme will be provided by the Associations, through supporting activities and staff transfers. Preparation will be undertaken for the final phase of JET (1995/96) with deuterium-tritium plasmas. A rigorous scientific, technical and safety assessment will be carried out as part of this preparation.
4. Support Programme (105.84 MECU): covering scientific support to the 'Next Step' and to JET, studies on alternative lines in toroidal magnetic confinement, and other approaches to controlled fusion.

9. Eligible Expenditure:

Eligible expenditure is outlined in the agreed contract.

10. Rate of Award:

The rate of award is agreed when the contract is drawn up.

11. Payment Procedure:

Payment procedure is outlined in the agreed contract.

12. Points to Note:

Council Decision EURATOM 678/91 adopting the programme was published in OJ L375; 31.12.91.

Other general objectives of the programme are: to continue demonstrating the safety and environmental feasibility of fusion power in parallel with the demonstration of its scientific and technological feasibility; to enlarge the involvement of European industry; to determine the reactor potential of toroidal magnetic configurations (concentrating on stellarators and reversed field pinches); to monitor other approaches to controlled fusion; to strengthen links between associated research bodies and the rest of the European scientific community; to make available to the EC the powerful source of neutrons necessary for the experiments; and to widen current knowledge and techniques regarding the treatment of waste and tritium, the first wall and the effects on humans of powerful magnetic fields.

13. Application Procedure:

Details of application procedure are available from the address below.

14. Further Information:

Mr P Kind
European Commission
DG XII
Rue de la Loi 200
B-1049 Brussels
Tel: (010 32 2) 299 1111
Fax: (010 32 2) 235 0145

Mr B Freeman
Department of Trade and Industry
1 Palace Street
London SW1E 5HE
Tel: (071) 238 3771

NUCLEAR FISSION SAFETY PROGRAMME

1. Summary:

The Nuclear Fission Safety programme supports collaborative shared-cost RTD contracts, concerted actions and accompanying measures in the following areas: 1. Radiation Protection (Human exposure to radiation and radioactivity; Effects of radiation exposure to man: their assessment, prevention and treatment; and Risks and management of radiation exposure) and 2. Reactor Safety (Accident progression analysis; Behaviour and qualification of the containment system; and Accident management and control).

Area 1 (Radiation protection) will be conducted mainly through shared-cost research projects. For Area 2 (Reactor Safety), activities will be carried out by means of concerted actions ie the Community will coordinate individual research activities carried out by Member States.

The programme is set to run from November 1991 to December 1994, with a budget allocation of 35.64 MECU.

2. Awarding Body:
Commission of the European Communities.

3. Location Restrictions:
Available in any Member State of the European Community. Organisations in non-Member States which have concluded cooperation agreements with the European Communities may participate in the programme, although they will not be eligible for Commission funding.

4. Sectoral Restrictions:
The programme is open to industrial firms, universities, research institutes and individuals, or any combination or association thereof, in particular European Economic Interest Groupings (EEIGs). Projects must be carried out by at least two independent partners established in different Member States.

5. Size Restrictions:
None.

6. Programme Duration:
The programme is set to run from 28 November 1991 to 31 December 1994.

7. Submission of Applications:
Application will normally be made within the deadlines specified in each of the Commission's calls for proposals, published in the Official Journal. A call for proposals was published in OJ C322; 13.12.91.
This call committed all remaining funds for shared-cost projects.

8. Other Restrictions:
The programme covers the following areas (budget allocation in brackets):

1. Radiation Protection (28.64 MECU): aiming to provide the scientific knowledge for an objective assessment of radiation effects and risks, as well as methods optimising radiation protection. Research will: define the extent of exposure and the ways in which it can occur from natural, medical and industrial sources; study health consequences, including the treatment of over-exposure; and assess, comparatively and quantitatively, the risks which radiation can pose to man and the environment. The following themes will be covered with a multidisciplinary approach: Human exposure to radiation and radioactivity; Effects of radiation exposure to man: their assessment, prevention and treatment; and Risks and management of radiation exposure.
2. Reactor Safety (7 MECU): contributing to the definition of what will be needed to satisfy safety requirements for future generations of nuclear power plants, and improving confidence in safety analyses, through an exercise promoting the concertation of parties from all EC Member States, whether or not they have a nuclear power programme. Action will include studies, inter-comparison of methods and tools (eg probabilistic safety analyses) and joint evaluations of research and development work. Key issues will be addressed under three main themes: accident progression analysis; behaviour and

qualification of the containment system; and accident management and control.

9. Eligible Expenditure:

For organisations other than universities, eligible expenditure covers: labour (actual cost or at approved rates), travel and subsistence, consumables, equipment, computing costs, external work (sub-contracts or services), reasonable overheads. The following are not allowable: profits; marketing, distribution, advertising expenses; any interest or return on capital employed; taxes (except in limited circumstances); cost of proposal preparation; patent protection costs. Specific arrangements exist to recover non-reclaimable VAT.

Universities and higher education establishments may elect to have their support calculated according to the marginal costs of the project (ie the actual additional direct costs of the research not met by normal recurrent expenditure, other financial sources or other third parties), unless their costing and recording systems enable them to submit and justify full costs. Each university is normally expected to operate on the basis of either marginal costs or full costs for all Community R & D programmes, and not reach a decision on a project-by-project basis. Marginal costs may include all the items listed above, although labour costs only relate to temporary additional staff specifically engaged for the research; routine and minor computing costs may not be charged; overheads may be fixed at a percentage, corresponding to a maximum of 20 percent of all expenditure, except associated contracts and VAT.

10. Rate of Award:

The rate of award is up to 50 percent of the full economic costs of the R & D project. Universities and higher education establishments may, however, attract a contribution of up to 100 percent of the actual marginal costs of the research project.

Concerted actions may be funded for up to 100 percent of coordinating expenditure.

11. Payment Procedure:

Payment is made in accordance with the agreed contract and takes the form of an advance payment following signature of the contract by all partners and the Commission, followed by periodic instalments on approval of progress reports and cost statements submitted as work progresses. Ten percent of the total financial contribution is retained (or, in the case of larger contracts, 500,000 ECUs, whichever is lower) and is paid, along with any other sums due, on approval of final technical reports and cost statements.

In all cases the Commission's contribution is made in ECUs and no liability is held for exchange losses incurred.

12. Points to Note:

Council Decision (EURATOM/626/91) adopting the programme was published in OJ L336; 7.12.91.

13. Application Procedure:

Application procedure is outlined when calls for proposals are published.

14. Further Information:

European Commission
DG XII/D-3
Rue de la Loi 200
B-1049 Brussels
Tel: (010 32 2) 235 4045

Mr J Verney (Reactor Safety)
Health & Safety Executive
Broad Lane
Sheffield S3 7HQ
Tel: (0742) 768141 Ext.3404
Fax: (0742) 700313

Dr H Walker (Radiation Protection)
Department of Health
Room 917a
Hannibal House
Elephant & Castle
London SE1 6TE
Tel: (071) 972 2157
Fax: (071) 703 9565

PART THREE

RESEARCH AND DEVELOPMENT/ INNOVATION

3.4 ENERGY

3.4.2 NON-NUCLEAR ENERGY

THERMIE 219
Coal Research Programme 221
Non-Nuclear Energies Programmes 223

3.4.2 NON-NUCLEAR ENERGY

THERMIE

1. Summary:

The THERMIE programme offers financial support for projects promoting energy technology (ie projects designed to develop and promote innovative technologies whose implementation entails a large element of risk). THERMIE covers the following fields of application: rational use of energy; renewable energy sources; coal and other solid fuels; and hydrocarbons. Support is available for innovatory projects, dissemination projects, and targeted projects instigated by the European Commission (see 8 for further details). THERMIE is set to run from 1990 to 1994, with a budget allocation of 350 MECU over the first 3 years. A further 350 MECU has been proposed for the final two years of the programme.

2. Awarding Body:

Commission of the European Communities.

3. Location Restrictions:

Available in any Member State of the European Community. Projects implemented in less developed regions are particularly encouraged.

Projects must generally be carried out within Community territory. However, if it is in the interests of the Community to have all or part of a project carried out in a non-Member State because of the special characteristics of the project, it may also qualify.

4. Sectoral Restrictions:

Preference is given to projects proposed by small and medium-sized enterprises or by an association of such enterprises. Projects must be proposed by persons prepared to disseminate the techniques, processes or products.

Projects costing over 6 MECU must, as a general rule, be submitted by two independent promoters in different Member States. Projects with a total cost of less than 6 MECU may be proposed by single organisations, although projects proposed by independent organisations in two or more Member States are also encouraged.

5. Size Restrictions:

None, however preference is given to projects proposed by SMEs or an association of SMEs.

6. Programme Duration:

THERMIE is set to run until 31 December 1994.

7. Submission of Applications:

Application is made within the deadlines specified in each of the Commission's invitations for proposals to be submitted, published in the Official Journal. A call for proposals was published in OJ C179; 16.7.92, covering all sectors of the programme. The deadline was 1 December 1992, except for targeted projects in the areas of low energy, low CO_2 buildings and integrated urban traffic management, where the deadline was 20 January 1993 (OJ C304; 21.11.92).

8. Other Restrictions:

Support may be granted for:

- Innovatory projects implementing innovatory techniques, processes or products for which the R & D stage has been completed, or new applications of established techniques, products or processes; projects should prove the viability of new technologies by applying them on a sufficiently large scale for the first time;
- Dissemination projects for the techniques, processes or products referred to above; projects must be designed to encourage preliminary applications of tested new technologies, either under different economic or geographic conditions or with technical modifications, provided they still entail some risk.
- Targeted projects: where the EC considers it necessary, and especially where a need is not being met or where a significant technological advance could be achieved, it will itself take the initiative to encourage or coordinate the setting-up of specific projects.

THERMIE covers the following fields and sectors of application:

- Rational Use of Energy: in buildings; industry; energy industry, electricity and heat; transport and urban infrastructure.
- Renewable Energy Sources: solar energy (thermal and photovoltaic applications); energy from biomass, agricultural products and waste; geothermal energy; hydroelectric energy; wind energy.
- Coal and Other Solid Fuels: combustion; conversion; waste; gasification integrated with a combined gas/steam cycle.
- Hydrocarbons: innovatory projects relating to onshore and offshore exploration, production, transportation and storage of oil and natural gas; refining projects are excluded, as are dissemination projects.

Projects must appear technically and economically viable, must offer appropriate solutions for protection of the environment and safety, be difficult to finance because of technical or economic risks and be designed to encourage propagation of the technology on the market.

9. Eligible Expenditure:

Support may be granted for an entire project, for novel elements of a project, or for different stages of a project.

10. Rate of Award:

The rates of award are determined separately for each project and may be up to 40 percent of eligible costs for Innovatory or Targeted projects, and up to 35 percent of eligible costs for Dissemination projects.

11. Payment Procedure:

Payment procedure is detailed in an Information Pack accompanying each call for proposals, but is normally 30 percent on signing of the contract, 50 percent phased throughout the project, and the final 20 percent on submission of a satisfactory final report.

12. Points to Note:

Council Decision (EEC) 2008/90 adopting THERMIE was published in OJ L185; 17.7.90.

The first general call was published in OJ C77; 27.3.90.

An invitation to tender for assistance with the implementation of THERMIE, encouraging the application and market penetration of energy technologies, was published in OJ C188; 28.7.90. The second general call was published in OJ C215; 30.8.90.

A call for proposals from the new German Lander was published in OJ C166; 26.6.91. The third general call was published in OJ C180; 11.7.91.

The Commission may undertake associated measures to encourage the application and marketing of energy technologies – eg evaluating and analysing market features and potential (including any feasibility studies); circulating information and results of projects; monitoring, auditing projects and sectoral energy units; areas of technological cooperation; encouraging industrial cooperation with third countries; training staff; using regional institutions to help with these activities.

The Commission may require all or part of the financial support granted to be repaid if the contractor responsible for implementing a project receiving assistance does not use the successful technique, process or product, or facilitate its use and allow the results obtained to be disseminated.

13. Application Procedure:

Application procedure is outlined in the Information Pack accompanying each call for proposals.

14. Further Information:

Michael Thomas Gowen
European Commission
DG XVII
Energy Technology
Rue de la Loi 200
B-1049 Brussels
Tel: (010 32 2) 236 0436
Fax: (010 32 2) 235 0150
Telex: 21877 COMEU-B

David Wallace
Department of Trade & Industry
1 Palace Street
London SW1E 5HE
Tel: (071) 238 3643

COAL RESEARCH PROGRAMME

1. Summary:

Under Article 55 of the ECSC Treaty, the European Commission is empowered to provide financial support for technical coal research projects relating to the production and increased use of coal and to occupational safety in the coal industry.

Within the Coal Research Programme, specific project areas are outlined in medium-term guidelines in order to direct support to projects of specific interest to the Community. Under the current guidelines covering the period 1990 to 1995, two major sectors of the coal industry have been selected for research projects: mining engineering, and product upgrading.

2. Awarding Body:
Commission of the European Communities.

3. Location Restrictions:
Available in any Member State of the European Community.

4. Sectoral Restrictions:
Available to any enterprise, research institute or individual. Applicants do not need to be directly connected with the coal industry but research projects must be of interest to a large number of undertakings in the coal sector.

5. Size Restrictions:
There are no formal restrictions, but projects should not exceed five years in duration.

6. Programme Duration:
There is no specified terminal date for this scheme.

7. Submission of Applications:
Applications should be submitted before 1 September each year in order to be effective the following year.

A call for proposals for a targeted project on gas cleaning was published in OJ C188; 25.7.92; the deadline was 31 August 1992.

8. Other Restrictions:
Under the 1990 to 1995 guidelines, eligible projects can relate to mining engineering or product upgrading. Within mining engineering, the following research fields are included: development work (relating to new pits or the extension of existing pits); mine gases, ventilation, climate; methods of working and techniques of coal-winning; mine infrastructure; modern management. Projects concerned with product upgrading may relate to: coal preparation; metallurgical uses of coal; combustion of coal; coal upgrading and conversion.

The criteria used for the selection of research projects are as follows: the objectives of the common energy policy and of the common general research policy (with particular reference to energy research); the interest of the research for the Community; the value of the research; the repercussions on the environment; the lead time between the completion of the research and its practical application.

9. Eligible Expenditure:
Eligible expenditure includes: the cost of equipment and apparatus (the rate of depreciation charged to research costs is generally 20 percent of the purchase price per estimated year of use); gross salaries and statutory charges on all staff directly employed (both full and part-time) on the research; operational costs directly chargeable to the project; a fixed allowance of 30 percent of gross personnel costs for other expenditure not specified elsewhere (eg travel, administrative etc).

10. Rate of Award:

As a general rule, the Commission contributes approximately 60 percent of estimated project costs. The extent of the contribution may vary from one project to another and will depend on the value of the research, its importance in the context of general objectives and on whether the research is initiated by the applicant or the Commission.

11. Payment Procedure:

The Commission will pay an advance on request, followed by half-yearly instalments, but normally not more than 90 percent of its total share until the closure of accounts.

12. Points to Note:

The general objectives of ECSC coal research are to: reduce production costs; concentrate R & D efforts on projects with the best prospects of technical and economic results; assure the optimal use of R & D resources through close collaboration/rapid dissemination of research results; maintain the technological lead position of engineering/mining machinery manufacturers; optimise colliery management through improved systems; transfer best practice to difficult geological situations; improve raw coal quality; increase the share of coal in the heat market; develop the coking plant of the year 2000; optimise coal utilisation processes to improve the public acceptance of coal; work towards the clean utilisation of coal.

The 1990–95 guidelines were published in Official Journal No C52; 1.03.89.

13. Application Procedure:

The procedure applicable to the lodging and consideration of applications, the terms and conditions of aid, and the obligations of the beneficiary as regards protection and dissemination of research results are outlined in a communication published in Official Journal No C159; 24.06.82.

14. Further Information:

James Keith Wilkinson
European Commission
Energy Technology Directorate
XVII/D/2
Rue de la Loi 200
B-1049 Brussels
Tel: (010 32 2) 235 5576

NON-NUCLEAR ENERGIES PROGRAMME

1. Summary:

The Non-Nuclear Energies Programme supports collaborative RTD projects, accompanying measures and concerted actions in the following areas: Analysis of Strategies and Modelling; Minimum Emission Power Production from Fossil Sources; Renewable Energy Sources; and Energy Utilisation and Conservation.

The programme is set to run for five years from 1991 to 1994, with a budget allocation of 155.5 MECU.

2. Awarding Body:
Commission of the European Communities.

3. Location Restrictions:
Available in any Member State of the European Community. Organisations in non-Member States which have concluded cooperation agreements with the European Communities may participate in the programme, although they will not be eligible for Commission funding.

4. Sectoral Restrictions:
The programme is open to industrial firms, universities, research institutes and individuals, or any combination or association thereof, in particular European Economic Interest Groupings (EEIGs). Projects must be carried out by at least two independent partners established in different Member States.

5. Size Restrictions:
None.

6. Programme Duration:
The programme is set to run for five years from 9 September 1991 to 31 December 1994.

7. Submission of Applications:
Application will normally be made within the deadlines specified in each of the Commission's calls for proposals, published in the Official Journal.

A call for proposals in relation to Area 1 of the programme – Analysis of Strategies and Modelling – was published in Official Journal No C201; 8.8.92; the deadline for proposals was 18 September 1992.

8. Other Restrictions:
The programme covers the following areas (budget allocation in brackets):

1. Analysis of Strategies and Modelling (9 MECU): defining energy R&D strategies and analysing national/Community policies dealing with energy and the environment. The programme will expand the existing capacity to elaborate energy forecasts and evaluate energy policies by introducing new environment and internal market dimensions. It will develop new concepts not envisaged or inadequately covered by previous actions. Work will cover two main areas: analysis of strategies; and development of new methods.
2. Minimum Emission Power Production from Fossil Sources (36 MECU): subject to the development and extension of projects already carried out under JOULE, research aims to optimise energy production from fossil sources and reduce the adverse effects on the environment from the widespread use of fossil fuels. Two main lines of activity are planned, energy production from fossil sources using advanced technologies; and reduction of emissions.

3. Renewable Energy Sources (57.5 MECU): accelerating technological readiness and preparing for early market integration of all the most promising technical options. Within a global systems approach, particular objectives are: to increase the conversion efficiency of solar, wind, mini-hydraulic, wave, tidal, biomass and geothermal systems, decrease their costs and improve their attractiveness to developers, industry and consumers. Research will cover: the solar house; renewable power plants; biomass; renewable energies for rural electricity, local fuel and water; and geothermal energy.
4. Energy Utilisation and Conservation (53 MECU): developing highly efficient and clean electrochemical energy conversion systems for electricity generation, cogeneration, hydrogen and methanol production, transport and industrial electrochemical reactors. Research will cover: technologies for energy saving; and energy efficiency in transport, including suitable substitutes for conventional fuels.

9. Eligible Expenditure:

For organisations other than universities, eligible expenditure covers: labour (actual cost or at approved rates), travel and subsistence, consumables, equipment, computing costs, external work (sub-contracts or services), reasonable overheads. The following are not allowable: profits; marketing, distribution, advertising expenses; any interest or return on capital employed; taxes (except in limited circumstances); cost of proposal preparation; patent protection costs. Specific arrangements exist to recover non-reclaimable VAT.

Universities and higher education establishments may elect to have their support calculated according to the marginal costs of the project (ie the actual additional direct costs of the research not met by normal recurrent expenditure, other financial sources or other third parties), unless their costing and recording systems enable them to submit and justify full costs. Each university is normally expected to operate on the basis of either marginal costs or full costs for all Community R & D programmes, and not reach a decision on a project-by-project basis. Marginal costs may include all the items listed above, although labour costs only relate to temporary additional staff specifically engaged for the research; routine and minor computing costs may not be charged; overheads may be fixed at a percentage, corresponding to a maximum of 20 percent of all expenditure, except associated contracts and VAT.

10. Rate of Award:

The rate of award is up to 50 percent of the full economic costs of the R & D project. Universities and higher education establishments may, however, attract a contribution of up to 100 percent of the actual marginal costs of the research project.

11. Payment Procedure:

Payment is made in accordance with the agreed contract and takes the form of an advance payment following signature of the contract by all partners and the Commission, followed by periodic instalments on approval of progress reports and cost statements submitted as work progresses. Ten percent of the total financial contribution is retained (or, in the case of larger contracts,

500,000 ECUs, whichever is lower) and is paid, along with any other sums due, on approval of final technical reports and cost statements.

In all cases the Commission's contribution is made in ECUs and no liability is held for exchange losses incurred.

12. Points to Note:

Council Decision (EEC) 484/91 adopting the programme was published in OJ L257; 14.9.91.

13. Application Procedure:

Application procedure is outlined when a call for proposals is published.

14. Further Information:

Mr D Irving
Department of Trade and Industry
1 Palace Street
London SW1E 5HE
Tel: (071) 238 3318
Fax: (071) 828 7969

Marcel Trousson
European Commission
DG XII-E
Rue de la Loi, 200
B-1049 Brussels
Tel: (010 32 2) 235 3978
Fax: (010 32 2) 236 3024
Telex: 21877 COMEU B

For a copy of the Information Pack:
Patricia Shand
ETSU
Building 156
Harwell
Oxfordshire OX11 0RA
Tel: (0235) 432377

PART THREE

RESEARCH AND DEVELOPMENT/ INNOVATION

3.5 ENVIRONMENTAL RESEARCH

Environment Programme 229

3.5 ENVIRONMENTAL RESEARCH

ENVIRONMENT PROGRAMME

1. Summary:

The RTD programme in the field of the Environment supports large projects which complement and strengthen the activities of ongoing environmental research programmes, allowing a rapid response to the scientific challenges arising from global change and providing continuity in scientific support to European Community environmental policy.

The programme is implemented through research projects, accompanying measures and concerted actions in the following fields: Participation in Global Change Programmes; Technologies and Engineering for the Environment; Research on Economic and Social Aspects of Environmental Issues; and Technological and Natural Risks.

The programme is set to run for five years from 1991 to 1994, with a budget allocation of 261 MECU.

2. Awarding Body:

Commission of the European Communities.

3. Location Restrictions:

Available in any Member State of the European Community. Organisations in non-Member States which have concluded cooperation agreements with the European Communities may participate in the programme, although they will not be eligible for Commission funding.

4. Sectoral Restrictions:

The programme is open to industrial firms, universities, research institutes and individuals, or any combination or association thereof, in particular European Economic Interest Groupings (EEIGs). Projects must be carried out by at least two independent partners established in different Member States.

5. Size Restrictions:

None.

6. Programme Duration:

The programme is set to run for five years, from 7 June 1991 to 31 December 1994.

7. Submission of Applications:

Application is normally made within the deadlines specified within each of the Commission's calls for proposals, published in the Official Journal. A call for proposals relating to Technologies and Engineering for the Environment was published in OJ C116; 7.5.92. The deadline was 15 July 1992.

8. Other Restrictions:

The programme covers the following fields (budget allocation in brackets):

1. Participation in Global Change Programmes (105 MECU): contributing to understanding the processes governing environmental change and assessing the impact of human activities. EC participation will

concentrate on problems having an impact on environment policy and in areas where the Community is best placed to ensure European coordination within the framework of large international programmes (taking national programmes into account). Topics covered include: natural climatic change; anthropogenic climate change; climate change impacts; stratospheric ozone; tropospheric physics and chemistry; biogeochemical cycles; and ecosystem dynamics.

2. Technologies and Engineering for the Environment (65 MECU): promoting better environmental quality standards by encouraging technological innovation at the pre-competitive level. The two main lines of research will be: assessment of environmental quality and monitoring; and technologies for protecting and rehabilitating the environment. Support for the activities of the European Environment Agency will be included in this research area.
3. Research on Economic and Social Aspects of Environmental Issues (16 MECU): to improve the understanding of the legal, economic, social, ethical and health aspects of environmental policy and management, including: socio-economic assessment of the changing environment; and socio-economic impact of environmental policies and research.
4. Technological and Natural Risks (76 MECU): to help solve broad problems of transnational interest through a systems approach and interdisciplinary research. Projects will cover the following fields: natural risks; technological risks; desertification in the Mediterranean area. An additional 150 MECU has been allocated to Joint Research Centre (JRC) environmental research activities:

9. Eligible Expenditure:

For organisations other than universities, eligible expenditure covers: labour (actual cost or at approved rates), travel and subsistence, consumables, equipment, computing costs, external work (sub-contracts or services), reasonable overheads. The following are not allowable: profits; marketing, distribution, advertising expenses; any interest or return on capital employed; taxes (except in limited circumstances); cost of proposal preparation; patent protection costs. Specific arrangements exist to recover non-reclaimable VAT.

Universities and higher education establishments may elect to have their support calculated according to the marginal costs of the project (ie the actual additional direct costs of the research not met by normal recurrent expenditure, other financial sources or other third parties), unless their costing and recording systems enable them to submit and justify full costs. Each university is normally expected to operate on the basis of either marginal costs or full costs for all Community R & D programmes, and not reach a decision on a project-by-project basis. Marginal costs may include all the items listed above, although labour costs only relate to temporary additional staff specifically engaged for the research; routine and minor computing costs may not be charged; overheads may be fixed at a percentage, corresponding to a maximum of 20 percent of all expenditure, except associated contracts and VAT.

10. Rate of Award:

The rate of award is up to 50 percent of the full economic costs of the R & D project. Universities and higher education establishments may, however, attract a contribution of up to 100 percent of the actual marginal costs of the research project.

11. Payment Procedure:

Payment is made in accordance with the agreed contract and takes the form of an advance payment following signature of the contract by all partners and the Commission, followed by periodic instalments on approval of progress reports and cost statements submitted as work progresses. Ten percent of the total financial contribution is retained (or, in the case of larger contracts, 500,000 ECUs, whichever is lower) and is paid, along with any other sums due, on approval of final technical reports and cost statements.

In all cases the Commission's contribution is made in ECUs and no liability is held for exchange losses incurred.

12. Points to Note:

Council Decision (EEC) 354/91 adopting the programme was published in OJ L192; 16.7.91.

A call for expressions of interest in technologies for protecting and rehabilitating the environment was published in OJ C291; 8.11.91; the deadline was 31 December 1991.

A call for proposals was published in OJ C184; 16.7.91; the deadlines varied according to the research area addressed and were 31 October; 30 November 1991; 31 January; and 31 March 1992.

13. Application Procedure:

Application procedure is outlined in a work programme available from the European Commission.

14. Further Information:

Heinrich Ott
European Commission
DG XII-E
Environment Programmes
Rue de la Loi 200
B-1049 Brussels
Tel: (010 32 2) 235 1182
Fax: (010 32 2) 236 3024
Telex: 21877 COMEU B

Mr D J A Davies
Department of the Environment
Romney House
43 Marsham Street
London SW1 3PY
Tel: (071) 276 8365
Fax: (071) 276 8355

Climate Changes:
Dr D K Carson
Director
Hadley Centre for Climate
Prediction and Research
Meteorological Office
London Road
Bracknell
Berkshire RG12 2SZ
Tel: (0344) 420242

Major Technological Hazards:
Mr J Skevington
Health and Safety Executive
Broad Lane
Sheffield S3 7HQ
Tel: (0742) 752539

PART THREE

RESEARCH AND DEVELOPMENT/ INNOVATION

3.6 BIOTECHNOLOGY/HEALTHCARE

Biotechnology Programme	235
Biomedicine and Health Programme	237

3.6 BIOTECHNOLOGY

BIOTECHNOLOGY PROGRAMME

1. Summary:

The Biotechnology Programme supports pre-normative research contributing to the strengthening of the science base through research centred on understanding biological information, transformation and control systems, whilst keeping in mind the ethical implications of such work.

The programme is implemented through shared cost research projects, cooperative research projects, concerted actions, and accompanying measures, covering the following topics: Molecular Approaches; Cellular and Organism Approaches; Ecology and Population Biology.

The programme is set to run from 26 March 1992 to 31 December 1994, with a budget allocation of 162.36 MECU.

2. Awarding Body:

Commission of the European Communities.

3. Location Restrictions:

Available in any Member State of the European Community. Organisations in non-Member States which have concluded cooperation agreements with the European Communities may participate in the programme, although they will not be eligible for Commission funding.

4. Sectoral Restrictions:

The programme is open to industrial firms, universities, research institutes and individuals, or any combination or association thereof, in particular European Economic Interest Groupings (EEIGs). Projects must be carried out by at least two independent partners established in different Member States.

5. Size Restrictions:

None.

6. Programme Duration:

The programme is set to run from 26 March 1992 to 31 December 1994.

7. Submission of Applications:

Application is made within the deadlines specified within each of the Commission's calls for proposals, published in the Official Journal. The first general call was published in OJ C127; 19.5.92; the deadline was 23 July 1992.

8. Other Restrictions:

Research is carried out at the level of molecules, cells, organisms and populations, covering the following topics (budget allocation in brackets);

1. Molecular Approaches (64 MECU): protein structure and function; structure of genes; expression of genes;
2. Cellular and Organism Approaches (81 MECU): cellular regeneration, reproduction and development of living organisms; metabolism of

animals, plants and microbes; essential physiological tracts; communication systems within living matter;

3. Ecology and Population Biology (17.36 MECU): ecological implications of biotechnology; conservation of genetic resources.

Information technology will be used throughout the programme for collecting, pooling, analysing, distributing or simulating data.

9. Eligible Expenditure:

For organisations other than universities, eligible expenditure covers: labour (actual cost or at approved rates), travel and subsistence, consumables, equipment, computing costs, external work (sub-contracts or services), reasonable overheads. The following are not allowable: profits; marketing, distribution, advertising expenses; any interest or return on capital employed; taxes (except in limited circumstances); cost of proposal preparation; patent protection costs. Specific arrangements exist to recover non-reclaimable VAT.

Universities and higher education establishments may elect to have their support calculated according to the marginal costs of the project (ie the actual additional direct costs of the research not met by normal recurrent expenditure, other financial sources or other third parties), unless their costing and recording systems enable them to submit and justify full costs. Each university is normally expected to operate on the basis of either marginal costs or full costs for all Community R & D programmes, and not reach a decision on a project-by-project basis. Marginal costs may include all the items listed above, although labour costs only relate to temporary additional staff specifically engaged for the research; routine and minor computing costs may not be charged; overheads may be fixed at a percentage, corresponding to a maximum of 20 percent of all expenditure, except associated contracts and VAT.

10. Rate of Award:

The rate of award for shared-cost projects is up to 50 percent of the full economic costs of the R & D project. Universities and higher education establishments may, however, attract a contribution of up to 100 percent of the actual marginal costs of the research project.

In the case of concerted actions, the EC funds up to 100 percent of coordinating expenditure, while participants pay the R & D costs.

In the case of cooperative research (see 12), the rate of award is 50 percent of research costs for a period of up to two years.

11. Payment Procedure:

Payment is made in accordance with the agreed contract and takes the form of an advance payment following signature of the contract by all partners and the Commission, followed by periodic instalments on approval of progress reports and cost statements submitted as work progresses. Ten percent of the total financial contribution is retained (or, in the case of larger contracts, 500,000 ECUs, whichever is lower) and is paid, along with any other sums due, on approval of final technical reports and cost statements.

In all cases the Commission's contribution is made in ECUs and no liability is held for exchange losses incurred.

12. Points to Note:

Council Decision (EEC) 218/92 adopting the Biotechnology Programme was published in OJ L107; 24.4.92.

The programme follows on from, and builds on, work done under the BRIDGE programme.

Contractors undertaking research projects will be requested to provide, when applicable, information necessary for the detailed evaluation of the social, ethical and ecological impact of their studies, and, where necessary, approval from the relevant authorities.

Cooperative research projects may be undertaken by groups of organisations (particularly small and medium-sized firms) which do not have their own research facilities, to resolve common technical problems. One or more outside organisations (research associations, universities or firms) will be appointed to carry out the research. Projects must be submitted by the organisations which are planning and piloting the research and implementing the results.

13. Application Procedure:

Application procedure is outlined when a call for proposals is issued.

14. Further Information:

European Commission
DG XII/F: Biotechnology Division
Rue de la Loi 200
B-1049 Brussels
Tel: (010 32 2) 235 0361
Fax: (010 32 2) 235 5365
Telex: 21877 COMEU B

Mr P Nolan
Department of Trade and Industry
Laboratory of the Government Chemist
Queens Road
Teddington
Middlesex TW11 0LY
Tel: (081) 943 7381
Fax: (081) 943 2767

Dr V Harrison
Agricultural and Food Research Council
Central Office
Polaris House
North Star Avenue
Swindon SN2 1EU
Tel: (0793) 413 200
Fax: (0793) 413 201

BIOMEDICINE AND HEALTH PROGRAMME

1. Summary:

The Biomedicine and Health programme aims to contribute to improving the efficacy of scientific and medical research programmes in Member States by developing coordinated research on prevention, care and health systems, and supporting collaborative research into major health problems and diseases of great socio-economic impact, human genome analysis, and biomedical ethics. The programme is set to run for five years from 1991 to 1994; with a budget allocation of 133 MECU.

2. Awarding Body:
Commission of the European Communities.

3. Location Restrictions:
Available in any Member State of the European Community. Organisations in non-Member States which have concluded cooperation agreements with the European Communities may participate in the programme, although they will not be eligible for Commission funding.

4. Sectoral Restrictions:
The programme is open to industrial firms, universities, research institutes and individuals, or any combination or association thereof, in particular European Economic Interest Groupings (EEIGs). Projects must be carried out by at least two independent partners established in different Member States.

5. Size Restrictions:
None.

6. Programme Duration:
The programme is set to run from 9 September 1991 to 31 December 1994.

7. Submission of Applications:
Application is made within the deadlines specified within each of the Commission's calls for proposals, published in the Official Journal. Two calls were published in OJ C324; 10.12.92; the deadlines were 26 February 1993 for Areas 1, 2 and 4, and 29 January 1993 for Area 3.

8. Other Restrictions:
The programme will cover the following areas (budget allocation in brackets):

1. Development of coordinated research on prevention, care and health systems (27.5 MECU): covering the harmonisation of methodologies and protocols in epidemiological, biological, clinical and technological research, including: pre-competitive drugs testing and the administration of medicines; risk factors, especially relating to occupational health; biomedical technology; harmonisation of protocols and approaches to health services;
2. Major Health Problems and Diseases of Great Socioeconomic Impact (72 MECU): covering AIDS (25 MECU), cancer, cardiovascular disease; mental illness and neurological disease; ageing, age-related health problems and handicaps;
3. Human genome analysis (27.5 MECU): research towards the completion and integration of the genetic and physical maps, the genetic basis for biological functions; and the setting-up of a coordinating mechanism to sequence portions of the genome of major biological interest.

Emphasis will be placed on medical applications which contribute to the well-being of patients. No research modifying, or seeking to modify, the genetic constitution of human beings by alteration of germ cells, or of any stage of embryo development which may make these alterations hereditary will be carried out under this programme.

4. Research on Biomedical Ethics (4.6 MECU): involving the study of problems related to the research carried out in Areas 1 to 3 of the programme, and the possible applications of research results.

9. Eligible Expenditure:

The Biomedical and Health Research Programme is implemented principally by Concerted Actions. Concerted Actions consist of action by the Community to coordinate the individual research activities carried out in the Member States.

The approved uses of Concerted Action funds include: the organisation of meetings of all sizes, from small workshops to plenary meetings of all participants; scientific support; short-term international exchanges of personnel; preparation and distribution of materials and reference products, ie for quality control; centralised data handling, storage and statistical analysis; and dissemination of information and results as early, as fully and as frequently as possible through a wide range of publication outlets. In addition, a 'centralised facility' can be provided, to ensure appropriate European resources or services if it is necessary for one or more Concerted Actions to have access to particular quality control products, experimental materials or specialised services, or if it has some other reference-type needs. Area 3 (Human Genome Analysis) is the only area of the Biomedical and Health Research Programme to be implemented by shared-cost research contracts. For organisations other than universities, eligible expenditure covers: labour (actual cost or at approved rates), travel and subsistence, consumables, equipment, computing costs, external work (sub-contracts or services), reasonable overheads. The following are not allowable: profits; marketing, distribution, advertising expenses; any interest or return on capital employed; taxes (except in limited circumstances); cost of proposal preparation; patent protection costs. Specific arrangements exist to recover non-reclaimable VAT.

Universities and higher education establishments may elect to have their support calculated according to the marginal costs of the project (ie the actual additional direct costs of the research not met by normal recurrent expenditure, other financial sources or other third parties), unless their costing and recording systems enable them to submit and justify full costs. Each university is normally expected to operate on the basis of either marginal costs or full costs for all Community R & D programmes, and not reach a decision on a project-by-project basis. Marginal costs may include all the items listed above, although labour costs only relate to temporary additional staff specifically engaged for the research; routine and minor computing costs may not be charged; overheads may be fixed at a percentage, corresponding to a maximum of 20 percent of all expenditure, except associated contracts and VAT.

10. Rate of Award:

The rate of the award for Concerted Actions is up to 100 percent of coordinating expenditure. For shared-cost research contracts the rate of the award is up to 50 percent of the full economic costs of the R & D project. Universities and higher education establishments may, however, attract a contribution of up to 100 percent of the actual marginal costs of the research project.

11. Payment Procedure:

In all cases the Commission's contribution is made in ECUs and no liability is held for exchange losses incurred.

12. Points to Note:

Council Decision (EEC) 505/91 adopting the programme was published in OJ L267; 24.9.91.

A call for proposals relating to areas 1, 2 and 4 was published in OJ C278; 25.10.91. The deadline was 31 January 1992. Research under the programme will be coordinated with that carried out under other EC research programmes, including Life Sciences and Technologies for Developing Countries, and Telematics Systems of General Interest (Healthcare), and also with the 'Europe against Cancer' and 'Europe against AIDS' programmes.

The programme will also continue work carried out under the Human Genome Analysis programme.

13. Application Procedure:

Application procedure is outlined when calls for proposals are issued. The UK mailing list for information on the programme is maintained by the Medical Research Council.

14. Further Information:

Dr Anthony Dickens
European Commission
DG XII
Rue de la Loi 200
B-1049 Brussels
Tel: (010 32 2) 235 0032
Fax: (010 32 2) 236 3024

Ms G Breen
Medical Research Council
20 Park Crescent
London W1N 4AL
Tel: (071) 636 5422
Fax: (071) 436 6179

PART THREE

RESEARCH AND DEVELOPMENT/ INNOVATION

3.7 AGRICULTURE AND FISHERIES RESEARCH

MAST II	243
Agriculture and Agro-Industries Programme (AIR)	246
Life Sciences and Technologies for Developing Countries	249

3.7 AGRICULTURE AND FISHERIES RESEARCH

MAST II

1. Summary:

The Marine Science and Technology programme (MAST II) supports shared cost research projects, concerted actions and accompanying measures in the following fields: 1. Marine Science; 2. Coastal Zone Science and Engineering; 3. Marine Technology; 4. Supporting Initiatives; and 5. Large-Scale Targeted Projects.

The programme is set to run for five years, from 1991 to 1994, with a budget allocation of 103 MECU.

2. Awarding Body:

Commission of the European Communities.

3. Location Restrictions:

Available in any Member State of the European Community. Organisations in non-Member States which have concluded cooperation agreements with the European Communities may participate in the programme, although they will not be eligible for Commission funding.

4. Sectoral Restrictions:

The programme is open to industrial firms, universities, research institutes and individuals, or any combination or association thereof, in particular European Economic Interest Groupings (EEIGs). Projects must be carried out by at least two independent partners established in different Member States.

5. Size Restrictions:

None.

6. Programme Duration:

The programme is set to run for five years, from 7 June 1991 to 31 December 1994.

7. Submission of Applications:

Application is normally made within the deadlines specified in each of the Commission's calls for proposals, published in the Official Journal. A call for expressions of interest to organise advanced study courses was published in OJ C314; 1.12.92; the deadline was 30 April 1993.

8. Other Restrictions:

The programme covers the following areas (budget allocation in brackets):

1. Marine Science (37 MECU): three main aims are: to achieve a better understanding of marine processes; to improve the ability to predict change; and to establish the scientific basis for the management, protection and exploration of the marine environment. Research will include: multidisciplinary research on processes and fluxes, using mathematical modelling where necessary; ocean circulation systems

and dynamics of water masses; biogeochemical processes; evaluation of rates of exchange of substances at interactive sites; mathematical modelling for biological processes and ecosystems; and marine geosciences. These activities will involve the Community in on-going international programmes (eg World Ocean Circulation Experiment, Joint Global Ocean Flux Studies, International Geosphere-Biosphere Programme etc). Work will be carried out in cooperation with related EC programmes on the marine environment eg STEP, EPOCH, FAR and Joint Research Centre (JRC) actions.

2. Coastal Zone Science and Engineering (15 MECU): research will build on work done under the MAST programme (1989–92). The objectives are: to gain an increased level of understanding of marine processes affecting the coastal zone and the behaviour of coastal structures, and of their interactions; to develop numerical modelling of coastal processes and the integration of process models for the purposes of coastal management in Europe; and to harmonise design concepts of coastal engineering works on a European scale.
3. Marine Technology (30 MECU): encouraging the necessary enabling technologies for the advancement of marine sciences and related industrial development, and to promote the development of new and existing instruments, particularly with a view to speeding up the introduction of automated long-term measuring systems, and contributing to the development of operational observation systems. Research will be coordinated with the EUREKA initiatives in marine science and technology and will supplement work done under the BRITE/EURAM and ESPRIT programmes in the materials testing, robotics and informatics aspects of instrument development.
4. Supporting Initiatives (5 MECU): continuing supporting activities commenced under MAST, including: the establishment of a European ocean data and information system; the preparation of norms and standards; a modelling coordination initiative; development of a pilot communication system for exchange of information on research cruises and research facilities; studies on the scientific and design requirements for new large scale facilities; and new approaches to mapping and standard bathymetric/hydrographic surveying. New ideas for supporting initiatives may be added.
5. Large-scale Targeted Projects (16 MECU): addressing particular problems which require a large-scale multidisciplinary coordinated research effort. These problems may be defined on the basis of scientific and technological requirements, or established on the basis of the scientific requirements of a particular geographical area.

9. Eligible Expenditure:

For organisations other than universities, eligible expenditure covers: labour (actual cost or at approved rates), travel and subsistence, consumables, equipment, computing costs, external work (sub-contracts or services), reasonable overheads. The following are not allowable: profits; marketing, distribution, advertising expenses; any interest or return on capital employed; taxes (except in limited circumstances); cost of proposal preparation; patent

protection costs. Specific arrangements exist to recover non-reclaimable VAT.

Universities and higher education establishments may elect to have their support calculated according to the marginal costs of the project (ie the actual additional direct costs of the research not met by normal recurrent expenditure, other financial sources or other third parties), unless their costing and recording systems enable them to submit and justify full costs. Each university is normally expected to operate on the basis of either marginal costs or full costs for all Community R & D programmes, and not reach a decision on a project-by-project basis. Marginal costs may include all the items listed above, although labour costs only relate to temporary additional staff specifically engaged for the research; routine and minor computing costs may not be charged; overheads may be fixed at a percentage, corresponding to a maximum of 20 percent of all expenditure, except associated contracts and VAT.

10. Rate of Award:

The rate of award is up to 50 percent of the full economic costs of the R & D project. Universities and higher education establishments may, however, attract a contribution of up to 100 percent of the actual marginal costs of the research project.

11. Payment Procedure:

Payment is made in accordance with the agreed contract and takes the form of an advance payment following signature of the contract by all partners and the Commission, followed by periodic instalments on approval of progress reports and cost statements submitted as work progresses. Ten percent of the total financial contribution is retained (or, in the case of larger contracts, 500,000 ECUs, whichever is lower) and is paid, along with any other sums due, on approval of final technical reports and cost statements.

In all cases the Commission's contribution is made in ECUs and no liability is held for exchange losses incurred.

12. Points to Note:

Council Decision (EEC) 351/91 adopting the programme was published in OJ L192; 16.7.91.

The programme develops activities started under the MAST (1989–92) programme, possibly expanding the geographical coverage. The general objectives are therefore similar, namely to contribute to establish a scientific and technological basis for the exploration, exploitation, management and protection of European coastal waters, and the seas surrounding Member States, and to add an EC dimension to on-going research activities.

A call for expressions of interest relating to a large scale targeted project in the North Atlantic was published in OJ C174; 5.7.91; the deadline was 30 September 1991.

The first general call for proposals was published in OJ C169; 28.6.91; the deadline was 15 November 1991 for areas 2 and 3, and 14 February 1992 for areas 1 and 5.

A further call relating to participation in the North Atlantic targeted project was published in OJ C284; 31.10.91. The deadline was also 14 February 1992.

A call concerning advanced study courses was published in OJ C15; 21.1.92. The deadline was 30 April 1992.

13. Application Procedure:
Application procedure is outlined in the work-programme, available from the European Commission.

14. Further Information:

Jean Boissonnas
European Commission
DG XII/E
Rue de la Loi 200
B-1049 Brussels
Tel: (010 32 2) 235 6787
Fax: (010 32 2) 236 3024

Dr R Paul
NERC
Polaris House
North Star Avenue
Swindon SN2 1EU
Tel: (0793) 411636
Fax: (0793) 411545

AGRICULTURE AND AGRO-INDUSTRY PROGRAMME (AIR)

1. Summary:
The Agriculture and Agro-Industry programme (AIR) supports shared-cost pre-competitive research contracts, demonstration projects, concerted actions and accompanying measures in four areas related to Agriculture, Horticulture, Forestry, Aquaculture and Fisheries: 1. Primary Production; 2. Inputs; 3. Processing of Biological Raw Materials; and 4. End-use and Products.
The programme is set to run from 1991 to 1994, with a budget allocation of 330 MECU.

2. Awarding Body:
Commission of the European Communities.

3. Location Restrictions:
Available in any Member State of the European Community. Organisations in non-Member States which have concluded cooperation agreements with the European Communities may participate in the programme, although they will not be eligible for Commission funding, and must contribute to general administrative costs.

4. Sectoral Restrictions:
The programme is open to industrial firms, universities, research institutes and individuals, or any combination or association thereof, in particular European Economic Interest Groupings (EEIGs). Projects must be carried out by at least two independent partners established in different Member States.

5. Size Restrictions:
None, but preference will be given to proposals involving at least one full working-year per annum for each of the main participants.

6. Programme Duration:

The programme is set to run from 9 September 1991 to 31 December 1994.

7. Submission of Applications:

Application is normally made within the deadlines specified in each of the Commission's calls for proposals, published in the Official Journal. The second (and final) call for proposals was published in OJ C154; 2.7.92; the deadline was 30 October 1992.

8. Other Restrictions:

The programme covers the following areas (budget allocation in brackets):

1. Primary production in (100 MECU): aiming to adapt primary production to the qualitative and quantitative demands of the market. Possible research topics include: improved product quality; better crop and animal husbandry; less intensive land-use systems; better assessment of resources (particularly of fish); diversification into alternative products for food and non-food uses; control of soil erosion, loss of fertility, and deforestation; and improvements in socio-economic conditions, particularly for areas lagging in development. In all cases protection of the environment and economically sustainable development will be sought.
2. Inputs (65 MECU): improving control of inputs and production costs. Possible research topics are: improved strains of plants, animals, and fish (for better pest resistance, yield, quality, adaptation to the environment); integrated and biological pest control systems; and new systems for monitoring and control.
3. Processing of biological raw materials (100 MECU): pre-competitive R & D providing the basic processes for new or improved products in the food, non-food and energy sectors. This includes new separation, extraction, and processing methods for raw materials, giving more useful products and less waste, particularly where they improve safety and maintain or increase the nutritional value of processed food.
4. End-use and Products (65 MECU): generating a better knowledge of the characteristics required in final products.

In relation to food, work will concentrate on the definition and satisfaction of consumer's nutritional needs, and on food toxicology, hygiene, and safety. In the non-food area, emphasis will be put on identification of new, more environmentally friendly types of products.

Pre-normative research will be supported under the programme in order to provide a sound scientific basis for the setting of standards and regulations related to the production and use of biological resources.

9. Eligible Expenditure:

For organisations other than universities, eligible expenditure covers: labour (actual cost or at approved rates), travel and subsistence, consumables, equipment, computing costs, external work (sub-contracts or services), reasonable overheads. The following are not allowable: profits; marketing, distribution, advertising expenses; any interest or return on capital employed; taxes (except in limited circumstances); cost of proposal preparation; patent

protection costs. Specific arrangements exist to recover non-reclaimable VAT.

Universities and higher education establishments may elect to have their support calculated according to the marginal costs of the project (ie the actual additional direct costs of the research not met by normal recurrent expenditure, other financial sources or other third parties), unless their costing and recording systems enable them to submit and justify full costs. Each university is normally expected to operate on the basis of either marginal costs or full costs for all Community R & D programmes, and not reach a decision on a project-by-project basis. Marginal costs may include all the items listed above, although labour costs only relate to temporary additional staff specifically engaged for the research; routine and minor computing costs may not be charged; overheads may be fixed at a percentage, corresponding to a maximum of 20 percent of all expenditure, except associated contracts and VAT.

10. Rate of Award:

The rate of award up to 50 percent of the full economic costs of research projects, and 30 percent for demonstration projects. Universities and higher education establishments may, however, attract a contribution of up to 100 percent of the additional marginal costs of the research or demonstration projects.

11. Payment Procedure:

Payment is made in accordance with the agreed contract and takes the form of an advance payment following signature of the contract by all partners and the Commission, followed by periodic instalments on approval of progress reports and cost statements submitted as work progresses. Ten percent of the total financial contribution is retained (or, in the case of larger contracts, 500,000 ECUs, whichever is lower) and is paid, along with any other sums due, on approval of final technical reports and cost statements.

In all cases the Commission's contribution is made in ECUs through the project coordinator, and no liability is held for exchange losses incurred.

12. Points to Note:

Council Decision (EEC) 504/91 adopting the programme was published in OJ L265; 21.9.91.

Under all research areas environmental benefits will be pursued, and measures taken to prevent negative effects on the environment.

The objective of demonstration projects is to show the technical and economic viability of a new product and/or technology, whose feasibility has been proven on a smaller scale. These projects must involve participation by both producers and users.

The first call for proposals was published in OJ C264; 10.10.91; the deadline was 31 January 1992.

13. Application Procedure:

Application procedure is outlined when a call for proposals is published.

14. Further Information:

European Commission
DG VI/F/11-3
Rue de la Loi 200
B-1049 Brussels
Tel: (010 32 2) 235 8612
Fax: (010 32 2) 236 4322
Telex: 22037 AGREC B

Mr D Woodward
Ministry of Agriculture, Fisheries and Food
Nobel House
17 Smith Square
London SW1P 3JR
Tel: (071) 238 5599
Fax: (071) 238 5597

For information packs contact:
Mrs A Dumoulin

For programme-related enquiries, contact:
Mr Dessylas (Agriculture)
Mr Rexen (Agro-Industry)
or Mr Brugge (Fisheries)

LIFE SCIENCES AND TECHNOLOGIES FOR DEVELOPING COUNTRIES

1. Summary:

The Life Sciences and Technologies for Developing Countries programme aims to promote increased scientific cooperation between the EC and developing countries in two fundamental areas: Improvement in Living Conditions (through Agricultural Research); and Improvements in Health. The environmental dimension, both in terms of environmental protection and the rational management of resources, will be taken into account. The programme is implemented through shared-cost research contracts and accompanying measures.

The programme is set to run from 1991 to 1994, with a budget allocation of 110 MECU.

2. Awarding Body:

Commission of the European Communities.

3. Location Restrictions:

Available in any Member State of the European Community, and in any developing country. Organisations in non-Member States, other than developing countries, which have concluded cooperation agreements with the European Communities may participate in the programme, although they will not be eligible for Commission funding.

4. Sectoral Restrictions:

The programme is open to industrial firms, higher education establishments, research institutes and individuals, or any combination or association thereof, in particular European Economic Interest Groupings (EEIGs). Projects must be carried out by at least two independent partners established in different Member States, as well as at least one partner established in a developing country.

5. Size Restrictions:
None.

6. Programme Duration:
The programme is set to run from 7 June 1991 to 31 December 1994.

7. Submission of Applications:
Application will normally be made within the deadlines specified in each of the Commission's calls for proposals, published in the Official Journal.

A call for proposals was published in OJ C198; 5.8.92; the deadline was 30 November 1992.

8. Other Restrictions:
The programme covers the following two sub-programmes (budget allocation in brackets):

1. Improvements in Living Conditions (71 MECU), covering the following subfields:
   - A. Reduction of food shortages: aiming to improve farm crop and livestock production for local use in regions where, for climatic, physical or human reasons, problems of food provision are the first priority.
   - B. Agriculture production of high economic value: providing a scientific and technical basis for agricultural activities (including the utilisation of forest and aquatic environments) that are of high economic value at local level, and for exportation in regions where there is no substantial food shortage. The work will cover: production systems and the marketing of cash crops; quantitative improvements; qualitative improvements; feasibility studies of local processing; and environmental protection.
2. Improvements in Health (38 MECU), covering the following subfields:
   - A. Prevention and treatment of the predominant diseases in the developing countries: reducing the impact of these diseases which continue to be the major public health problem in most of the developing countries;
   - B. Healthcare systems appropriate to the rural or urban environment of developing countries: studying ways of organising healthcare, taking into account the specific constraints and the socio-economic context of the developing countries (financial, human and material resources) and the new opportunities offered by the results of biomedical research. A number of themes will be covered: the selection, evaluation and validation of health strategies; the management and financing of health services; the study of the optimum development of human resources; the prerequisites for the transfer of existing and new technologies; and research on the factors which determine the participation of the population;
   - C. Nutrition: developing the scientific basis necessary for improving the nutritional condition of underprivileged populations, by means of a multidisciplinary approach between medicine, agronomy, eco-

nomics and the social sciences. This will cover research on nutritional interventions, specific shortages, and protection mechanisms in the event of food shortage at the individual, family and community level.

9. Eligible Expenditure:

For organisations other than higher education establishments, eligible expenditure covers: labour (actual cost or at approved rates), travel and subsistence, consumables, equipment, computing costs, external work (subcontracts or services), reasonable overheads. The following are not allowable: profits; marketing, distribution, advertising expenses; any interest or return on capital employed; taxes (except in limited circumstances); cost of proposal preparation; patent protection costs. Specific arrangements exist to recover non-reclaimable VAT.

Higher education establishments and all developing country institutions may elect to have their support calculated according to the marginal costs of the project (ie the actual additional direct costs of the research not met by normal recurrent expenditure, other financial sources or other third parties), unless their costing and recording systems enable them to submit and justify full costs. Each higher education establishment/developing country institution is normally expected to operate on the basis of either marginal costs or full costs for all Community R & D programmes, and not reach a decision on a project-by-project basis. Marginal costs may include all the items listed above, although labour costs only relate to temporary additional staff specifically engaged for the research; routine and minor computing costs may not be charged; overheads may be fixed at a percentage, corresponding to a maximum of 20 percent of all expenditure, except associated contracts and VAT.

10. Rate of Award:

The rate of award is up to 50 percent of the full economic costs of the R & D project. Higher education establishments and developing country institutions may, however, attract a contribution of up to 100 percent of the actual marginal costs of the research project.

11. Payment Procedure:

Payment is made in accordance with the agreed contract and takes the form of an advance payment following signature of the contract by all partners and the Commission, followed by periodic instalments on approval of progress reports and cost statements submitted as work progresses. Ten percent of the total financial contribution is retained (or, in the case of larger contracts, 500,000 ECUs, whichever is lower) and is paid, along with any other sums due, on approval of final technical reports and cost statements.

In all cases the Commission's contribution is made in ECUs and no liability is held for exchange losses incurred.

12. Points to Note:

Council Decision (EEC) 366/91 adopting the programme was published in OJ L196; 19.7.91.

Programme results will be disseminated to all developing countries. A call for proposals was published in OJ C186; 18.7.91. The deadline for the first phase was 16 September 1991, and 16 December 1991 for the second.

13. Application Procedure:

Application procedure is outlined in an Information Package available from the European Commission.

14. Further Information:

European Commission
DG XII/G-4
75, rue Montoyer
B-1040 Brussels
Tel: (010 32 2) 235 1731
Fax: (010 32 2) 236 3308/6252
Telex: 21877 COMEU B

Mr G Porter/Ms A Siddall
Overseas Development Administration
94 Victoria Street
London SW1E 5JL
Tel: (071) 917 0299/0699
Fax: (071) 917 0128

PART THREE

RESEARCH AND DEVELOPMENT/ INNOVATION

3.8 PROGRAMMES WITH FULLY ALLOCATED BUDGETS

Decommissioning of Nuclear Installations	255
EPOCH	255
EURET	255
MONITOR	256
Management and Storage of Radioactive Waste	256

3.8 PROGRAMMES WITH FULLY ALLOCATED BUDGETS

DECOMMISSIONING OF NUCLEAR INSTALLATIONS

1. Summary:

Under the research and technological development programme concerned with the Decommissioning of Nuclear Installations, financial support was available for: A. selected R&D projects; B. projects concerned with the identification of guiding principles in relation to a number of key areas; and C. testing of new techniques in practice.

The aim of the programme is to promote the joint development of a system of management of decommissioned nuclear installations and of the radioactive wastes produced in their dismantling which will provide the best possible protection for mankind and the environment throughout the decommissioning process. The programme was implemented through research contracts, concerted actions, studies, coordination activities; secondment, training and mobility grants were also available.

The programme has been agreed to run from 1 January 1989 to 31 December 1993 with a budget allocation of 31.5 MECU.

Funding under the Decommissioning of Nuclear Installations programme has been fully allocated. A follow-up programme may be launched in 1994.

EPOCH (CLIMATOLOGY & NATURAL HAZARDS)

1. Summary:

EPOCH (Climatology and Natural Hazards) supported research projects in the following areas: 1. Past climates and climate change; 2. Climate processes and models; 3. Climatic impacts and climate-related hazards; and 4. Seismic hazard.

EPOCH is set to run from 20 November 1989 to 19 November 1993 with a budget allocation of 40 MECU. EPOCH's budget has now been fully committed and no further calls for proposals are expected.

Similar topics are covered by the Environment programme.

EURET (TRANSPORT RESEARCH)

1. Summary:

The EURET programme supports research and technological development projects in the field of transport. Research should contribute towards the standardisation of equipment and systems, have an added Community dimension, and be in one of the following fields: optimum network exploitation; logistics; and the reduction of harmful externalities (eg pollution, accidents). The programme was implemented by means of shared-cost research contracts and concerted actions.

EURET is set to run from 1 March 1990 to 28 February 1994, with a budget allocation of 25 MECU. The EURET budget has now been fully allocated and no further calls for proposals are expected.

MONITOR (STRATEGIC ANALYSIS, FORECASTING AND EVALUATION)

1. Summary:

The MONITOR programme supports strategic analysis, forecasting and evaluation projects concerned with new developments in the area of research and technology. The programme's broad aim is to identify new directions and priorities for Community research and technological development policy and to help highlight the relationship between R & D and other common policies. MONITOR comprises three activities: SAST – strategic analysis; FAST – forecasting and technology assessment; and SPEAR – activities in support of the evaluation of R & D programmes.

MONITOR is implemented through transnational collaborative projects carried out by experts and organisations on contract, or through scientific and professional networks.

MONITOR will run from 1989 until June 1993 with a total budget allocation of 22 MECU.

The MONITOR budget has now been fully allocated, and no new projects will be undertaken under the current programme. Activities under MONITOR are now directed at the completion of the research and dissemination of the results.

MANAGEMENT AND STORAGE OF RADIOACTIVE WASTE

1. Summary:

The research and technological development programme in the field of Management and Storage of Radioactive Waste is aimed at perfecting and demonstrating a system for managing the radioactive waste produced by the nuclear industry ensuring, at the various stages, the best possible protection of man and environment. Part A covers waste management and associated R & D actions, Part B covers the construction and/or operation of underground facilities open to Community joint activities.

The programme is carried out by means of research contracts, study contracts, coordination projects and training and mobility grants, and is set to run for five years from 1 January 1990, with a budget allocation of 79.6 MECU. The budget for the Management and Storage of Radioactive Waste programme has been fully allocated. No further calls for proposals will be published.

INDEX OF EC PROGRAMMES

Access to Large Scale Facilities, 149
Agriculture and Agro-Industries Programme, 246

BRITE/EURAM II (Industrial Technology and Advanced Materials), 197
Biomedicine and Health Programme, 237
Biotechnology Programme, 235

COMETT II (Education and Training for Technology), 124
Coal Research Programme, 221
Controlled Thermonuclear Fusion Programme, 211

Decommissioning of Nuclear Installations, 255

EAGGF: Processing and Marketing of Agricultural Products, 65
EAGGF: Processing and Marketing of Fishery and Aquaculture Products, 68
ECSC Conversion Loans, 15
ECSC: Industrial Loans to Promote Coal Consumption, 61
ECSC: Industrial Loans to Promote Steel Consumption, 63
ENVIREG (Environmental Protection to the Regions), 31
EPOCH (Climatology and Natural Hazards), 255
ERASMUS (Mobility Programme for University Studies), 128
ESPRIT III (Information Technologies), 179
EURATOM Loans, 71
EURET (Transport Research), 255
EUROFORM (Vocational Training and Employment), 118
EUROTECH Capital and INNVEST, 75
EUROTECNET (Vocational Training and Technological Change), 130
Environment Programme, 229
European Investment Bank (EIB), 23
European Regional Development Fund (ERDF), 25
European Social Fund, 115
Exchange Risk Guarantee Scheme, 21
Executive Training in Japan, 139

FORCE (Continuing Vocational Training), 131

HORIZON (Employment/Training for the Disabled/Disadvantaged), 120
Human Capital and Mobility Programme, 149

IMPACT II (Information Services), 179
INNVEST, 75
INTERREG (Development of Border Areas), 33
International Investment Partners (Joint Ventures), 77

JOPP (Joint Ventures in Eastern Europe), 88

KALEIDOSCOPE (Cultural Events), 101

LEADER (Rural Development), 35

LIFE (Financial Instrument for the Environment), 95
LINGUA (Foreign Language Training, 134
Life Sciences and Technologies for Developing Countries, 249

MAST II (Marine Science and Technology), 243
MEDIA (Audio-visual Production), 103
MONITOR (Strategic Analysis, Forecasting and Evaluation), 256
Management and Storage of Radioactive Waste, 256
Measurements and Testing Programme, 203

NOW (New Opportunities for Women), 122
Non-Nuclear Energies Programme, 223
Nuclear Fission Safety Programme, 213

PETRA II (Vocational Training for Young People), 137
PHARE (Aid for Eastern Europe), 85
PRISMA (Preparing for the Single Market), 39
Pilot Conservation Projects (Architectural Heritage), 106

R & D Euroconferences, 151
RACE II (Advanced Communications), 184
RECHAR (Coal Producing Areas), 41
RENAVAL (Shipbuilding Areas), 44
RESIDER (Steel Producing Areas), 47
RETEX (Textile Producing Areas), 49
Regional and Urban Energy Planning Programme, 97
Research Training Fellowships, 152

S & T Fellowships in Japan, 158
SPRINT (Innovation and Technology Transfer), 171
STA Fellowships in Japan, 156
STRIDE (Regional Research and Development), 51
Scientific and Technical Research Networks, 154
Steel Research Programme, 200
Support Programme for Employment Creation (SPEC), 141

TEDIS II (Trade Electronic Data Interchange Systems), 187
TELEMAN (Nuclear Safety), 209
TELEMATIQUE (Advanced Telecoms Services), 54
TEMPUS (Eastern European Mobility Programme), 88
THERMIE (Energy Technology), 219
Telematic Systems Programme, 189
Transport Infrastructure Programme, 55

VALUE II (Research Dissemination and Utilisation), 173
Venture Consort Pilot Scheme, 81

Women's Local Employment Initiatives, 143